Python

Python Distilled

David M. Beazley

✦✦ Addison-Wesley

Boston • Columbus • New York • San Francisco • Amsterdam • Cape Town
Dubai • London • Madrid • Milan • Munich • Paris • Montreal • Toronto • Delhi • Mexico City
São Paulo • Sydney • Hong Kong • Seoul • Singapore • Taipei • Tokyo

Library of Congress Control Number: 2021943288

ISBN-13: 978-0-13-417327-6
ISBN-10: 0-13-417327-9

1 2021

Contents

8 Modules and Packages 225

Preface

More than 20 years have passed since I authored the *Python Essential Reference*. At that time, Python was a much smaller language and it came with a useful set of batteries in its standard library. It was something that could mostly fit in your brain. The *Essential Reference* reflected that era. It was a small book that you could take with you to write some Python code on a desert island or inside a secret vault. Over the three subsequent revisions, the *Essential Reference* stuck with this vision of being a compact but complete language reference—because if you're going to code in Python on vacation, why not use all of it?

Today, more than a decade since the publication of the last edition, the Python world is much different. No longer a niche language, Python has become one of the most popular programming languages in the world. Python programmers also have a wealth of information at their fingertips in the form of advanced editors, IDEs, notebooks, web pages, and more. In fact, there's probably little need to consult a reference book when almost any reference material you might want can be conjured to appear before your eyes with the touch of a few keys.

If anything, the ease of information retrieval and the scale of the Python universe presents a different kind of challenge. If you're just starting to learn or need to solve a new problem, it can be overwhelming to know where to begin. It can also be difficult to separate the features of various tools from the core language itself. These kinds of problems are the rationale for this book.

Python Distilled is a book about programming in Python. It's not trying to document everything that's possible or has been done in Python. Its focus is on presenting a modern yet curated (or distilled) core of the language. It has been informed by my years of teaching Python to scientists, engineers, and software professionals. However, it's also a product of writing software libraries, pushing the edges of what makes Python tick, and finding out what's most useful.

For the most part, the book focuses on Python programming itself. This includes abstraction techniques, program structure, data, functions, objects, modules, and so forth—topics that will well serve programmers working on Python projects of any size. Pure reference material that can be easily obtained via an IDE (such as lists of functions, names of commands, arguments, etc.) is generally omitted. I've also made a conscious choice to not describe the fast-changing world of Python tooling—editors, IDEs, deployment, and related matters.

Perhaps controversially, I don't generally focus on language features related to large-scale software project management. Python is sometimes used for big and serious things—comprised of millions upon millions of lines of code. Such applications require specialized tooling, design, and features. They also involve committees, and meetings, and decisions to be made about very important matters. All this is too much for this small book. But perhaps the honest answer is that I don't use Python to write such applications—and neither should you. At least not as a hobby.

In writing a book, there is always a cut-off for the ever-evolving language features. This book was written during the era of Python 3.9. As such, it does not include some of the major additions planned for later releases—for example, structural pattern matching. That's a topic for a different time and place.

Last, but not least, I think it's important that programming remains fun. I hope that my book will not only help you become a productive Python programmer but also capture some of the magic that has inspired people to use Python for exploring the stars, flying helicopters on Mars, and spraying squirrels with a water cannon in the backyard.

Acknowledgments

I'd like to thank the technical reviewers, Shawn Brown, Sophie Tabac, and Pete Fein, for their helpful comments. I'd also like to thank my long-time editor Debra Williams Cauley for her work on this and past projects. The many students who have taken my classes have had a major if indirect impact on the topics covered in this book. Last, but not least, I'd like to thank Paula, Thomas, and Lewis for their support and love.

About the Author

David Beazley is the author of the *Python Essential Reference, Fourth Edition* (Addison-Wesley, 2010) and *Python Cookbook, Third Edition* (O'Reilly, 2013). He currently teaches advanced computer science courses through his company Dabeaz LLC (www.dabeaz.com). He's been using, writing, speaking, and teaching about Python since 1996.

1

Python Basics

This chapter gives an overview of the core of the Python language. It covers variables, data types, expressions, control flow, functions, classes, and input/output. The chapter concludes with a discussion of modules, script writing, packages, and a few tips on organizing larger programs. This chapter is not trying to provide comprehensive coverage of every feature, nor does it concern itself with all of the tooling that might surround a larger Python project. However, experienced programmers should be able to extrapolate from the material here to write more advanced programs. Newcomers are encouraged to try the examples in a simple environment, such as a terminal window and a basic text editor.

1.1 Running Python

Python programs are executed by an interpreter. There are many different environments in which the Python interpreter might run—an IDE, a browser, or a terminal window. However, underneath all that, the core of the interpreter is a text-based application that can be started by typing `python` in a command shell such as `bash`. Since Python 2 and Python 3 might both be installed on the same machine, you might need to type `python2` or `python3` to pick a version. This book assumes Python 3.8 or newer.

When the interpreter starts, a prompt appears where you can type programs into a so-called "read-evaluation-print loop" (or REPL). For example, in the following output, the interpreter displays its copyright message and presents the user with the `>>>` prompt, at which the user types a familiar "Hello World" program:

```
Python 3.8.0 (default, Feb  3 2019, 05:53:21)
[GCC 4.2.1 Compatible Apple LLVM 8.0.0 (clang-800.0.38)] on darwin
Type "help", "copyright", "credits" or "license" for more information.
>>> print('Hello World')
Hello World
>>>
```

Certain environments may display a different prompt. The following output is from `ipython` (an alternate shell for Python):

```
Python 3.8.0 (default, Feb 4, 2019, 07:39:16)
Type 'copyright', 'credits' or 'license' for more information
IPython 6.5.0 -- An enhanced Interactive Python. Type '?' for help.

In [1]: print('Hello World')
Hello World

In [2]:
```

Regardless of the exact form of output you see, the underlying principle is the same. You type a command, it runs, and you immediately see the output.

Python's interactive mode is one of its most useful features because you can type any valid statement and immediately see the result. This is useful for debugging and experimentation. Many people, including the author, use interactive Python as their desktop calculator. For example:

```
>>> 6000 + 4523.50 + 134.25
10657.75
>>> _ + 8192.75
18850.5
>>>
```

When you use Python interactively, the variable _ holds the result of the last operation. This is useful if you want to use that result in subsequent statements. This variable only gets defined when working interactively, so don't use it in saved programs.

You can exit the interactive interpreter by typing `quit()` or the EOF (end of file) character. On UNIX, EOF is Ctrl+D; on Windows, it's Ctrl+Z.

1.2 Python Programs

If you want to create a program that you can run repeatedly, put statements in a text file. For example:

```
# hello.py
print('Hello World')
```

Python source files are UTF-8-encoded text files that normally have a `.py` suffix. The `#` character denotes a comment that extends to the end of the line. International (Unicode) characters can be freely used in the source code as long as you use the UTF-8 encoding (this is the default in most editors, but it never hurts to check your editor settings if you're unsure).

To execute the `hello.py` file, provide the filename to the interpreter as follows:

```
shell % python3 hello.py
Hello World
shell %
```

It is common to use `#!` to specify the interpreter on the first line of a program, like this:

```
#!/usr/bin/env python3
print('Hello World')
```

On UNIX, if you give this file execute permissions (for example, by `chmod +x hello.py`), you can run the program by typing `hello.py` into your shell.

On Windows, you can double-click on a `.py` file or type the name of the program into the Run command on the Windows Start menu to launch it. The `#!` line, if given, is used to pick the interpreter version (Python 2 versus 3). Execution of a program might take place in a console window that disappears immediately after the program completes—often before you can read its output. For debugging, it's better to run the program within a Python development environment.

The interpreter runs statements in order until it reaches the end of the input file. At that point, the program terminates and Python exits.

1.3   Primitives, Variables, and Expressions

Python provides a collection of primitive types such as integers, floats, and strings:

```
42              # int
4.2             # float
'forty-two'     # str
True            # bool
```

A variable is a name that refers to a value. A value represents an object of some type:

```
x = 42
```

Sometimes you might see a type explicitly attached to a name. For example:

```
x: int = 42
```

The type is merely a hint to improve code readability. It can be used by third-party code-checking tools. Otherwise, it is completely ignored. It does not prevent you from assigning a different kind of value later.

An expression is a combination of primitives, names, and operators that produces a value:

```
2 + 3 * 4       # -> 14
```

The following program uses variables and expressions to perform a compound-interest calculation:

```python
# interest.py

principal = 1000        # Initial amount
rate = 0.05             # Interest rate
numyears = 5            # Number of years
year = 1
while year <= numyears:
    principal = principal * (1 + rate)
    print(year, principal)
    year += 1
```

When executed, it produces the following output:

```
1 1050.0
2 1102.5
3 1157.625
4 1215.5062500000001
5 1276.2815625000003
```

The `while` statement tests the conditional expression that immediately follows. If the tested condition is true, the body of the `while` statement executes. The condition is then retested and the body executed again until the condition becomes false. The body of the loop is denoted by indentation. Thus, the three statements following `while` in `interest.py` execute on each iteration. Python doesn't specify the amount of required indentation, as long as it's consistent within a block. It is most common to use four spaces per indentation level.

One problem with the `interest.py` program is that the output isn't very pretty. To make it better, you could right-align the columns and limit the precision of principal to two digits. Change the `print()` function to use a so-called *f-string* like this:

```python
print(f'{year:>3d} {principal:0.2f}')
```

In the f-string, variable names and expressions can be evaluated by enclosing them in curly braces. Optionally, each substitution can have a formatting specifier attached to it. `'>3d'` means a three-digit decimal number, right aligned. `'0.2f'` means a floating-point number with two decimal places of accuracy. More information about these formatting codes can be found in Chapter 9.

Now the output of the program looks like this:

```
1 1050.00
2 1102.50
3 1157.62
4 1215.51
5 1276.28
```

1.4 Arithmetic Operators

Python has a standard set of mathematical operators, shown in Table 1.1. These operators have the same meaning they do in most other programming languages.

Table 1.1   Arithmetic Operators

Operation	Description
x + y	Addition
x - y	Subtraction
x * y	Multiplication
x / y	Division
x // y	Truncating division
x ** y	Power (x to the y power)
x % y	Modulo (x mod y). Remainder.
−x	Unary minus
+x	Unary plus

The division operator (/) produces a floating-point number when applied to integers. Therefore, 7/4 is 1.75. The truncating division operator //, also known as floor division, truncates the result to an integer and works with both integers and floating-point numbers. The modulo operator returns the remainder of the division x // y. For example, 7 % 4 is 3. For floating-point numbers, the modulo operator returns the floating-point remainder of x // y, which is x - (x // y) * y.

In addition, the built-in functions in Table 1.2 provide a few more commonly used numerical operations.

Table 1.2   Common Mathematic Functions

Function	Description
abs(x)	Absolute value
divmod(x,y)	Returns (x // y, x % y)
pow(x,y [,modulo])	Returns (x ** y) % modulo
round(x,[n])	Rounds to the nearest multiple of 10 to the nth power.

The round() function implements "banker's rounding." If the value being rounded is equally close to two multiples, it is rounded to the nearest even multiple (for example, 0.5 is rounded to 0.0, and 1.5 is rounded to 2.0).

Integers provide a few additional operators to support bit manipulation, shown in Table 1.3.

Table 1.3   Bit Manipulation Operators

Operation	Description
x << y	Left shift
x >> y	Right shift
x & y	Bitwise and
x | y	Bitwise or
x ^ y	Bitwise xor (exclusive or)
~x	Bitwise negation

One would commonly use these with binary integers. For example:

```
a = 0b11001001
mask = 0b11110000
x = (a & mask) >> 4    # x = 0b1100 (12)
```

In this example, 0b11001001 is how you write an integer value in binary. You could have written it as decimal 201 or hexadecimal 0xc9, but if you're fiddling with bits, binary makes it easier to visualize what you're doing.

The semantics of the bitwise operators assumes that the integers use a two's complement binary representation and that the sign bit is infinitely extended to the left. Some care is required if you are working with raw bit patterns that are intended to map to native integers on the hardware. This is because Python does not truncate the bits or allow values to overflow—instead, the result will grow arbitrarily large in magnitude. It's up to you to make sure the result is properly sized or truncated if needed.

To compare numbers, use the comparison operators in Table 1.4.

Table 1.4   Comparison Operators

Operation	Description
x == y	Equal to
x != y	Not equal to
x < y	Less than
x > y	Greater than
x >= y	Greater than or equal to
x <= y	Less than or equal to

The result of a comparison is a Boolean value True or False.

The and, or, and not operators (not to be confused with the bit-manipulation operators above) can form more complex Boolean expressions. The behavior of these operators is as shown in Table 1.5.

A value is considered false if it is literally False, None, numerically zero, or empty. Otherwise, it's considered true.

Table 1.5 Logical Operators

Operator	Description
x or y	If x is false, return y; otherwise, return x.
x and y	If x is false, return x; otherwise, return y.
not x	If x is false, return True; otherwise, return False.

It is common to write an expression that updates a value. For example:

```
x = x + 1
y = y * n
```

For these, you can write the following shortened operation instead:

```
x += 1
y *= n
```

This shortened form of update can be used with any of the +, -, *, **, /, //, %, &, |, ^, <<, >> operators. Python does not have increment (++) or decrement (--) operators found in some other languages.

1.5 Conditionals and Control Flow

The while, if and else statements are used for looping and conditional code execution. Here's an example:

```
if a < b:
    print('Computer says Yes')
else:
    print('Computer says No')
```

The bodies of the if and else clauses are denoted by indentation. The else clause is optional. To create an empty clause, use the **pass** statement, as follows:

```
if a < b:
    pass        # Do nothing
else:
    print('Computer says No')
```

To handle multiple-test cases, use the elif statement:

```
if suffix == '.htm':
    content = 'text/html'
elif suffix == '.jpg':
    content = 'image/jpeg'
```

```
elif suffix == '.png':
    content = 'image/png'
else:
    raise RuntimeError(f'Unknown content type {suffix!r}')
```

If you are assigning a value in combination with a test, use a conditional expression:

```
maxval = a if a > b else b
```

This is the same as the longer:

```
if a > b:
    maxval = a
else:
    maxval = b
```

Sometimes, you may see the assignment of a variable and a conditional combined together using the := operator. This is known as an assignment expression (or more colloquially as the "walrus operator" because := looks like a walrus tipped over on its side—presumably playing dead). For example:

```
x = 0
while (x := x + 1) < 10:    # Prints 1, 2, 3, ..., 9
    print(x)
```

The parentheses used to surround an assignment expression are always required.

The `break` statement can be used to abort a loop early. It only applies to the innermost loop. For example:

```
x = 0
while x < 10:
    if x == 5:
        break  # Stops the loop. Moves to Done below
    print(x)
    x += 1

print('Done')
```

The `continue` statement skips the rest of the loop body and goes back to the top of the loop. For example:

```
x = 0
while x < 10:
    x += 1
    if x == 5:
        continue  # Skips the print(x). Goes back to loop start.
    print(x)

print('Done')
```

1.6 Text Strings

To define a string literal, enclose it in single, double, or triple quotes as follows:

```
a = 'Hello World'
b = "Python is groovy"
c = '''Computer says no.'''
d = """Computer still says no."""
```

The same type of quote used to start a string must be used to terminate it. Triple-quoted strings capture all the text until the terminating triple quote—as opposed to single- and double-quoted strings which must be specified on one logical line. Triple-quoted strings are useful when the contents of a string literal span multiple lines of text:

```
print('''Content-type: text/html

<h1> Hello World </h1>
Click <a href="http://www.python.org">here</a>.
''')
```

Immediately adjacent string literals are concatenated into a single string. Thus, the above example could also be written as:

```
print(
'Content-type: text/html\n'
'\n'
'<h1> Hello World </h1>\n'
'Clock <a href="http://www.python.org">here</a>\n'
)
```

If the opening quotation mark of a string is prefaced by an f, escaped expressions within a string are evaluated. For example, in earlier examples, the following statement was used to output values of a calculation:

```
print(f'{year:>3d} {principal:0.2f}')
```

Although this is only using simple variable names, any valid expression can appear. For example:

```
base_year = 2020
...
print(f'{base_year + year:>4d} {principal:0.2f}')
```

As an alternative to f-strings, the `format()` method and `%` operator are also sometimes used to format strings. For example:

```
print('{0:>3d} {1:0.2f}'.format(year, principal))
print('%3d %0.2f' % (year, principal))
```

More information about string formatting is found in Chapter 9.

Strings are stored as sequences of Unicode characters indexed by integers, starting at zero. Negative indices index from the end of the string. The length of a string s is computed using `len(s)`. To extract a single character, use the indexing operator `s[i]` where i is the index.

```
a = 'Hello World'
print(len(a))          # 11
b = a[4]               # b = 'o'
c = a[-1]              # c = 'd'
```

To extract a substring, use the slicing operator `s[i:j]`. It extracts all characters from s whose index k is in the range `i <= k < j`. If either index is omitted, the beginning or end of the string is assumed, respectively:

```
c = a[:5]              # c = 'Hello'
d = a[6:]              # d = 'World'
e = a[3:8]             # e = 'lo Wo'
f = a[-5:]             # f = 'World'
```

Strings have a variety of methods for manipulating their contents. For example, the `replace()` method performs a simple text replacement:

```
g = a.replace('Hello', 'Hello Cruel')   # f = 'Hello Cruel World'
```

Table 1.6 shows a few common string methods. Here and elsewhere, arguments enclosed in square brackets are optional.

Table 1.6 Common String Methods

Method	Description
s.endswith(prefix [,start [,end]])	Checks whether a string ends with prefix.
s.find(sub [, start [,end]])	Finds the first occurrence of the specified substring sub or -1 if not found.
s.lower()	Converts to lowercase.
s.replace(old, new [,maxreplace])	Replaces a substring.
s.split([sep [,maxsplit]])	Splits a string using sep as a delimiter. maxsplit is the maximum number of splits to perform.
s.startswith(prefix [,start [,end]])	Checks whether a string starts with prefix.
s.strip([chrs])	Removes leading and trailing whitespace or characters supplied in chrs.
s.upper()	Converts a string to uppercase.

Strings are concatenated with the plus (+) operator:

```
g = a + 'ly'    # g = 'Hello Worldly'
```

Python never implicitly interprets the contents of a string as numerical data. Thus, + always concatenates strings:

```
x = '37'
y = '42'
z = x + y      # z = '3742' (String Concatenation)
```

To perform mathematical calculations, a string first has to be converted into a numeric value using a function such as int() or float(). For example:

```
z = int(x) + int(y)   # z = 79  (Integer Addition)
```

Non-string values can be converted into a string representation by using the str(), repr(), or format() functions. Here's an example:

```
s = 'The value of x is ' + str(x)
s = 'The value of x is ' + repr(x)
s = 'The value of x is ' + format(x, '4d')
```

Although str() and repr() both create strings, their output is often different. str() produces the output that you get when you use the print() function, whereas repr() creates a string that you type into a program to exactly represent the value of an object. For example:

```
>>> s = 'hello\nworld'
>>> print(str(s))
hello
world
>>> print(repr(s))
'hello\nworld'
>>>
```

When debugging, use repr(s) to produce output because it shows you more information about a value and its type.

The format() function is used to convert a single value to a string with a specific formatting applied. For example:

```
>>> x = 12.34567
>>> format(x, '0.2f')
'12.35'
>>>
```

The format code given to format() is the same code you would use with f-strings when producing formatted output. For example, the above code could be replaced by the following:

```
>>> f'{x:0.2f}'
'12.35'
>>>
```

1.7   File Input and Output

The following program opens a file and reads its contents line by line as text strings:

```
with open('data.txt') as file:
    for line in file:
        print(line, end='')  # end='' omits the extra newline
```

The open() function returns a new file object. The with statement that precedes it declares a block of statements (or context) where the file (file) is going to be used. Once control leaves this block, the file is automatically closed. If you don't use the with statement, the code would need to look like this:

```
file = open('data.txt')
for line in file:
    print(line, end='')  # end='' omits the extra newline
file.close()
```

It's easy to forget the extra step of calling close() so it's better to use the with statement and have the file closed for you.

The for loop iterates line-by-line over the file until no more data is available.

If you want to read the file in its entirety as a string, use the read() method like this:

```
with open('data.txt') as file:
    data = file.read()
```

If you want to read a large file in chunks, give a size hint to the read() method as follows:

```
with open('data.txt') as file:
    while (chunk := file.read(10000)):
        print(chunk, end='')
```

The := operator used in this example assigns to a variable and returns its value so that it can be tested by the while loop to break out. When the end of a file is reached, read() returns an empty string. An alternate way to write the above function is using break:

```
with open('data.txt') as file:
    while True:
        chunk = file.read(10000)
        if not chunk:
            break
        print(chunk, end='')
```

To make the output of a program go to a file, supply a file argument to the print() function:

```
with open('out.txt', 'wt') as out:
    while year <= numyears:
```

```
        principal = principal * (1 + rate)
        print(f'{year:>3d} {principal:0.2f}', file=out)
        year += 1
```

In addition, file objects support a `write()` method that can be used to write string data. For example, the `print()` function in the previous example could have been written this way:

```
out.write(f'{year:3d} {principal:0.2f}\n')
```

By default, files contain text encoded as UTF-8. If you're working with a different text encoding, use the extra `encoding` argument when opening the file. For example:

```
with open('data.txt', encoding='latin-1') as file:
    data = file.read()
```

Sometimes you might want to read data typed interactively in the console. To do that, use the `input()` function. For example:

```
name = input('Enter your name : ')
print('Hello', name)
```

The `input()` function returns all of the typed text up to the terminating newline, which is not included.

1.8 Lists

Lists are an ordered collection of arbitrary objects. Create a list by enclosing values in square brackets:

```
names = [ 'Dave', 'Paula', 'Thomas', 'Lewis' ]
```

Lists are indexed by integers, starting with zero. Use the indexing operator to access and modify individual items of the list:

```
a = names[2]        # Returns the third item of the list, 'Thomas'
names[2] = 'Tom'    # Changes the third item to 'Tom'
print(names[-1])    # Print the last item ('Lewis')
```

To append new items to the end of a list, use the `append()` method:

```
names.append('Alex')
```

To insert an item in the list at a specific position, use the `insert()` method:

```
names.insert(2, 'Aya')
```

To iterate over the items in a list, use a `for` loop:

```
for name in names:
    print(name)
```

You can extract or reassign a portion of a list by using the slicing operator:

```
b = names[0:2]       # b -> ['Dave', 'Paula']
c = names[2:]        # c -> ['Aya', 'Tom', 'Lewis', 'Alex']
names[1] = 'Becky'   # Replaces 'Paula' with 'Becky'
names[0:2] = ['Dave', 'Mark', 'Jeff'] # Replace the first two items
                                      # with ['Dave','Mark','Jeff']
```

Use the plus (+) operator to concatenate lists:

```
a = ['x','y'] + ['z','z','y']  # Result is ['x','y','z','z','y']
```

An empty list is created in one of two ways:

```
names = []         # An empty list
names = list()     # An empty list
```

Specifying [] for an empty list is more idiomatic. list is the name of the class associated with the list type. It's more common to see it used when performing conversions of data to a list. For example:

```
letters = list('Dave')     # letters = ['D', 'a', 'v', 'e']
```

Most of the time, all of the items in a list are of the same type (for example, a list of numbers or a list of strings). However, lists can contain any mix of Python objects, including other lists, as in the following example:

```
a = [1, 'Dave', 3.14, ['Mark', 7, 9, [100, 101]], 10]
```

Items contained in nested lists are accessed by applying more than one indexing operation:

```
a[1]            # Returns 'Dave'
a[3][2]         # Returns 9
a[3][3][1]      # Returns 101
```

The following program pcost.py illustrates how to read data into a list and perform a simple calculation. In this example, lines are assumed to contain comma-separated values. The program computes the sum of the product of two columns.

```
# pcost.py
#
# Reads input lines of the form 'NAME,SHARES,PRICE'.
# For example:
#
#     SYM,123,456.78
```

```
import sys
if len(sys.argv) != 2:
    raise SystemExit(f'Usage: {sys.argv[0]} filename')

rows = []
with open(sys.argv[1], 'rt') as file:
    for line in file:
        rows.append(line.split(','))

# rows is a list of this form
# [
#   ['SYM', '123', '456.78']
#   ...
# ]

total = sum([ int(row[1]) * float(row[2]) for row in rows ])
print(f'Total cost: {total:0.2f}')
```

The first line of this program uses the import statement to load the sys module from the Python library. This module is used to obtain command-line arguments which are found in the list sys.argv. The initial check makes sure that a filename has been provided. If not, a SystemExit exception is raised with a helpful error message. In this message, sys.argv[0] inserts the name of the program that's running.

The open() function uses the filename that was specified on the command line. The for line in file loop is reading the file line by line. Each line is split into a small list using the comma character as a delimiter. This list is appended to rows. The final result, rows, is a list of lists—remember that a list can contain anything including other lists.

The expression [int(row[1]) * float(row[2]) for row in rows] constructs a new list by looping over all of the lists in rows and computing the product of the second and third items. This useful technique for constructing a list is known as a list comprehension. The same computation could have been expressed more verbosely as follows:

```
values = []
for row in rows:
    values.append(int(row[1]) * float(row[2]))
total = sum(values)
```

As a general rule, list comprehensions are a preferred technique for performing simple calculations. The built-in sum() function computes the sum for all items in a sequence.

1.9 Tuples

To create simple data structures, you can pack a collection of values into an immutable object known as a tuple. You create a tuple by enclosing a group of values in parentheses:

```
holding = ('GOOG', 100, 490.10)
address = ('www.python.org', 80)
```

For completeness, 0- and 1-element tuples can be defined, but have special syntax:

```
a = ()          # 0-tuple (empty tuple)
b = (item,)     # 1-tuple (note the trailing comma)
```

The values in a tuple can be extracted by numerical index just like a list. However, it is more common to unpack tuples into a set of variables, like this:

```
name, shares, price = holding
host, port = address
```

Although tuples support most of the same operations as lists (such as indexing, slicing, and concatenation), the elements of a tuple cannot be changed after creation—that is, you cannot replace, delete, or append new elements to an existing tuple. A tuple is best viewed as a single immutable object that consists of several parts, not as a collection of distinct objects like a list.

Tuples and lists are often used together to represent data. For example, this program shows how you might read a file containing columns of data separated by commas:

```
# File containing lines of the form ``name,shares,price"
filename = 'portfolio.csv'

portfolio = []
with open(filename) as file:
    for line in file:
        row = line.split(',')
        name = row[0]
        shares = int(row[1])
        price = float(row[2])
        holding = (name, shares, price)
        portfolio.append(holding)
```

The resulting portfolio list created by this program looks like a two-dimensional array of rows and columns. Each row is represented by a tuple and can be accessed as follows:

```
>>> portfolio[0]
('AA', 100, 32.2)
>>> portfolio[1]
('IBM', 50, 91.1)
>>>
```

Individual items of data can be accessed like this:

```
>>> portfolio[1][1]
50
```

```
>>> portfolio[1][2]
91.1
>>>
```

Here's how to loop over all of the records and unpack fields into a set of variables:

```
total = 0.0
for name, shares, price in portfolio:
    total += shares * price
```

Alternatively, you could use a list comprehension:

```
total = sum([shares * price for _, shares, price in portfolio])
```

When iterating over tuples, the variable _ can be used to indicate a discarded value. In the above calculation, it means we're ignoring the first item (the name).

1.10 Sets

A set is an unordered collection of unique objects. Sets are used to find distinct values or to manage problems related to membership. To create a set, enclose a collection of values in curly braces or give an existing collection of items to set(). For example:

```
names1 = { 'IBM', 'MSFT', 'AA' }
names2 = set(['IBM', 'MSFT', 'HPE', 'IBM', 'CAT'])
```

The elements of a set are typically restricted to immutable objects. For example, you can make a set of numbers, strings, or tuples. However, you can't make a set containing lists. Most common objects will probably work with a set, however—when in doubt, try it.

Unlike lists and tuples, sets are unordered and cannot be indexed by numbers. Moreover, the elements of a set are never duplicated. For example, if you inspect the value of names2 from the preceding code, you get the following:

```
>>> names2
{'CAT', 'IBM', 'MSFT', 'HPE'}
>>>
```

Notice that 'IBM' only appears once. Also, the order of items can't be predicted; the output may vary from what's shown. The order might even change between interpreter runs on the same computer.

If working with existing data, you can also create a set using a set comprehension. For example, this statement turns all of the stock names from the data in the previous section into a set:

```
names = { s[0] for s in portfolio }
```

To create an empty set, use `set()` with no arguments:

```
r = set()    # Initially empty set
```

Sets support a standard collection of operations including union, intersection, difference, and symmetric difference. Here's an example:

```
a = t | s       # Union {'MSFT', 'CAT', 'HPE', 'AA', 'IBM'}
b = t & s       # Intersection {'IBM', 'MSFT'}
c = t - s       # Difference { 'CAT', 'HPE' }
d = s - t       # Difference { 'AA' }
e = t ^ s       # Symmetric difference { 'CAT', 'HPE', 'AA' }
```

The difference operation `s - t` gives items in `s` that aren't in `t`. The symmetric difference `s ^ t` gives items that are in either `s` or `t` but not in both.

New items can be added to a set using `add()` or `update()`:

```
t.add('DIS')                    # Add a single item
s.update({'JJ', 'GE', 'ACME'}) # Adds multiple items to s
```

An item can be removed using `remove()` or `discard()`:

```
t.remove('IBM')    # Remove 'IBM' or raise KeyError if absent.
s.discard('SCOX')  # Remove 'SCOX' if it exists.
```

The difference between `remove()` and `discard()` is that `discard()` doesn't raise an exception if the item isn't present.

1.11 Dictionaries

A dictionary is a mapping between keys and values. You create a dictionary by enclosing the key-value pairs, each separated by a colon, in curly braces ({ }), like this:

```
s = {
    'name' : 'GOOG',
    'shares' : 100,
    'price' : 490.10
    }
```

To access members of a dictionary, use the indexing operator as follows:

```
name = s['name']
cost = s['shares'] * s['price']
```

Inserting or modifying objects works like this:

```
s['shares'] = 75
s['date'] = '2007-06-07'
```

A dictionary is a useful way to define an object that consists of named fields. However, dictionaries are also commonly used as a mapping for performing fast lookups on unordered data. For example, here's a dictionary of stock prices:

```
prices = {
    'GOOG' : 490.1,
    'AAPL' : 123.5,
    'IBM' : 91.5,
    'MSFT' : 52.13
}
```

Given such a dictionary, you can look up a price:

```
p = prices['IBM']
```

Dictionary membership is tested with the in operator:

```
if 'IBM' in prices:
    p = prices['IBM']
else:
    p = 0.0
```

This particular sequence of steps can also be performed more compactly using the get() method:

```
p = prices.get('IBM', 0.0)    # prices['IBM'] if it exists, else 0.0
```

Use the del statement to remove an element of a dictionary:

```
del prices['GOOG']
```

Although strings are the most common type of key, you can use many other Python objects, including numbers and tuples. For example, tuples are often used to construct composite or multipart keys:

```
prices = { }
prices[('IBM', '2015-02-03')] = 91.23
prices['IBM', '2015-02-04'] = 91.42        # Parens omitted
```

Any kind of object can be placed into a dictionary, including other dictionaries. However, mutable data structures such as lists, sets, and dictionaries cannot be used as keys.

Dictionaries are often used as building blocks for various algorithms and data–handling problems. One such problem is tabulation. For example, here's how you could count the total number of shares for each stock name in earlier data:

```
portfolio = [
  ('ACME', 50, 92.34),
  ('IBM', 75, 102.25),
  ('PHP', 40, 74.50),
```

```
    ('IBM', 50, 124.75)
]

total_shares = { s[0]: 0 for s in portfolio }
for name, shares, _ in portfolio:
    total_shares[name] += shares

# total_shares = {'IBM': 125, 'ACME': 50, 'PHP': 40}
```

In this example, `{ s[0]: 0 for s in portfolio }` is an example of a dictionary comprehension. It creates a dictionary of key-value pairs from another collection of data. In this case, it's making an initial dictionary mapping stock names to 0. The `for` loop that follows iterates over the dictionary and adds up all of the held shares for each stock symbol.

Many common data processing tasks such as this one have already been implemented by library modules. For example, the `collections` module has a `Counter` object that can be used for this task:

```
from collections import Counter

total_shares = Counter()
for name, shares, _ in portfolio:
    total_shares[name] += shares

# total_shares = Counter({'IBM': 125, 'ACME': 50, 'PHP': 40})
```

An empty dictionary is created in one of two ways:

```
prices = {}        # An empty dict
prices = dict()    # An empty dict
```

It is more idiomatic to use {} for an empty dictionary—although caution is required since it might look like you are trying to create an empty set (use `set()` instead). `dict()` is commonly used to create dictionaries from key-value values. For example:

```
pairs = [('IBM', 125), ('ACME', 50), ('PHP', 40)]
d = dict(pairs)
```

To obtain a list of dictionary keys, convert a dictionary to a list:

```
syms = list(prices)     # syms = ['AAPL', 'MSFT', 'IBM', 'GOOG']
```

Alternatively, you can obtain the keys using `dict.keys()`:

```
syms = prices.keys()
```

The difference between these two methods is that `keys()` returns a special "keys view" that is attached to the dictionary and actively reflects changes made to the dictionary. For example:

```
>>> d = { 'x': 2, 'y':3 }
>>> k = d.keys()
>>> k
dict_keys(['x', 'y'])
>>> d['z'] = 4
>>> k
dict_keys(['x', 'y', 'z'])
>>>
```

The keys always appear in the same order as the items were initially inserted into the dictionary. The list conversion above will preserve this order. This can be useful when dicts are used to represent key-value data read from files and other data sources. The dictionary will preserve the input order. This might help readability and debugging. It's also nice if you want to write the data back to a file. Prior to Python 3.6, however, this ordering was not guaranteed, so you cannot rely upon it if compatibility with older versions of Python is required. Order is also not guaranteed if multiple deletions and insertions have taken place.

To obtain the values stored in a dictionary, use the `dict.values()` method. To obtain key-value pairs, use `dict.items()`. For example, here's how to iterate over the entire contents of a dictionary as key-value pairs:

```
for sym, price in prices.items():
    print(f'{sym} = {price}')
```

1.12 Iteration and Looping

The most widely used looping construct is the `for` statement that iterates over a collection of items. One common form of iteration is to loop over all the members of a sequence—such as a string, list, or tuple. Here's an example:

```
for n in [1, 2, 3, 4, 5, 6, 7, 8, 9]:
    print(f'2 to the {n} power is {2**n}')
```

In this example, the variable n will be assigned successive items from the list [1, 2, 3, 4, ..., 9] on each iteration. Since looping over ranges of integers is quite common, there is a shortcut:

```
for n in range(1, 10):
    print(f'2 to the {n} power is {2**n}')
```

The `range(i, j [,step])` function creates an object that represents a range of integers with values from i up to, but not including, j. If the starting value is omitted, it's taken to be zero. An optional stride can also be given as a third argument. Here are some examples:

```
a = range(5)        # a = 0, 1, 2, 3, 4
b = range(1, 8)     # b = 1, 2, 3, 4, 5, 6, 7
c = range(0, 14, 3) # c = 0, 3, 6, 9, 12
d = range(8, 1, -1) # d = 8, 7, 6, 5, 4, 3, 2
```

The object created by range() computes the values it represents on demand when lookups are requested. Thus, it's efficient to use even with a large range of numbers.

The for statement is not limited to sequences of integers. It can be used to iterate over many kinds of objects including strings, lists, dictionaries, and files. Here's an example:

```
message = 'Hello World'
# Print out the individual characters in message
for c in message:
    print(c)

names = ['Dave', 'Mark', 'Ann', 'Phil']
# Print out the members of a list
for name in names:
    print(name)

prices = { 'GOOG' : 490.10, 'IBM' : 91.50, 'AAPL' : 123.15 }
# Print out all of the members of a dictionary
for key in prices:
    print(key, '=', prices[key])

# Print all of the lines in a file
with open('foo.txt') as file:
    for line in file:
        print(line, end='')
```

The for loop is one of Python's most powerful language features because you can create custom iterator objects and generator functions that supply it with sequences of values. More details about iterators and generators can be found later in Chapter 6.

1.13 Functions

Use the def statement to define a function:

```
def remainder(a, b):
    q = a // b        # // is truncating division.
    r = a - q * b
    return r
```

To invoke a function, use its name followed by its arguments in parentheses, for example result = remainder(37, 15).

It is common practice for a function to include a documentation string as the first statement. This string feeds the help() command and may be used by IDEs and other development tools to assist the programmer. For example:

```
def remainder(a, b):
    '''
```

```
    Computes the remainder of dividing a by b
    '''
    q = a // b
    r = a - q * b
    return r
```

If the inputs and outputs of a function aren't clear from their names, they might be annotated with types:

```
def remainder(a: int, b: int) -> int:
    '''
    Computes the remainder of dividing a by b
    '''
    q = a // b
    r = a - q * b
    return r
```

Such annotations are merely informational and are not actually enforced at runtime. Someone could still call the above function with non-integer values, such as `result = remainder(37.5, 3.2)`.

Use a tuple to return multiple values from a function:

```
def divide(a, b):
    q = a // b        # If a and b are integers, q is integer
    r = a - q * b
    return (q, r)
```

When multiple values are returned in a tuple, they can be unpacked into separate variables like this:

```
quotient, remainder = divide(1456, 33)
```

To assign a default value to a function parameter, use assignment:

```
def connect(hostname, port, timeout=300):
    # Function body
    ...
```

When default values are given in a function definition, they can be omitted from subsequent function calls. An omitted argument will take on the supplied default value. Here's an example:

```
connect('www.python.org', 80)
connect('www.python.org', 80, 500)
```

Default arguments are often used for optional features. If there are many such arguments, readability can suffer. It's therefore recommended to specify such arguments using keyword arguments. For example:

```
connect('www.python.org', 80, timeout=500)
```

If you know the names of the arguments, all of them can be named when calling a
function. When named, the order in which they are listed doesn't matter. For example,
this is fine:

```
connect(port=80, hostname='www.python.org')
```

When variables are created or assigned inside a function, their scope is local. That is,
the variable is only defined inside the body of the function and is destroyed when the
function returns. Functions can also access variables defined outside of a function as long as
they are defined in the same file. For example:

```
debug = True       # Global variable

def read_data(filename):
    if debug:
        print('Reading', filename)
    ...
```

Scoping rules are described in more detail in Chapter 5.

1.14 Exceptions

If an error occurs in your program, an exception is raised and a traceback message appears:

```
Traceback (most recent call last):
  File "readport.py", line 9, in <module>
    shares = int(row[1])
ValueError: invalid literal for int() with base 10: 'N/A'
```

The traceback message indicates the type of error that occurred, along with its location.
Normally, errors cause a program to terminate. However, you can catch and handle
exceptions using try and except statements, like this:

```
portfolio = []
with open('portfolio.csv') as file:
    for line in file:
        row = line.split(',')
        try:
            name = row[0]
            shares = int(row[1])
            price = float(row[2])
            holding = (name, shares, price)
            portfolio.append(holding)
        except ValueError as err:
```

```
print('Bad row:', row)
print('Reason:', err)
```

In this code, if a `ValueError` occurs, details concerning the cause of the error are placed in `err` and control passes to the code in the `except` block. If some other kind of exception is raised, the program crashes as usual. If no errors occur, the code in the `except` block is ignored. When an exception is handled, program execution resumes with the statement that immediately follows the last `except` block. The program does not return to the location where the exception occurred.

The `raise` statement is used to signal an exception. You need to give the name of an exception. For instance, here's how to raise `RuntimeError`, a built-in exception:

```
raise RuntimeError('Computer says no')
```

Proper management of system resources such as locks, files, and network connections is often tricky when combined with exception handling. Sometimes there are actions that must be performed no matter what happens. For this, use `try-finally`. Here is an example involving a lock that must be released to avoid deadlock:

```
import threading
lock = threading.Lock()
...
lock.acquire()
# If a lock has been acquired, it MUST be released
try:
    ...
    statements
    ...
finally:
    lock.release()        # Always runs
```

To simplify such programming, most objects that involve resource management also support the `with` statement. Here is a modified version of the above code:

```
with lock:
    ...
    statements
    ...
```

In this example, the `lock` object is automatically acquired when the `with` statement executes. When execution leaves the context of the with block, the lock is automatically released. This is done regardless of what happens inside the `with` block. For example, if an exception occurs, the lock is released when control leaves the context of the block.

The `with` statement is normally only compatible with objects related to system resources or the execution environment—such as files, connections, and locks. However, user-defined objects can have their own custom processing, as described further in Chapter 3.

1.15   Program Termination

A program terminates when no more statements exist to execute in the input program or when an uncaught `SystemExit` exception is raised. If you want to force a program to quit, here's how to do it:

```
raise SystemExit()                        # Exit with no error message
raise SystemExit("Something is wrong")    # Exit with error
```

On exit, the interpreter makes a best effort to garbage-collect all active objects. However, if you need to perform a specific cleanup action (remove files, close a connection), you can register it with the `atexit` module as follows:

```
import atexit

# Example
connection = open_connection("deaddot.com")

def cleanup():
    print "Going away..."
    close_connection(connection)

atexit.register(cleanup)
```

1.16   Objects and Classes

All values used in a program are objects. An object consists of internal data and methods that perform various kinds of operations involving that data. You have already used objects and methods when working with the built-in types such as strings and lists. For example:

```
items = [37, 42]      # Create a list object
items.append(73)      # Call the append() method
```

The `dir()` function lists the methods available on an object. It is a useful tool for interactive experimentation when no fancy IDE is available. For example:

```
>>> items = [37, 42]
>>> dir(items)
['__add__', '__class__', '__contains__', '__delattr__', '__delitem__',
...
 'append', 'count', 'extend', 'index', 'insert', 'pop',
 'remove', 'reverse', 'sort']
>>>
```

When inspecting objects, you will see familiar methods such as `append()` and `insert()` listed. However, you will also see special methods whose names begin and end with a double underscore. These methods implement various operators. For example, the __add__() method is used to implement the + operator. These methods are explained in more detail in later chapters.

```
>>> items.__add__([73, 101])
[37, 42, 73, 101]
>>>
```

The `class` statement is used to define new types of objects and for object-oriented programming. For example, the following class defines a stack with `push()` and `pop()` operations:

```
class Stack:
    def __init__(self):              # Initialize the stack
        self._items = [ ]

    def push(self, item):
        self._items.append(item)

    def pop(self):
        return self._items.pop()

    def __repr__(self):
        return f'<{type(self).__name__} at 0x{id(self):x}, size={len(self)}>'

    def __len__(self):
        return len(self._items)
```

Inside the class definition, methods are defined using the `def` statement. The first argument in each method always refers to the object itself. By convention, `self` is the name used for this argument. All operations involving the attributes of an object must explicitly refer to the `self` variable.

Methods with leading and trailing double underscores are special methods. For example, `__init__` is used to initialize an object. In this case, `__init__` creates an internal list for storing the stack data.

To use a class, write code such as this:

```
s = Stack()               # Create a stack
s.push('Dave')            # Push some things onto it
s.push(42)
s.push([3, 4, 5])
x = s.pop()               # x gets [3,4,5]
y = s.pop()               # y gets 42
```

Within the class, you will notice that the methods use an internal _items variable. Python does not have any mechanism for hiding or protecting data. However, there is a programming convention wherein names preceded by a single underscore are taken to be "private." In this example, _items should be treated (by you) as internal implementation and not used outside the Stack class itself. Be aware that there is no actual enforcement of this convention—if you want to access _items, you can do so at any time. You'll just have to answer to your coworkers when they review your code.

The __repr__() and __len__() methods are there to make the object play nicely with the rest of the environment. Here, __len__() makes a Stack work with the built-in len() function and __repr__() changes the way that a Stack is displayed and printed. It's a good idea to always define __repr__() as it can simplify debugging.

```
>>> s = Stack()
>>> s.push('Dave')
>>> s.push(42)
>>> len(s)
2
>>> s
<Stack at 0x10108c1d0, size=2>
>>>
```

A major feature of objects is that you can add to or redefine the capabilities of existing classes via inheritance.

Suppose you wanted to add a method to swap the top two items on the stack. You might write a class like this:

```
class MyStack(Stack):
    def swap(self):
        a = self.pop()
        b = self.pop()
        self.push(a)
        self.push(b)
```

MyStack is identical to Stack except that it has a new method, swap().

```
>>> s = MyStack()
>>> s.push('Dave')
>>> s.push(42)
>>> s.swap()
>>> s.pop()
'Dave'
>>> s.pop()
42
>>>
```

Inheritance can also be used to change the behavior of an existing method. Suppose you want to restrict the stack to only hold numeric data. Write a class like this:

```
class NumericStack(Stack):
    def push(self, item):
```

```
    if not isinstance(item, (int, float)):
        raise TypeError('Expected an int or float')
    super().push(item)
```

In this example, the `push()` method has been redefined to add extra checking. The `super()` operation is a way to invoke the prior definition of `push()`. Here's how this class would work:

```
>>> s = NumericStack()
>>> s.push(42)
>>> s.push('Dave')
Traceback (most recent call last):
    ...
TypeError: Expected an int or float
>>>
```

Often, inheritance is not the best solution. Suppose you wanted to define a simple stack-based 4-function calculator that worked like this:

```
>>> # Calculate 2 + 3 * 4
>>> calc = Calculator()
>>> calc.push(2)
>>> calc.push(3)
>>> calc.push(4)
>>> calc.mul()
>>> calc.add()
>>> calc.pop()
14
>>>
```

You might look at this code, see the use of `push()` and `pop()`, and think that `Calculator` could be defined by inheriting from `Stack`. Although that would work, it is probably better to define `Calculator` as a completely separate class:

```
class Calculator:
    def __init__(self):
        self._stack = Stack()

    def push(self, item):
        self._stack.push(item)

    def pop(self):
        return self._stack.pop()

    def add(self):
        self.push(self.pop() + self.pop())
```

```
    def mul(self):
        self.push(self.pop() * self.pop())

    def sub(self):
        right = self.pop()
        self.push(self.pop() - right)

    def div(self):
        right = self.pop()
        self.push(self.pop() / right)
```

In this implementation, a `Calculator` contains a `Stack` as an internal implementation detail. This is an example of *composition*. The `push()` and `pop()` methods delegate to the internal `Stack`. The main reason for taking this approach is that you don't really think of the `Calculator` as a `Stack`. It's a separate concept—a different kind of object. By analogy, your phone contains a central processing unit (CPU) but you don't usually think of your phone as a type of CPU.

1.17 Modules

As your programs grow in size, you will want to break them into multiple files for easier maintenance. To do this, use the `import` statement. To create a module, put the relevant statements and definitions into a file with a `.py` suffix and the same name as the module. Here's an example:

```
# readport.py
#
# Reads a file of 'NAME,SHARES,PRICE' data

def read_portfolio(filename):
    portfolio = []
    with open(filename) as file:
        for line in file:
            row = line.split(',')
            try:
                name = row[0]
                shares = int(row[1])
                price = float(row[2])
                holding = (name, shares, price)
                portfolio.append(holding)
            except ValueError as err:
                print('Bad row:', row)
                print('Reason:', err)
    return portfolio
```

To use your module in other files, use the import statement. For example, here is a module pcost.py that uses the above read_portfolio() function:

```
# pcost.py

import readport

def portfolio_cost(filename):
    '''
    Compute the total shares*price of a portfolio
    '''
    port = readport.read_portfolio(filename)
    return sum(shares * price for _, shares, price in port)
```

The import statement creates a new namespace (or environment) and executes all the statements in the associated .py file within that namespace. To access the contents of the namespace after import, use the name of the module as a prefix, as in readport.read_portfolio() in the preceding example.

If the import statement fails with an ImportError exception, you need to check a few things in your environment. First, make sure you created a file called readport.py. Next, check the directories listed on sys.path. If your file isn't saved in one of those directories, Python won't be able to find it.

If you want to import a module under a different name, supply the import statement with an optional as qualifier:

```
import readport as rp
port = rp.read_portfolio('portfolio.dat')
```

To import specific definitions into the current namespace, use the from statement:

```
from readport import read_portfolio
port = read_portfolio('portfolio.dat')
```

As with objects, the dir() function lists the contents of a module. It is a useful tool for interactive experimentation.

```
>>> import readport
>>> dir(readport)
['__builtins__', '__cached__', '__doc__', '__file__', '__loader__',
  '__name__', '__package__', '__spec__', 'read_portfolio']
...
>>>
```

Python provides a large standard library of modules that simplify certain programming tasks. For example, the csv module is a standard library for dealing with files of comma-separated values. You could use it in your program as follows:

```
# readport.py
#
# Reads a file of 'NAME,SHARES,PRICE' data

import csv

def read_portfolio(filename):
    portfolio = []
    with open(filename) as file:
        rows = csv.reader(file)
        for row in rows:
            try:
                name = row[0]
                shares = int(row[1])
                price = float(row[2])
                holding = (name, shares, price)
                portfolio.append(holding)
            except ValueError as err:
                print('Bad row:', row)
                print('Reason:', err)
    return portfolio
```

Python also has a vast number of third-party modules that can be installed to solve almost any imaginable task (including the reading of CSV files). See https://pypi.org.

1.18 Script Writing

Any file can execute either as a script or as a library imported with import. To better support imports, script code is often enclosed with a conditional check against the module name:

```
# readport.py
#
# Reads a file of 'NAME,SHARES,PRICE' data

import csv

def read_portfolio(filename):
    ...

def main():
    portfolio = read_portfolio('portfolio.csv')
    for name, shares, price in portfolio:
        print(f'{name:>10s} {shares:10d} {price:10.2f}')
```

```
if __name__ == '__main__':
    main()
```

__name__ is a built-in variable that always contains the name of the enclosing module. If a program is run as the main script with a command such as `python readport.py`, the __name__ variable is set to `'__main__'`. Otherwise, if the code is imported using a statement such as `import readport`, the __name__ variable is set to `'readport'`.

As shown, the program is hardcoded to use a filename `'portfolio.csv'`. Instead, you may want to prompt the user for a filename or accept the filename as a command-line argument. To do this, use the built-in `input()` function or the `sys.argv` list. For example, here is a modified version of the `main()` function:

```
def main(argv):
    if len(argv) == 1:
        filename = input('Enter filename: ')
    elif len(argv) == 2:
        filename = argv[1]
    else:
        raise SystemExit(f'Usage: {argv[0]} [ filename ]')
    portfolio = read_portfolio(filename)
    for name, shares, price in portfolio:
        print(f'{name:>10s} {shares:10d} {price:10.2f}')

if __name__ == '__main__':
    import sys
    main(sys.argv)
```

This program can be run in two different ways from the command line:

```
bash % python readport.py
Enter filename: portfolio.csv
...
bash % python readport.py portfolio.csv
...
bash % python readport.py a b c
Usage: readport.py [ filename ]
bash %
```

For very simple programs, it is often enough to process arguments in `sys.argv` as shown. For more advanced usage, the `argparse` standard library module can be used.

1.19 Packages

In large programs, it's common to organize code into packages. A package is a hierarchical collection of modules. On the filesystem, put your code as a collection of files in a directory like this:

```
tutorial/
    __init__.py
    readport.py
    pcost.py
    stack.py
    . . .
```

The directory should have an __init__.py file, which may be empty. Once you've done this, you should be able to make nested import statements. For example:

```
import tutorial.readport

port = tutorial.readport.read_portfolio('portfolio.dat')
```

If you don't like the long names, you can shorten things using an import like this:

```
from tutorial.readport import read_portfolio

port = read_portfolio('portfolio.dat')
```

One tricky issue with packages is imports between files within the same package. In an earlier example, a pcost.py module was shown that started with an import like this:

```
# pcost.py
import readport
...
```

If the pcost.py and readport.py files are moved into a package, this import statement breaks. To fix it, you must use a fully qualified module import:

```
# pcost.py
from tutorial import readport
...
```

Alternatively, you can use a package-relative import like this:

```
# pcost.py
from . import readport
...
```

The latter form has the benefit of not hardcoding the package name. This makes it easier to later rename a package or move it around within your project.

Other subtle details concerning packages are covered later (see Chapter 8).

1.20 Structuring an Application

As you start to write more Python code, you may find yourself working on larger applications that include a mix of your own code as well as third-party dependencies.

Managing all of this is a complex topic that continues to evolve. There are also many conflicting opinions about what constitutes "best practice." However, there are a few essential facets to it that you should know.

First, it is standard practice to organize large code bases into packages (that is, directories of .py files that include the special __init__.py file). When doing this, pick a unique package name for the top-level directory name. The primary purpose of the package directory is to manage import statements and the namespaces of modules used while programming. You want your code isolated from everyone else's code.

In addition to your main project source code, you might additionally have tests, examples, scripts, and documentation. This additional material usually lives in a separate set of directories than the package containing your source code. Thus, it is common to create an enclosing top-level directory for your project and to put all of your work under that. For example, a fairly typical project organization might look like this:

```
tutorial-project/
    tutorial/
        __init__.py
        readport.py
        pcost.py
        stack.py
        ...
    tests/
        test_stack.py
        test_pcost.py
        ...
    examples/
        sample.py
        ...
    doc/
        tutorial.txt
        ...
```

Keep in mind that there is more than one way to do it. The nature of the problem you're solving might dictate a different structure. Nevertheless, as long as your main set of source code files lives in a proper package (again, the directory with the __init__.py file), you should be fine.

1.21 Managing Third-Party Packages

Python has a large library of contributed packages that can be found at the Python Package Index (https://pypi.org). You may need to depend on some of these packages in your own code. To install a third-party package, use a command such as pip:

```
bash % python3 -m pip install somepackage
```

Installed packages are placed into a special `site-packages` directory that you can find if you inspect the value of `sys.path`. For example, on a UNIX machine, packages might be placed in `/usr/local/lib/python3.8/site-packages`. If you are ever left wondering where a package is coming from, inspect the `__file__` attribute of a package after importing it in the interpreter:

```
>>> import pandas
>>> pandas.__file__
'/usr/local/lib/python3.8/site-packages/pandas/__init__.py'
>>>
```

One potential problem with installing a package is that you might not have permission to change the locally installed version of Python. Even if you had permission, it still might not be a good idea. For example, many systems already have Python installed for use by various system utilities. Altering the installation of that version of Python is often a bad idea.

To make a sandbox where you can install packages and work without worrying about breaking anything, create a *virtual environment* by a command like this:

```
bash % python3 -m venv myproject
```

This will set up a dedicated Python installation for you in a directory called `myproject/`. Within that directory, you'll find an interpreter executable and library where you can safely install packages. For example, if you run `myproject/bin/python3`, you'll get an interpreter configured for your personal use. You can install packages into this interpreter without worrying about breaking any part of the default Python installation. To install a package, use `pip` as before but make sure to specify the correct interpreter:

```
bash % ./myproject/bin/python3 -m pip install somepackage
```

There are various tools that aim to simplify the use of `pip` and `venv`. Such matters might also be handled automagically by your IDE. As this is a fluid and ever-evolving part of Python, no further advice is given here.

1.22 Python: It Fits Your Brain

In the early days of Python, "it fits your brain" was a common motto. Even today, the core of Python is a small programming language along with a useful collection of built-in objects—lists, sets, and dictionaries. A vast array of practical problems can be solved using nothing more than the basic features presented in this chapter. This is a good thing to keep in mind as you begin your Python adventure—although there are always more complicated ways to solve a problem, there might also be a simple way to do it with the basic features Python already provides. When in doubt, you'll probably thank your past self for doing just that.

2

Operators, Expressions, and Data Manipulation

This chapter describes Python's expressions, operators, and evaluation rules related to data manipulation. Expressions are at the heart of performing useful computations. Moreover, third-party libraries can customize Python's behavior to provide a better user experience. This chapter describes expressions at a high level. Chapter 3 describes the underlying protocols that can be used to customize the behavior of the interpreter.

2.1 Literals

A literal is a value typed directly into a program such as 42, 4.2, or 'forty-two'.

Integer literals represent a signed integer value of arbitrary size. It's possible to specify integers in binary, octal, or hexadecimal:

```
42          # Decimal integer
0b101010    # Binary integer
0o52        # Octal integer
0x2a        # Hexadecimal integer
```

The base is not stored as part of the integer value. All of the above literals will display as 42 if printed. You can use the built-in functions bin(x), oct(x), or hex(x) to convert an integer to a string representing its value in different bases.

Floating-point numbers can be written by adding a decimal point or by using scientific notation where an e or E specifies an exponent. All of the following are floating-point numbers:

```
4.2
42.
.42
4.2e+2
4.2E2
-4.2e-2
```

Internally, floating-point numbers are stored as IEEE 754 double-precision (64-bit) values.

In numeric literals, a single underscore (_) can be used as a visual separator between digits. For example:

```
123_456_789
0x1234_5678
0b111_00_101
123.789_012
```

The digit separator is not stored as part of the number—it's only used to make large numeric literals easier to read in source code.

Boolean literals are written as `True` and `False`.

String literals are written by enclosing characters with single, double, or triple quotes. Single- and double-quoted strings must appear on the same line. Triple-quoted strings can span multiple lines. For example:

```
'hello world'
"hello world"
'''hello world'''
"""hello world"""
```

Tuple, liss, set, and dictionary literals are written as follows:

```
(1, 2, 3)               # tuple
[1, 2, 3]               # list
{1, 2, 3}               # set
{'x':1, 'y':2, 'z':3}   # dict
```

2.2 Expressions and Locations

An expression represents a computation that evaluates to a concrete value. It consists of a combination of literals, names, operators, and function or method calls. An expression can always appear on the right-hand side of an assignment statement, be used as an operand in operations in other expressions, or be passed as a function argument. For example:

```
value = 2 + 3 * 5 + sqrt(6+7)
```

Operators, such as + (addition) or * (multiplication), represent an operation performed on objects provided as operands. `sqrt()` is a function that is applied to input arguments.

The left hand side of an assignment represents a location where a reference to an object is stored. That location, as shown in the previous example, might be a simple identifier such as `value`. It could also be an attribute of an object or an index within a container. For example:

```
a = 4 + 2
b[1] = 4 + 2
c['key'] = 4 + 2
d.value = 4 + 2
```

Reading a value back from a location is also an expression. For example:

```
value = a + b[1] + c['key']
```

The assignment of a value and the evaluation of an expression are separate concepts. In particular, you can't include the assignment operator as part of an expression:

```
while line=file.readline():        # Syntax Error
    print(line)
```

However, an "assignment expression" operator (:=) can be used to perform this combined action of expression evaluation and assignment. For example:

```
while (line:=file.readline()):
    print(line)
```

The := operator is usually used in combination with statements such as if and while. In fact, using it as a normal assignment operator results in a syntax error unless you put parentheses around it.

2.3 Standard Operators

Python objects can be made to work with any of the operators in Table 2.1.

Usually these have a numeric interpretation. However, there are notable special cases. For example, the + operator is also used to concatenate sequences, * operator replicates sequences, - is used for set differences, and % performs string formatting:

```
[1,2,3] + [4,5]    # [1,2,3,4,5]
[1,2,3] * 4        # [1,2,3,1,2,3,1,2,3,1,2,3]
'%s has %d messages' % ('Dave', 37)
```

Checking of operators is a dynamic process. Operations involving mixed data types will often "work" if there is an intuitive sense for the operation to work. For example, you can add integers and fractions:

```
>>> from fractions import Fraction
>>> a = Fraction(2, 3)
>>> b = 5
>>> a + b
Fraction(17, 3)
>>>
```

Table 2.1   Standard Operators

Operation	Description
x + y	Addition
x - y	Subtraction
x * y	Multiplication
x / y	Division
x // y	Truncating division
x @ y	Matrix multiplication
x ** y	Power (x to the y power)
x % y	Modulo (x mod y). Remainder.
x << y	Left shift
x >> y	Right shift
x & y	Bitwise and
x | y	Bitwise or
x ^ y	Bitwise xor (exclusive or)
~x	Bitwise negation
−x	Unary minus
+x	Unary plus
abs(x)	Absolute value
divmod(x,y)	Returns (x // y, x % y)
pow(x,y [,modulo])	Returns (x ** y) % modulo
round(x,[n])	Rounds to the nearest multiple of 10-n

However, it's not always foolproof. For example, it doesn't work with decimals.

```
>>> from decimal import Decimal
>>> from fractions import Fraction
>>> a = Fraction(2, 3)
>>> b = Decimal('5')
>>> a + b
Traceback (most recent call last):
  File "<stdin>", line 1, in <module>
TypeError: unsupported operand type(s) for +: 'Fraction' and 'decimal.Decimal'
>>>
```

For most combinations of numbers, however, Python follows a standard numeric hierarchy of Booleans, integers, fractions, floats, and complex numbers. Mixed-type operations will simply work—you don't have to worry about it.

2.4   In-Place Assignment

Python provides the "in-place" or "augmented" assignment operations in Table 2.2.

Table 2.2   Augmented Assignment Operators

Operation	Description
x += y	x = x + y
x -= y	x = x - y
x *= y	x = x * y
x /= y	x = x / y
x //= y	x = x // y
x **= y	x = x ** y
x %= y	x = x % y
x @= y	x = x @ y
x &= y	x = x & y
x |= y	x = x | y
x ^= y	x = x ^ y
x >>= y	x = x >> y
x <<= y	x = x << y

These are not considered to be expressions. Instead, they are a syntactic convenience for updating a value in place. For example:

```
a = 3
a = a + 1          # a = 4
a += 1             # a = 5
```

Mutable objects can use these operators to perform an in-place mutation of the data as an optimization. Consider this example:

```
>>> a = [1, 2, 3]
>>> b = a         # Creates a new reference to a
>>> a += [4, 5]   # In-place update (doesn't create a new list)
>>> a
[1, 2, 3, 4, 5]
>>> b
[1, 2, 3, 4, 5]
>>>
```

In this example, a and b are references to the same list. When a += [4, 5] is performed, it updates the list object in place without creating a new list. Thus, b also sees this update. This is often surprising.

2.5 Object Comparison

The equality operator (x == y) tests the values of x and y for equality. In the case of lists and tuples, they must be of equal size, have equal elements, and be in the same order. For dictionaries, `True` is returned only if x and y have the same set of keys and all the objects with the same key have equal values. Two sets are equal if they have the same elements.

An equality comparison between objects of incompatible types, such as a file and a floating-point number, does not trigger an error but returns `False`. However, sometimes a comparison between objects of different types will produce `True`. For example, comparing an integer and a floating-point number of the same value:

```
>>> 2 == 2.0
True
>>>
```

The identity operators (x is y and x is not y) test two values to see whether they refer to literally the same object in memory (e.g., `id(x) == id(y)`). In general, it may be the case that x == y, but x is not y. For example:

```
>>> a = [1, 2, 3]
>>> b = [1, 2, 3]
>>> a is b
False
>>> a == b
True
>>>
```

In practice, comparing objects with the `is` operator is almost never what you want. Use the == operator for all comparisons unless you have a good reason to expect the two objects to have the same identity.

2.6 Ordered Comparison Operators

The ordered comparison operators in Table 2.3 have the standard mathematical interpretation for numbers. They return a Boolean value.

Table 2.3   Ordered Comparison Operators

Operation	Description
x < y	Less than
x > y	Greater than
x >= y	Greater than or equal to
x <= y	Less than or equal to

For sets, x < y tests if x is strict subset of y (i.e., has fewer elements, but is not equal to y).

When comparing two sequences, the first elements of each sequence are compared. If they differ, this determines the result. If they're the same, the comparison moves to the second element of each sequence. This process continues until two different elements are found or no more elements exist in either of the sequences. If the end of both sequences is reached, the sequences are considered equal. If a is a subsequence of b, then a < b.

Strings and bytes are compared using lexicographical ordering. Each character is assigned a unique numerical index determined by the character set (such as ASCII or Unicode). A character is less than another character if its index is less.

Not all types support the ordered comparisons. For example, trying to use < on dictionaries is undefined and results in a TypeError. Similarly, applying ordered comparisons to incompatible types (such as a string and a number) will result in a TypeError.

2.7 Boolean Expressions and Truth Values

The and, or, and not operators can form complex Boolean expressions. The behavior of these operators is shown in Table 2.4.

Table 2.4 Logical Operators

Operator	Description
x or y	If x is false, return y; otherwise, return x.
x and y	If x is false, return x; otherwise, return y.
not x	If x is false, return True; otherwise, return False.

When you use an expression to determine a true or false value, True, any nonzero number, a nonempty string, list, tuple, or dictionary is taken to be true. False, zero, None, and empty lists, tuples, and dictionaries evaluate as false.

Boolean expressions are evaluated from left to right and consume the right operand only if it's needed to determine the final value. For example, a and b evaluates b only if a is true. This is known as short-circuit evaluation. It can be useful to simplify code involving a test and a subsequent operation. For example:

```
if y != 0:
    result = x / y
else:
    result = 0


# Alternative
result = y and x / y
```

In the second version, the x / y division is only performed if y is nonzero.

Relying on implicit "truthiness" of objects may lead to difficult-to-find bugs. For example, consider this function:

```
def f(x, items=None):
    if not items:
        items = []
    items.append(x)
    return items
```

This function has an optional argument that, if not given, causes a new list to be created and returned. For example,

```
>>> foo(4)
[4]
>>>
```

However, the function has really strange behavior if you give it an existing empty list as an argument:

```
>>> a = []
>>> foo(3, a)
[3]
>>> a            # Notice how a did NOT update
[]
>>>
```

This is a truth-checking bug. Empty lists evaluate to `False` so the code created a new list instead of using the one (a) that was passed in as an argument. To fix this, you need to be more precise in your checking against `None`:

```
def f(x, items=None):
    if items is None:
        items = []
    items.append(x)
    return items
```

It's always good practice to be precise when writing conditional checks.

2.8 Conditional Expressions

A common programming pattern is assigning a value conditionally based on the result of an expression. For example:

```
if a <= b:
    minvalue = a
else:
    minvalue = b
```

This code can be shortened using a conditional expression. For example:

```
minvalue = a if a <= b else b
```

In such expressions, the condition in the middle is evaluated first. The expression to the left of the if is then evaluated if the result is True. Otherwise, the expression after the else is evaluated. The else clause is always required.

2.9 Operations Involving Iterables

Iteration is an important Python feature supported by all of Python's containers (lists, tuples, dicts, and so on), files, as well as generator functions. The operations in Table 2.5 can be applied to any iterable object s.

Table 2.5 Operations on Iterables

Operation	Description
for vars in s:	Iteration
v1, v2, ... = s	Variable unpacking
x in s, x not in s	Membership
[a, *s, b], (a, *s, b), {a, *s, b}	Expansion in list, tuple, or set literals

The most essential operation on an iterable is the for loop. This is how you iterate through the values one by one. All the other operations build upon this.

The x in s operator tests whether the object x appears as one of the items produced by the iterable s and returns True or False. The x not in s operator is the same as not (x in s). For strings, the in and not in operators accept substrings. For example, 'hello' in 'hello world' produces True. Note that the in operator does not support wildcards or any kind of pattern matching.

Any object supporting iteration can have its values unpacked into a series of locations. For example:

```
items = [ 3, 4, 5 ]
x, y, z = items        # x = 3, y = 4, z = 5

letters = "abc"
x, y, z = letters      # x = 'a', y = 'b', z = 'c'
```

The locations on the left don't have to be simple variable names. Any valid location that could appear on the left-hand side of an equal sign is acceptable. So, you could write code like this:

```
items = [3, 4, 5]
d = { }
d['x'], d['y'], d['z'] = items
```

When unpacking values into locations, the number of locations on the left must exactly match the number of items in the iterable on the right. For nested data structures, match locations and data by following the same structural pattern. Consider this example of unpacking two nested 3-tuples:

```
datetime = ((5, 19, 2008), (10, 30, "am"))
(month, day, year), (hour, minute, am_pm) = datetime
```

Sometimes, the _ variable is used to indicate a throw-away value when unpacking. For example, if you only care about the day and the hour, you can use:

```
(_, day, _), (hour, _, _) = datetime
```

If the number of items being unpacked isn't known, you can use an extended form of unpacking by including a starred variable, such as *extra in the following example:

```
items = [1, 2, 3, 4, 5]
a, b, *extra = items      # a = 1, b = 2, extra = [3,4,5]
*extra, a, b              # extra = [1,2,3], a = 4, b = 5
a, *extra, b              # a = 1, extra = [2,3,4], b = 5
```

In this example, *extra receives all of the extra items. It is always a list. No more than one starred variable can be used when unpacking a single iterable. However, multiple starred variables could be used when unpacking more complex data structures involving different iterables. For example:

```
datetime = ((5, 19, 2008), (10, 30, "am"))

(month, *_), (hour, *_) = datetime
```

Any iterable can be expanded when writing out list, tuple, and set literals. This is also done using the star (*). For example:

```
items = [1, 2, 3]
a = [10, *items, 11]      # a = [10, 1, 2, 3, 11]        (list)
b = (*items, 10, *items)  # b = [1, 2, 3, 10, 1, 2, 3]   (tuple)
c = {10, 11, *items}      # c = {1, 2, 3, 10, 11}        (set)
```

In this example, the contents of items are simply pasted into the list, tuple, or set being created as if you typed it in place at that location. This expansion is known as "splatting." You can include as many * expansions as you like when defining a literal. However, many iterable objects (such as files or generators) only support one-time iteration. If you use *-expansion, the contents will be consumed and the iterable won't produce any more values on subsequent iterations.

A variety of built-in functions accept any iterable as input. Table 2.6 shows some of these operations.

Table 2.6 Functions consuming iterables

Function	Description
`list(s)`	Create a list from s
`tuple(s)`	Create a tuple from s
`set(s)`	Create a set from s
`min(s [,key])`	Minimum item in s
`max(s [,key])`	Maximum item in s
`any(s)`	Return True if any item in s is true
`all(s)`	Return True if all items in s are true
`sum(s [, initial])`	Sum of items with an optional initial value
`sorted(s [, key])`	Create a sorted list

This applies to many other library functions as well—for example, functions in the statistics module.

2.10 Operations on Sequences

A sequence is an iterable container that has a size and allows items to be accessed by an integer index starting at 0. Examples include strings, lists, and tuples. In addition to all of the operations involving iteration, the operators in Table 2.7 can be applied to a sequence.

Table 2.7 Operations on Sequences

Operation	Description
`s + r`	Concatenation
`s * n, n * s`	Makes n copies of s, where n is an integer
`s[i]`	Indexing
`s[i:j]`	Slicing
`s[i:j:stride]`	Extended slicing
`len(s)`	Length

The + operator concatenates two sequences of the same type. For example:

```
>>> a = [3, 4, 5]
>>> b = [6, 7]
>>> a + b
[3, 4, 5, 6, 7]
>>>
```

The s * n operator makes n copies of a sequence. However, these are shallow copies that replicate elements by reference only. Consider the following code:

```
>>> a = [3, 4, 5]
>>> b = [a]
>>> c = 4 * b
>>> c
[[3, 4, 5], [3, 4, 5], [3, 4, 5], [3, 4, 5]]
>>> a[0] = -7
>>> c
[[-7, 4, 5], [-7, 4, 5], [-7, 4, 5], [-7, 4, 5]]
>>>
```

Notice how the change to a modifies every element of the list c. In this case, a reference to the list a was placed in the list b. When b was replicated, four additional references to a were created. Finally, when a was modified, this change was propagated to all the other copies of a. This behavior of sequence multiplication is often not the intent of the programmer. One way to work around the problem is to manually construct the replicated sequence by duplicating the contents of a. Here's an example:

```
a = [ 3, 4, 5 ]
c = [list(a) for _ in range(4)]   # list() makes a copy of a list
```

The indexing operator s[n] returns the nth object from a sequence; s[0] is the first object. Negative indices can be used to fetch characters from the end of a sequence. For example, s[-1] returns the last item. Otherwise, attempts to access elements that are out of range result in an IndexError exception.

The slicing operator s[i:j] extracts a subsequence from s consisting of the elements with index k, where i <= k < j. Both i and j must be integers. If the starting or ending index is omitted, the beginning or end of the sequence is assumed, respectively. Negative indices are allowed and assumed to be relative to the end of the sequence.

The slicing operator may be given an optional stride, s[i:j:stride], that causes the slice to skip elements. However, the behavior is somewhat more subtle. If a stride is supplied, i is the starting index, j is the ending index, and the produced subsequence is the elements s[i], s[i+stride], s[i+2*stride], and so forth until index j is reached (which is not included). The stride may also be negative. If the starting index i is omitted, it is set to the beginning of the sequence if stride is positive or the end of the sequence if stride is negative. If the ending index j is omitted, it is set to the end of the sequence if stride is positive or the beginning of the sequence if stride is negative. Here are some examples:

```
a = [0, 1, 2, 3, 4, 5, 6, 7, 8, 9]

a[2:5]      # [2, 3, 4]
a[:3]       # [0, 1, 2]
a[-3:]      # [7, 8, 9]
a[::2]      # [0, 2, 4, 6, 8 ]
a[::-2]     # [9, 7, 5, 3, 1 ]
a[0:5:2]    # [0, 2, 4]
a[5:0:-2]   # [5, 3, 1]
```

```
a[:5:1]     # [0, 1, 2, 3, 4]
a[:5:-1]    # [9, 8, 7, 6]
a[5::1]     # [5, 6, 7, 8, 9]
a[5::-1]    # [5, 4, 3, 2, 1, 0]
a[5:0:-1]   # [5, 4, 3, 2, 1]
```

Fancy slices may result in code that is hard to understand later. Thus, some judgment is probably warranted. Slices can be named using slice(). For example:

```
firstfive = slice(0, 5)
s = 'hello world'
print(s[firstfive])        # Prints 'hello'
```

2.11   Operations on Mutable Sequences

Strings and tuples are immutable and cannot be modified after creation. The contents of a list or other mutable sequence can be modified in-place with the operators in Table 2.8.

Table 2.8   Mutable Sequence Operations

Operation	Description
s[i] = x	Index assignment
s[i:j] = r	Slice assignment
s[i:j:stride] = r	Extended slice assignment
del s[i]	Deletes an element
del s[i:j]	Deletes a slice
del s[i:j:stride]	Deletes an extended slice

The s[i] = x operator changes element i of a sequence to refer to object x, increasing the reference count of x. Negative indices are relative to the end of the list and attempts to assign a value to an out-of-range index result in an IndexError exception. The slicing assignment operator s[i:j] = r replaces elements k, where i <= k < j, with elements from sequence r. Indices have the same meaning as for slicing. If necessary, the sequence s may be expanded or reduced in size to accommodate all the elements in r. Here's an example:

```
a = [1, 2, 3, 4, 5]
a[1] = 6               # a = [1, 6, 3, 4, 5]
a[2:4] = [10, 11]      # a = [1, 6, 10, 11, 5]
a[3:4] = [-1, -2, -3]  # a = [1, 6, 10, -1, -2, -3, 5]
a[2:] = [0]            # a = [1, 6, 0]
```

A slicing assignment may be supplied with an optional stride argument. However, the behavior is then more restricted in that the argument on the right side must have exactly the same number of elements as the slice that's being replaced. Here's an example:

```
a = [1, 2, 3, 4, 5]
a[1::2] = [10, 11]       # a = [1, 10, 3, 11, 5]
a[1::2] = [30, 40, 50]   # ValueError. Only two elements in slice on left.
```

The del s[i] operator removes element i from a sequence and decrements its reference count. del s[i:j] removes all the elements in a slice. A stride may also be supplied, as in del s[i:j:stride].

The semantics described here apply to the built-in list type. Operations involving sequence slicing is a rich area for customization in third-party packages. You may find that slices on non-list objects have different rules concerning reassignment, deletion, and sharing of objects. For example, the popular numpy package has different slicing semantics than Python lists.

2.12 Operations on Sets

A set is an unordered collection of unique values. The operations in Table 2.9 can be performed on sets.

Table 2.9   Operations on Sets

Operation	Description
s | t	Union of s and t
s & t	Intersection of s and t
s – t	Set difference (items in s, not in t)
s ^ t	Symmetric difference (items not in both s or t)
len(s)	Number of items in the set
item in s, item not in s	Membership test
s.add(item)	Add an item to set s
s.remove(item)	Remove an item from s if it exists (otherwise an error)
s.discard(item)	Discard an item from s if it exists

Here are some examples:

```
>>> a = {'a', 'b', 'c' }
>>> b = {'c', 'd'}
>>> a | b
{'a', 'b', 'c', 'd'}
>>> a & b
>>> {'c' }
>>> a - b
{'a', 'b'}
>>> b - a
{'d'}
```

```
>>> a ^ b
{'a', 'b', 'd'}
>>>
```

Set operations also work on the key-view and item-view objects of dictionaries. For example, to find out which keys two dictionaries have in common, do this:

```
>>> a = { 'x': 1, 'y': 2, 'z': 3 }
>>> b = { 'z': 3, 'w': 4, 'q': 5 }
>>> a.keys() & b.keys()
{ 'z' }
>>>
```

2.13 Operations on Mappings

A mapping is an association between keys and values. The built-in `dict` type is an example. The operations in Table 2.10 may be applied to mappings.

Table 2.10 Operations on Mappings

Operation	Description
x = m[k]	Indexing by key
m[k] = x	Assignment by key
del m[k]	Deletes an item by key
k in m	Membership testing
len(m)	Number of items in the mapping
m.keys()	Return the keys
m.values()	Return the values
m.items()	Return (key, value) pairs

Key values can be any immutable object, such as strings, numbers, and tuples. When using a tuple as the key, you can omit the parentheses and write comma-separated values like this:

```
d = { }
d[1,2,3] = "foo"
d[1,0,3] = "bar"
```

In this case, the key values represent a tuple, making these assignments equivalent to the following:

```
d[(1,2,3)] = "foo"
d[(1,0,3)] = "bar"
```

Using a tuple as a key is a common technique for creating composite keys in a mapping. For example, a key may consist of a "first name" and "last name."

2.14   List, Set, and Dictionary Comprehensions

One of the most common operations involving data is transforming a collection of data into another data structure. For example, here we take all the items in a list, apply an operation, and create a new list:

```
nums = [1, 2, 3, 4, 5]
squares = []
for n in nums:
    nums.append(n * n)
```

Since this kind of operation is so common, it is available as an operator known as a list comprehension. Here is a more compact version of this code:

```
nums = [1, 2, 3, 4, 5]
squares = [n * n for n in nums]
```

It is also possible to apply a filter to the operation:

```
squares = [n * n for n in nums if n > 2]    # [9, 16, 25]
```

The general syntax for a list comprehension is as follows:

```
[expression for item1 in iterable1 if condition1
            for item2 in iterable2 if condition2
            ...
            for itemN in iterableN if conditionN ]
```

This syntax is equivalent to the following code:

```
result = []
for item1 in iterable1:
    if condition1:
        for item2 in iterable2:
            if condition2:
                ...
                for itemN in iterableN:
                    if conditionN:
                        result.append(expression)
```

List comprehensions are a very useful way to process list data of various forms. Here are some practical examples:

```
# Some data (a list of dictionaries)
portfolio = [
   {'name': 'IBM', 'shares': 100, 'price': 91.1 },
   {'name': 'MSFT', 'shares': 50, 'price': 45.67 },
   {'name': 'HPE', 'shares': 75, 'price': 34.51 },
   {'name': 'CAT', 'shares': 60, 'price': 67.89 },
   {'name': 'IBM', 'shares': 200, 'price': 95.25 }
]

# Collect all names ['IBM', 'MSFT', 'HPE', 'CAT', 'IBM' ]
names = [s['name'] for s in portfolio]

# Find all entries with more than 100 shares ['IBM']
more100 = [s['name'] for s in portfolio if s['shares'] > 100 ]

# Find the total shares*price
cost = sum([s['shares']*s['price'] for s in portfolio])

# Collect (name, shares) tuples
name_shares = [ (s['name'], s['shares']) for s in portfolio ]
```

All of the variables used inside a list comprehension are private to the comprehension. You don't need to worry about such variables overwriting other variables with the same name. For example:

```
>>> x = 42
>>> squares = [x*x for x in [1,2,3]]
>>> squares
[1, 4, 9]
>>> x
42
>>>
```

Instead of creating a list, you can also create a set by changing the brackets into curly braces. This is known as a set comprehension. A set comprehension will give you a set of distinct values. For example:

```
# Set comprehension
names = { s['name'] for s in portfolio }
# names = { 'IBM', 'MSFT', 'HPE', 'CAT' }
```

If you specify key:value pairs, you'll create a dictionary instead. This is known as a dictionary comprehension. For example:

```
prices = { s['name']:s['price'] for s in portfolio }
# prices = { 'IBM': 95.25, 'MSFT': 45.67, 'HPE': 34.51, 'CAT': 67.89 }
```

When creating sets and dictionaries, be aware that later entries might overwrite earlier entries. For example, in the `prices` dictionary you get the last price for `'IBM'`. The first price is lost.

Within a comprehension, it's not possible to include any sort of exception handling. If this is a concern, consider wrapping exceptions with a function, as shown here:

```
def toint(x):
    try:
        return int(x)
    except ValueError:
        return None


values = [ '1', '2', '-4', 'n/a', '-3', '5' ]
data1 = [ toint(x) for x in values ]
# data1 = [1, 2, -4, None, -3, 5]

data2 = [ toint(x) for x in values if toint(x) is not None ]
# data2 = [1, 2, -4, -3, 5]
```

The double evaluation of `toint(x)` in the last example can be avoided by using the `:=` operator. For example:

```
data3 = [ v for x in values if (v:=toint(x)) is not None ]
# data3 = [1, 2, -4, -3, 5]

data4 = [ v for x in values if (v:=toint(x)) is not None and v >= 0 ]
# data4 = [1, 2, 5]
```

2.15   Generator Expressions

A generator expression is an object that carries out the same computation as a list comprehension but produces the result iteratively. The syntax is the same as for a list comprehension except that you use parentheses instead of square brackets. Here's an example:

```
nums = [1,2,3,4]
squares = (x*x for x in nums)
```

Unlike a list comprehension, a generator expression does not actually create a list or immediately evaluate the expression inside the parentheses. Instead, it creates a generator object that produces the values on demand via iteration. If you look at the result of the above example, you'll see the following:

```
>>> squares
<generator object at 0x590a8>
>>> next(squares)
```

```
1
>>> next(squares)
4
...
>>> for n in squares:
...     print(n)
9
16
>>>
```

A generator expression can only be used once. If you try to iterate a second time, you'll get nothing:

```
>>> for n in squares:
...     print(n)
...
>>>
```

The difference between list comprehensions and generator expressions is important but subtle. With a list comprehension, Python actually creates a list that contains the resulting data. With a generator expression, Python creates a generator that merely knows how to produce data on demand. In certain applications, this can greatly improve performance and memory use. Here's an example:

```
# Read a file
f = open('data.txt')                        # Open a file
lines = (t.strip() for t in f)              # Read lines, strip
                                            # trailing/leading whitespace
comments = (t for t in lines if t[0] == '#') # All comments
for c in comments:
    print(c)
```

In this example, the generator expression that extracts lines and strips whitespace does not actually read and hold the entire file in memory. The same is true of the expression that extracts comments. Instead, the lines of the file are read one-by-one when the program starts iterating in the for loop that follows. During this iteration, the lines of the file are produced upon demand and filtered accordingly. In fact, at no time will the entire file be loaded into memory during this process. This is therefore a highly efficient way to extract comments from a gigabyte-sized Python source file.

Unlike a list comprehension, a generator expression does not create an object that works like a sequence. It can't be indexed, and none of the usual list operations (such as append()) will work. However, the items produced by a generator expression can be converted into a list using list():

```
clist = list(comments)
```

When passed as a single function argument, one set of parentheses can be removed. For example, the following statements are equivalent:

```
sum((x*x for x in values))
sum(x*x for x in values)      # Extra parens removed
```

In both cases, a generator (x*x for x in values) is created and passed to the sum() function.

2.16   The Attribute (.) Operator

The dot (.) operator is used to access the attributes of an object. Here's an example:

```
foo.x = 3
print(foo.y)
a = foo.bar(3,4,5)
```

More than one dot operator can appear in a single expression, for example foo.y.a.b. The dot operator can also be applied to the intermediate results of functions, as in a = foo.bar(3,4,5).spam. Stylistically, however, it is not so common for programs to create long chains of attribute lookups.

2.17   The Function Call () Operator

The f(args) operator is used to make a function call on f. Each argument to a function is an expression. Prior to calling the function, all of the argument expressions are fully evaluated from left to right. This is known as applicative order evaluation. More information about functions can be found in Chapter 5.

2.18   Order of Evaluation

Table 2.11 lists the order of operation (precedence rules) for Python operators. All operators except the power (**) operator are evaluated from left to right and are listed in the table from highest to lowest precedence. That is, operators listed first in the table are evaluated before operators listed later. Operators included together within subsections, such as x * y, x / y, x // y, x @ y, and x % y, have equal precedence.

The order of evaluation in Table 2.11 does not depend on the types of x and y. So, even though user-defined objects can redefine individual operators, it is not possible to customize the underlying evaluation order, precedence, and associativity rules.

Table 2.11   Order of Evaluation (Highest Precedence to Lowest)

Operator	Name
(...), [...], {...}	Tuple, list, and dictionary creation
s[i], s[i:j]	Indexing and slicing
s.attr	Attribute lookup
f(...)	Function calls
+x, -x, ~x	Unary operators
x ** y	Power (right associative)
x * y, x / y, x // y, x % y, x @ y	Multiplication, division, floor division, modulo, matrix multiplication
x + y, x - y	Addition, subtraction
x << y, x >> y	Bit-shifting
x & y	Bitwise and
x ^ y	Bitwise exclusive or
x | y	Bitwise or
x < y, x <= y, x > y, x >= y, x == y, x !=y, x is y, x is not y, x in y, x not in y	Comparison, identity, and sequence membership tests
not x	Logical negation
x and y	Logical and
x or y	Logical or
lambda args: expr	Anonymous function
expr if expr else expr	Conditional expression
name := expr	Assignment expression

A common confusion with precedence rules is when bitwise-and (&) and bitwise-or (|) operators are used to mean logical-and (and) and logical-or (or). For example:

```
>>> a = 10
>>> a <= 10 and 1 < a
True
>>> a <= 10 & 1 < a
False
>>>
```

The latter expression gets evaluated as a <= (10 & 1) < a or a <= 0 < a. You can fix it by adding parentheses:

```
>>> (a <= 10) & (1 < a)
True
>>>
```

This might seem like an esoteric edge case, but it arises with some frequency in data-oriented packages such as numpy and pandas. The logical operators and and or can't be customized so the bitwise operators are used instead—even though they have a higher precedence level and evaluate differently when used in Boolean relations.

2.19 Final Words: The Secret Life of Data

One of the most frequent uses of Python is in applications involving data manipulation and analysis. Here, Python provides a kind of "domain language" for thinking about your problem. The built-in operators and expressions are at the core of that language and everything else builds from it. Thus, once you build a kind of intuition around Python's built-in objects and operations, you will find that your intuition applies everywhere.

As an example, suppose you're working with a database and you want to iterate over the records returned by a query. Chances are, you will use the for statement to do just that. Or, suppose you're working with numeric arrays and want to perform element-by-element mathematics on arrays. You might think that the standard math operators would work— and your intuition would be correct. Or, suppose you're using a library to fetch data over HTTP and you want to access the contents of the HTTP headers. There's a good chance that data will be presented in a way that looks like a dictionary.

More information about Python's internal protocols and how to customize them is given in Chapter 4.

3

Program Structure and Control Flow

This chapter covers the details of program structure and control flow. Topics include conditionals, looping, exceptions, and context managers.

3.1 Program Structure and Execution

Python programs are structured as a sequence of statements. All language features, including variable assignment, expressions, function definitions, classes, and module imports, are statements that have equal status with all other statements—meaning that any statement can be placed almost anywhere in a program (although certain statements such as `return` can only appear inside a function). For example, this code defines two different versions of a function inside a conditional:

```
if debug:
    def square(x):
        if not isinstance(x,float):
            raise TypeError('Expected a float')
        return x * x
else:
    def square(x):
        return x * x
```

When loading source files, the interpreter executes statements in the order they appear until there are no more statements to execute. This execution model applies both to files you run as the main program and to library files that are loaded via `import`.

3.2 Conditional Execution

The `if`, `else`, and `elif` statements control conditional code execution. The general format of a conditional statement is

```
if expression:
     statements
elif expression:
     statements
elif expression:
     statements
...
else:
     statements
```

If no action is to be taken, you can omit both the `else` and `elif` clauses of a conditional. Use the `pass` statement if no statements exist for a particular clause:

```
if expression:
     pass              # To do: please implement
else:
     statements
```

3.3 Loops and Iteration

You implement loops using the `for` and `while` statements. Here's an example:

```
while expression:
     statements


for i in s:
     statements
```

The `while` statement executes statements until the associated expression evaluates to false. The `for` statement iterates over all the elements of s until no more elements are available. The `for` statement works with any object that supports iteration. This includes the built-in sequence types such as lists, tuples, and strings, but also any object that implements the iterator protocol.

In the statement `for i in s`, the variable i is known as the iteration variable. On each iteration of the loop, it receives a new value from s. The scope of the iteration variable is not private to the `for` statement. If a previously defined variable has the same name, that value will be overwritten. Moreover, the iteration variable retains the last value after the loop has completed.

If the elements produced by iteration are iterables of identical size, you can unpack their values into separate iteration variables using a statement such as this:

```
s = [ (1, 2, 3), (4, 5, 6) ]


for x, y, z in s:
     statements
```

In this example, s must contain or produce iterables, each with three elements. On each iteration, the contents of the variables x, y, and z are assigned the items of the corresponding iterable. Although it is most common to see this used when s is a sequence of tuples, unpacking works when the items in s are any kind of iterable, including lists, generators, and strings.

Sometimes a throw-away variable such as _ is used while unpacking. For example:

```
for x, _, z in s:
    statements
```

In this example, a value is still placed into the _ variable, but the variable's name implies that it's not interesting or of use in the statements that follow.

If the items produced by an iterable have varying sizes, you can use wildcard unpacking to place multiple values into a variable. For example:

```
s = [ (1, 2), (3, 4, 5), (6, 7, 8, 9) ]

for x, y, *extra in s:
    statements         # x = 1, y = 2, extra = []
                       # x = 3, y = 4, extra = [5]
                       # x = 6, y = 7, extra = [8, 9]
                       # ...
```

In this example, at least two values x and y are required, but *extra receives any extra values that might also be present. These values are always placed in a list. At most, only one starred variable can appear in a single unpacking, but it can appear in any position. So, both of these variants are legal:

```
for *first, x, y in s:
    ...

for x, *middle, y in s:
    ...
```

When looping, it is sometimes useful to keep track of a numerical index in addition to the data values. Here's an example:

```
i = 0
for x in s:
    statements
    i += 1
```

Python provides a built-in function, enumerate(), that can be used to simplify this code:

```
for i, x in enumerate(s):
    statements
```

`enumerate(s)` creates an iterator that produces tuples `(0, s[0])`, `(1, s[1])`, `(2, s[2])`, and so on. A different starting value for the count can be provided with the `start` keyword argument to `enumerate()`:

```
for i, x in enumerate(s, start=100):
    statements
```

In this case, tuples of the form `(100, s[0])`, `(101, s[1])`, and so on will be produced.

Another common looping problem is iterating in parallel over two or more iterables—for example, writing a loop where you take items from different sequences on each iteration:

```
# s and t are two sequences
i = 0
while i < len(s) and i < len(t):
    x = s[i]        # Take an item from s
    y = t[i]        # Take an item from t
    statements
    i += 1
```

This code can be simplified using the `zip()` function. For example:

```
# s and t are two sequences
for x, y in zip(s, t):
    statements
```

`zip(s, t)` combines iterables `s` and `t` into an iterable of tuples `(s[0], t[0])`, `(s[1], t[1])`, `(s[2], t[2])`, and so forth, stopping with the shortest of `s` and `t` should they be of unequal length. The result of `zip()` is an iterator that produces the results when iterated. If you want the result converted to a list, use `list(zip(s, t))`.

To break out of a loop, use the `break` statement. For example, this code reads lines of text from a file until an empty line of text is encountered:

```
with open('foo.txt') as file:
    for line in file:
        stripped = line.strip()
        if not stripped:
            break            # A blank line, stop reading
        # process the stripped line
        ...
```

To jump to the next iteration of a loop (skipping the remainder of the loop body), use the `continue` statement. This statement is useful when reversing a test and indenting another level would make the program too deeply nested or unnecessarily complicated. As an example, the following loop skips all of the blank lines in a file:

```
with open('foo.txt') as file:
    for line in file:
        stripped = line.strip()
        if not stripped:
            continue       # Skip the blank line
        # process the stripped line
        ...
```

The break and continue statements apply only to the innermost loop being executed. If you need to break out of a deeply nested loop structure, you can use an exception. Python doesn't provide a "goto" statement. You can also attach the else statement to loop constructs, as in the following example:

```
# for-else
with open('foo.txt') as file:
    for line in file:
        stripped = line.strip()
        if not stripped:
            break
        # process the stripped line
        ...
    else:
        raise RuntimeError('Missing section separator')
```

The else clause of a loop executes only if the loop runs to completion. This either occurs immediately (if the loop wouldn't execute at all) or after the last iteration. If the loop is terminated early using the break statement, the else clause is skipped.

The primary use case for the looping else clause is in code that iterates over data but needs to set or check some kind of flag or condition if the loop breaks prematurely. For example, if you didn't use else, the previous code might have to be rewritten with a flag variable as follows:

```
found_separator = False

with open('foo.txt') as file:
    for line in file:
        stripped = line.strip()
        if not stripped:
            found_separator = True
            break
        # process the stripped line
        ...
    if not found_separator:
        raise RuntimeError('Missing section separator')
```

3.4   Exceptions

Exceptions indicate errors and break out of the normal control flow of a program. An exception is raised using the `raise` statement. The general format of the `raise` statement is `raise Exception([value])`, where `Exception` is the exception type and `value` is an optional value giving specific details about the exception. Here's an example:

```
raise RuntimeError('Unrecoverable Error')
```

To catch an exception, use the `try` and `except` statements, as shown here:

```
try:
    file = open('foo.txt', 'rt')
except FileNotFoundError as e:
    statements
```

When an exception occurs, the interpreter stops executing statements in the `try` block and looks for an `except` clause that matches the exception type that has occurred. If one is found, control is passed to the first statement in the except clause. After the except clause is executed, control continues with the first statement that appears after the entire `try-except` block.

It is not necessary for a `try` statement to match all possible exceptions that might occur. If no matching `except` clause can be found, an exception continues to propagate and might be caught in a different `try-except` block that can actually handle the exception elsewhere. As a matter of programming style, you should only catch exceptions from which your code can actually recover. If recovery is not possible, it's often better to let the exception propagate.

If an exception works its way up to the top level of a program without being caught, the interpreter aborts with an error message.

If the `raise` statement is used by itself, the last exception generated is raised again. This works only while handling a previously raised exception. For example:

```
try:
    file = open('foo.txt', 'rt')
except FileNotFoundError:
    print("Well, that didn't work.")
    raise        # Reraises current exception
```

Each `except` clause may be used with an `as var` modifier that gives the name of a variable into which an instance of the exception type is placed if an exception occurs. Exception handlers can examine this value to find out more about the cause of the exception. For example, you can use `isinstance()` to check the exception type.

Exceptions have a few standard attributes that might be useful in code that needs to perform further actions in response to an error:

`e.args`
> The tuple of arguments supplied when raising the exception. In most cases, this is a one-item tuple with a string describing the error. For `OSError` exceptions, the value

is a 2-tuple or 3-tuple containing an integer error number, string error message, and an optional filename.

e.__cause__

Previous exception if the exception was intentionally raised in response to handling another exception. See the later section on chained exceptions.

e.__context__

Previous exception if the exception was raised while handling another exception.

e.__traceback__

Stack traceback object associated with the exception.

The variable used to hold an exception value is only accessible inside the associated except block. Once control leaves the block, the variable becomes undefined. For example:

```
try:
    int('N/A')                  # Raises ValueError
except ValueError as e:
    print('Failed:', e)


print(e)     # Fails -> NameError. 'e' not defined.
```

Multiple exception-handling blocks can be specified using multiple except clauses:

```
try:
    do something
except TypeError as e:
    # Handle Type error
    ...
except ValueError as e:
    # Handle Value error
    ...
```

A single handler clause can catch multiple exception types like this:

```
try:
    do something
except (TypeError, ValueError) as e:
    # Handle Type or Value errors
    ...
```

To ignore an exception, use the pass statement as follows:

```
try:
    do something
except ValueError:
    pass                 # Do nothing (shrug)
```

Silently ignoring errors is often dangerous and a source of hard-to-find mistakes. Even if ignored, it is often wise to optionally report the error in a log or some other place where you can inspect it later.

To catch all exceptions except those related to program exit, use `Exception` like this:

```
try:
    do something
except Exception as e:
    print(f'An error occurred : {e!r}')
```

When catching all exceptions, you should take great care to report accurate error information to the user. For example, in the previous code, an error message and the associated exception value are being printed. If you don't include any information about the exception value, it can make it very difficult to debug code that is failing for reasons you don't expect.

The `try` statement also supports an `else` clause, which must follow the last `except` clause. This code is executed if the code in the `try` block doesn't raise an exception. Here's an example:

```
try:
    file = open('foo.txt', 'rt')
except FileNotFoundError as e:
    print(f'Unable to open foo : {e}')
    data = ''
else:
    data = file.read()
    file.close()
```

The `finally` statement defines a cleanup action that must execute regardless of what happens in a `try-except` block. Here's an example:

```
file = open('foo.txt', 'rt')
try:
    # Do some stuff
    ...
finally:
    file.close()
    # File closed regardless of what happened
```

The `finally` clause isn't used to catch errors. Rather, it's used for code that must always be executed, regardless of whether an error occurs. If no exception is raised, the code in the `finally` clause is executed immediately after the code in the `try` block. If an exception occurs, a matching `except` block (if any) is executed first and then control is passed to the first statement of the `finally` clause. If, after this code has executed, an exception is still pending, that exception is reraised to be caught by another exception handler.

3.4.1 The Exception Hierarchy

One challenge of working with exceptions is managing the vast number of exceptions that might potentially occur in your program. For example, there are more than 60 built-in exceptions alone. Factor in the rest of the standard library and it turns into hundreds of possible exceptions. Moreover, there is often no way to easily determine in advance what kind of exceptions any portion of code might raise. Exceptions aren't recorded as part of a function's calling signature nor is there any sort of compiler to verify correct exception handling in your code. As a result, exception handling can sometimes feel haphazard and disorganized.

It helps to realize that exceptions are organized into a hierarchy via inheritance. Instead of targeting specific errors, it might be easier to focus on more general categories of errors. For example, consider the different errors that might arise when looking values up in a container:

```
try:
    item = items[index]
except IndexError:       # Raised if items is a sequence
    ...
except KeyError:         # Raised if items is a mapping
    ...
```

Instead of writing code to handle two highly specific exceptions, it might be easier to do this:

```
try:
    item = items[index]
except LookupError:
    ...
```

LookupError is a class that represents a higher-level grouping of exceptions. IndexError and KeyError both inherit from LookupError, so this except clause would catch either one. Yet, LookupError isn't so broad as to include errors unrelated to the lookup.

Table 3.1 describes the most common categories of built-in exceptions.

The BaseException class is rarely used directly in exception handling because it matches all possible exceptions whatsoever. This includes special exceptions that affect the control flow such as SystemExit, KeyboardInterrupt, and StopIteration. Catching these is rarely what you want. Instead, all normal program-related errors inherit from Exception. ArithmeticError is the base for all math-related errors such as ZeroDivisionError, FloatingPointError, and OverflowError. ImportError is a base for all import-related errors. LookupError is a base for all container lookup-related errors. OSError is a base for all errors originating from the operating system and environment. OSError encompasses a wide range of exceptions related to files, network connections, permissions, pipes, timeouts, and more. The ValueError exception is commonly raised when a bad input value is given to an operation. UnicodeError is a subclass of ValueError grouping all Unicode-related encoding and decoding errors.

Table 3.1   Exception Categories

Exception Class	Description
BaseException	The root class for all exceptions
Exception	Base class for all program-related errors
ArithmeticError	Base class for all math-related errors
ImportError	Base class for import-related errors
LookupError	Base class for all container lookup errors
OSError	Base class for all system-related errors. IOError and EnvironmentError are aliases.
ValueError	Base class for value-related errors, including Unicode
UnicodeError	Base class for a Unicode string encoding-related errors

Table 3.2 shows some common built-in exceptions that inherit directly from Exception but aren't part of a larger exception group.

Table 3.2   Other Built-in Exceptions

Exception Class	Description
AssertionError	Failed assert statement
AttributeError	Bad attribute lookup on an object
EOFError	End of file
MemoryError	Recoverable out-of-memory error
NameError	Name not found in the local or global namespace
NotImplementedError	Unimplemented feature
RuntimeError	A generic "something bad happened" error
TypeError	Operation applied to an object of the wrong type
UnboundLocalError	Usage of a local variable before a value is assigned

3.4.2   Exceptions and Control Flow

Normally, exceptions are reserved for the handling of errors. However, a few exceptions are used to alter the control flow. These exceptions, shown in Table 3.3, inherit from BaseException directly.

Table 3.3   Exceptions Used for Control Flow

Exception Class	Description
SystemExit	Raised to indicate program exit
KeyboardInterrupt	Raised when a program is interrupted via Control-C
StopIteration	Raised to signal the end of iteration

The `SystemExit` exception is used to make a program terminate on purpose. As an argument, you can either provide an integer exit code or a string message. If a string is given, it is printed to `sys.stderr` and the program is terminated with an exit code of 1. Here is a typical example:

```
import sys

if len(sys.argv) != 2:
    raise SystemExit(f'Usage: {sys.argv[0]} filename)

filename = sys.argv[1]
```

The `KeyboardInterrupt` exception is raised when the program receives a `SIGINT` signal (typically by pressing Control-C in a terminal). This exception is a bit unusual in that it is asynchronous—meaning that it could occur at almost any time and on any statement in your program. The default behavior of Python is to simply terminate when this happens. If you want to control the delivery of `SIGINT`, the `signal` library module can be used (see Chapter 9).

The `StopIteration` exception is part of the iteration protocol and signals the end of iteration.

3.4.3 Defining New Exceptions

All the built-in exceptions are defined in terms of classes. To create a new exception, create a new class definition that inherits from `Exception`, such as the following:

```
class NetworkError(Exception):
    pass
```

To use your new exception, use the `raise` statement as follows:

```
raise NetworkError('Cannot find host')
```

When raising an exception, the optional values supplied with the `raise` statement are used as the arguments to the exception's class constructor. Most of the time, this is a string containing some kind of error message. However, user-defined exceptions can be written to take one or more exception values, as shown in this example:

```
class DeviceError(Exception):
    def __init__(self, errno, msg):
        self.args = (errno, msg)
        self.errno = errno
        self.errmsg = msg

# Raises an exception (multiple arguments)
raise DeviceError(1, 'Not Responding')
```

When you create a custom exception class that redefines __init__(), it is important to assign a tuple containing the arguments of __init__() to the attribute self.args as shown. This attribute is used when printing exception traceback messages. If you leave it undefined, users won't be able to see any useful information about the exception when an error occurs.

Exceptions can be organized into a hierarchy using inheritance. For instance, the NetworkError exception defined earlier could serve as a base class for a variety of more specific errors. Here's an example:

```python
class HostnameError(NetworkError):
    pass

class TimeoutError(NetworkError):
    pass

def error1():
    raise HostnameError('Unknown host')

def error2():
    raise TimeoutError('Timed out')

try:
    error1()
except NetworkError as e:
    if type(e) is HostnameError:
        # Perform special actions for this kind of error
        ...
```

In this case, the except NetworkError clause catches any exception derived from NetworkError. To find the specific type of error that was raised, examine the type of the execution value with type().

3.4.4 Chained Exceptions

Sometimes, in response to an exception, you might want to raise a different exception. To do this, raise a chained exception:

```python
class ApplicationError(Exception):
    pass

def do_something():
    x = int('N/A')       # raises ValueError

def spam():
    try:
        do_something()
```

```
    except Exception as e:
        raise ApplicationError('It failed') from e
```

If an uncaught ApplicationError occurs, you will get a message that includes both exceptions. For example:

```
>>> spam()
Traceback (most recent call last):
  File "c.py", line 9, in spam
    do_something()
  File "c.py", line 5, in do_something
    x = int('N/A')
ValueError: invalid literal for int() with base 10: 'N/A'

The above exception was the direct cause of the following exception:

Traceback (most recent call last):
  File "<stdin>", line 1, in <module>
  File "c.py", line 11, in spam
    raise ApplicationError('It failed') from e
__main__.ApplicationError: It failed
>>>
```

If you catch an ApplicationError, the __cause__ attribute of the resulting exception will contain the other exception. For example:

```
try:
    spam()
except ApplicationError as e:
    print('It failed. Reason:', e.__cause__)
```

If you want to raise a new exception without including the chain of other exceptions, raise an error from None like this:

```
def spam():
    try:
        do_something()
    except Exception as e:
        raise ApplicationError('It failed') from None
```

A programming mistake that appears in an except block will also result in a chained exception, but that works in a slightly different way. For example, suppose you have some buggy code like this:

```
def spam():
    try:
        do_something()
```

```
    except Exception as e:
        print('It failed:', err)      # err undefined (typo)
```

The resulting exception traceback message is slightly different:

```
>>> spam()
Traceback (most recent call last):
  File "d.py", line 9, in spam
    do_something()
  File "d.py", line 5, in do_something
    x = int('N/A')
ValueError: invalid literal for int() with base 10: 'N/A'

During handling of the above exception, another exception occurred:

Traceback (most recent call last):
  File "<stdin>", line 1, in <module>
  File "d.py", line 11, in spam
    print('It failed. Reason:', err)
NameError: name 'err' is not defined
>>>
```

If an unexpected exception is raised while handling another exception, the __context__ attribute (instead of __cause__) holds information about the exception that was being handled when the error occurred. For example:

```
try:
    spam()
except Exception as e:
    print('It failed. Reason:', e)
    if e.__context__:
        print('While handling:', e.__context__)
```

There is an important distinction between expected and unexpected exceptions in exception chains. In the first example, the code was written so that the possibility of an exception was anticipated. For example, code was explicitly wrapped in a try-except block:

```
try:
    do_something()
except Exception as e:
    raise ApplicationError('It failed') from e
```

In the second case, there was a programming mistake in the except block:

```
try:
    do_something()
```

```
except Exception as e:
    print('It failed:', err)      # err undefined
```

The difference between these two cases is subtle but important. That is why exception chaining information is placed into either the __cause__ or the __context__ attribute. The __cause__ attribute is reserved for when you're expecting the possibility of a failure. The __context__ attribute is set in both cases, but would be the only source of information for an unexpected exception raised while handling another exception.

3.4.5 Exception Tracebacks

Exceptions have an associated stack traceback that provides information about where an error occurred. The traceback is stored in the __traceback__ attribute of an exception. For the purposes of reporting or debugging, you might want to produce the traceback message yourself. The traceback module can be used to do this. For example:

```
import traceback

try:
    spam()
except Exception as e:
    tblines = traceback.format_exception(type(e), e, e.__traceback__)
    tbmsg = ''.join(tblines)
    print('It failed:')
    print(tbmsg)
```

In this code, format_exception() produces a list of strings containing the output Python would normally produce in a traceback message. As input, you provide the exception type, value, and traceback.

3.4.6 Exception Handling Advice

Exception handling is one of the most difficult things to get right in larger programs. However, there are a few rules of thumb that make it easier.

The first rule is to not catch exceptions that can't be handled at that specific location in the code. Consider a function like this:

```
def read_data(filename):
    with open(filename, 'rt') as file:
        rows = []
        for line in file:
            row = line.split()
            rows.append((row[0], int(row[1]), float(row[2])))
    return rows
```

Suppose the open() function fails due to a bad filename. Is this an error that should be caught with a try-except statement in this function? Probably not. If the caller gives a bad filename, there is no sensible way to recover. There is no file to open, no data to read, and nothing else that's possible. It's better to let the operation fail and report an exception back to the caller. Avoiding an error check in read_data() doesn't mean that the exception would never be handled anywhere—it just means that it's not the role of read_data() to do it. Perhaps the code that prompted a user for a filename would handle this exception.

This advice might seem contrary to the experience of programmers accustomed to languages that rely upon special error codes or wrapped result types. In those languages, great care is made to make sure you always check return codes for errors on all operations. You don't do this in Python. If an operation can fail and there's nothing you can do to recover, it's better to just let it fail. The exception will propagate to upper levels of the program where it is usually the responsibility of some other code to handle it.

On the other hand, a function might be able to recover from bad data. For example:

```python
def read_data(filename):
    with open(filename, 'rt') as file:
        rows = []
        for line in file:
            row = line.split()
            try:
                rows.append((row[0], int(row[1]), float(row[2])))
            except ValueError as e:
                print('Bad row:', row)
                print('Reason:', e)
    return rows
```

When catching errors, try to make your except clauses as narrow as reasonable. The above code could have been written to catch all errors by using except Exception. However, doing that would make the code catch legitimate programming errors that probably shouldn't be ignored. Don't do that—it will make debugging difficult.

Finally, if you're explicitly raising an exception, consider making your own exception types. For example:

```python
class ApplicationError(Exception):
    pass


class UnauthorizedUserError(ApplicationError):
    pass


def spam():
    ...
    raise UnauthorizedUserError('Go away')
    ...
```

One of the more challenging problems in large code bases is assigning blame for program failures. If you make your own exceptions, you'll be better able to distinguish between intentionally raised errors and legitimate programming mistakes. If your program crashes with some kind of `ApplicationError` defined above, you'll know immediately why that error got raised—because you wrote the code to do it. On the other hand, if the program crashes with one of Python's built-in exceptions (such as `TypeError` or `ValueError`), that might indicate a more serious problem.

3.5 Context Managers and the `with` Statement

Proper management of system resources such as files, locks, and connections is often a tricky problem when combined with exceptions. For example, a raised exception can cause control flow to bypass statements responsible for releasing critical resources, such as a lock.

The `with` statement allows a series of statements to execute inside a runtime context that is controlled by an object serving as a context manager. Here is an example:

```
with open('debuglog', 'wt') as file:
    file.write('Debugging\n')
    statements
    file.write('Done\n')

import threading
lock = threading.Lock()
with lock:
    # Critical section
    statements
    # End critical section
```

In the first example, the `with` statement automatically causes the opened file to be closed when the control flow leaves the block of statements that follow. In the second example, the `with` statement automatically acquires and releases a lock when control enters and leaves the block of statements that follow.

The `with obj` statement allows the object `obj` to manage what happens when the control flow enters and exits the associated block of statements that follow. When the `with obj` statement executes, it calls the method `obj.__enter__()` to signal that a new context is being entered. When control flow leaves the context, the method `obj.__exit__(type, value, traceback)` executes. If no exception has been raised, the three arguments to `__exit__()` are all set to `None`. Otherwise, they contain the type, value, and traceback associated with the exception that has caused the control flow to leave the context. If the `__exit__()` method returns `True`, it indicates that the raised exception was handled and should no longer be propagated. Returning `None` or `False` will cause the exception to propagate.

The `with obj` statement accepts an optional `as var` specifier. If given, the value returned by `obj.__enter__()` is placed into `var`. This value is commonly the same as `obj` because this allows an object to be constructed and used as a context manager in the same step. For example, consider this class:

```
class Manager:
    def __init__(self, x):
        self.x = x

    def yow(self):
        pass

    def __enter__(self):
        return self

    def __exit__(self, ty, val, tb):
        pass
```

With it, you can create and use an instance as a context manager in a single step:

```
with Manager(42) as m:
    m.yow()
```

Here is a more interesting example involving list transactions:

```
class ListTransaction:
    def __init__(self,thelist):
        self.thelist = thelist

    def __enter__(self):
        self.workingcopy = list(self.thelist)
        return self.workingcopy

    def __exit__(self, type, value, tb):
        if type is None:
            self.thelist[:] = self.workingcopy
        return False
```

This class allows you to make a sequence of modifications to an existing list. However, the modifications only take effect if no exceptions occur. Otherwise, the original list is left unmodified. For example:

```
items = [1,2,3]

with ListTransaction(items) as working:
    working.append(4)
    working.append(5)
print(items)         # Produces [1,2,3,4,5]

try:
    with ListTransaction(items) as working:
        working.append(6)
```

```
        working.append(7)
        raise RuntimeError("We're hosed!")
except RuntimeError:
    pass

print(items)   # Produces [1,2,3,4,5]
```

The `contextlib` standard library module contains functionality related to more advanced uses of context managers. If you find yourself regularly creating context managers, it might be worth a look.

3.6 Assertions and __debug__

The `assert` statement can introduce debugging code into a program. The general form of `assert` is

```
assert test [, msg]
```

where `test` is an expression that should evaluate to `True` or `False`. If `test` evaluates to `False`, `assert` raises an `AssertionError` exception with the optional message `msg` supplied to the `assert` statement. Here's an example:

```
def write_data(file, data):
    assert file, 'write_data: file not defined!'
    ...
```

The `assert` statement should not be used for code that must be executed to make the program correct, because it won't be executed if Python is run in optimized mode (specified with the -O option to the interpreter). In particular, it's an error to use `assert` to check user input or the success of some important operation. Instead, `assert` statements are used to check invariants that should always be true; if one is violated, it represents a bug in the program, not an error by the user.

For example, if the function `write_data()`, shown previously, were intended for use by an end user, the `assert` statement should be replaced by a conventional `if` statement and the desired error handling.

A common use of `assert` is in testing. For example, you might use it to include a minimal test of a function:

```
def factorial(n):
    result = 1
    while n > 1:
        result *= n
        n -= 1
    return result

assert factorial(5) == 120
```

The purpose of such a test is not to be exhaustive, but to serve as a kind of "smoke test." If something obvious is broken in the function, the code will crash immediately with a failed assertion upon import.

Assertions can also be useful in specifying a kind of programming contract on expected inputs and outputs. For example:

```python
def factorial(n):
    assert n > 0, "must supply a positive value"
    result = 1
    while n > 1:
        result *= n
        n -= 1
    return result
```

Again, this is not meant to check for user input. It's more of a check for internal program consistency. If some other code tries to compute negative factorials, the assertion will fail and point at the offending code so that you could debug it.

3.7 Final Words

Although Python supports a variety of different programming styles involving functions and objects, the fundamental model of program execution is that of imperative programming. That is, programs are made up of statements that execute one after the other in the order they appear within a source file. There are only three basic control flow constructs: the `if` statement, the `while` loop, and the `for` loop. There are few mysteries when it comes to understanding how Python executes your program.

By far the most complicated and potentially error-prone feature is the exceptions. In fact, much of this chapter focused on how to properly think about exception handling. Even if you follow this advice, exceptions remain a delicate part of designing libraries, frameworks, and APIs. Exceptions can also play havoc with proper management of resources—this is a problem addressed via the use of context managers and the `with` statement.

Not covered in this chapter are the techniques that can be used to customize almost every Python language feature—including the built-in operators and even aspects of the control flow described in this chapter. Although Python programs often appear superficially simple in structure, a surprising amount of magic can often be at work behind the scenes. Much of this is described in the next chapter.

4

Objects, Types, and Protocols

Python programs manipulate objects of various types. There are a variety of built-in types such as numbers, strings, lists, sets, and dictionaries. In addition, you can make your own types using classes. This chapter describes the underlying Python object model and mechanisms that make all objects work. Particular attention is given to the "protocols" that define the core behavior of various objects.

4.1 Essential Concepts

Every piece of data stored in a program is an object. Each object has an identity, a type (also known as its class), and a value. For example, when you write `a = 42`, an integer object is created with the value of 42. The identity of the object is a number representing its location in memory; `a` is a label that refers to this specific location although the label is not part of the object itself.

The type of an object, also known as the object's class, defines the object's internal data representation as well as supported methods. When an object of a particular type is created, that object is called an *instance* of that type. After an instance is created, its identity does not change. If an object's value can be modified, the object is said to be mutable. If the value cannot be modified, the object is said to be immutable. An object that holds references to other objects is said to be a container.

Objects are characterized by their attributes. An attribute is a value associated with an object that is accessed using the dot operator (.). An attribute might be a simple data value such as a number. However, an attribute could also be a function that is invoked to carry out some operation. Such functions are called methods. The following example illustrates access to attributes:

```
a = 34              # Create an integer
n = a.numerator     # Get the numerator (an attribute)

b = [1, 2, 3]       # Create a list
b.append(7)         # Add a new element using the append method
```

Objects may also implement various operators, such as the + operator. For example:

```
c = a + 10          # c = 34 + 10
d = b + [4, 5]      # d = [1, 2, 3, 7, 4, 5]
```

Although operators use a different syntax, they are ultimately mapped to methods. For example, writing a + 10 executes a method a.__add__(10).

4.2 Object Identity and Type

The built-in function id() returns the identity of an object. The identity is an integer that usually corresponds to the object's location in memory. The is and is not operators compare the identities of two objects. type() returns the type of an object. Here's an example of different ways you might compare two objects:

```
# Compare two objects
def compare(a, b):
    if a is b:
        print('same object')
    if a == b:
        print('same value')
    if type(a) is type(b):
        print('same type')
```

Here is how this function works:

```
>>> a = [1, 2, 3]
>>> b = [1, 2, 3]
>>> compare(a, a)
same object
same value
same type
>>> compare(a, b)
same value
same type
>>> compare(a, [4,5,6])
same type
>>>
```

The type of an object is itself an object, known as object's class. This object is uniquely defined and is always the same for all instances of a given type. Classes usually have names (list, int, dict, and so on) that can be used to create instances, perform type checking, and provide type hints. For example:

```
items = list()

if isinstance(items, list):
    items.append(item)
```

```
def removeall(items: list, item) -> list:
    return [i for i in items if i != item]
```

A *subtype* is a type defined by inheritance. It carries all of the features of the original type plus additional and/or redefined methods. Inheritance is discussed in more detail in Chapter 7, but here is an example of defining a subtype of list with a new method added to it:

```
class mylist(list):
    def removeall(self, val):
        return [i for i in self if i != val]

# Example
items = mylist([5, 8, 2, 7, 2, 13, 9])
x = items.removeall(2)
print(x)       # [5, 8, 7, 13, 9]
```

The isinstance(instance, type) function is the preferred way to check a value against a type because it is aware of subtypes. It can also check against many possible types. For example:

```
if isinstance(items, (list, tuple)):
    maxval = max(items)
```

Although type checks can be added to a program, this is often not as useful as you might imagine. For one, excessive checking impacts performance. Second, programs don't always define objects that neatly fit into a nice type hierarchy. For instance, if the purpose of the isinstance(items, list) statement above is to test whether items is "list-like," it won't work with objects that have the same programming interface as a list but don't directly inherit from the built-in list type (one example is deque from the collections module).

4.3 Reference Counting and Garbage Collection

Python manages objects through automatic garbage collection. All objects are reference-counted. An object's reference count is increased whenever it's assigned to a new name or placed in a container such as a list, tuple, or dictionary:

```
a = 37        # Creates an object with value 37
b = a         # Increases reference count on 37
c = []
c.append(b)   # Increases reference count on 37
```

This example creates a single object containing the value 37. a is a name that initially refers to the newly created object. When b is assigned a, b becomes a new name for the same object, and the object's reference count increases. When you place b into a list, the object's reference count increases again. Throughout the example, only one object corresponds to 37. All other operations are creating references to that object.

An object's reference count is decreased by the `del` statement or whenever a reference goes out of scope or is reassigned. Here's an example:

```
del a       # Decrease reference count of 37
b = 42      # Decrease reference count of 37
c[0] = 2.0  # Decrease reference count of 37
```

The current reference count of an object can be obtained using the `sys.getrefcount()` function. For example:

```
>>> a = 37
>>> import sys
>>> sys.getrefcount(a)
7
>>>
```

The reference count is often much higher than you might expect. For immutable data such as numbers and strings, the interpreter aggressively shares objects between different parts of the program in order to conserve memory. You just don't notice that because the objects are immutable.

When an object's reference count reaches zero, it is garbage-collected. However, in some cases a circular dependency may exist in a collection of objects that are no longer in use. Here's an example:

```
a = { }
b = { }
a['b'] = b     # a contains reference to b
b['a'] = a     # b contains reference to a
del a
del b
```

In this example, the `del` statements decrease the reference count of a and b and destroy the names used to refer to the underlying objects. However, since each object contains a reference to the other, the reference count doesn't drop to zero and the objects remain allocated. The interpreter won't leak memory, but the destruction of the objects will be delayed until a cycle detector executes to find and delete the inaccessible objects. The cycle-detection algorithm runs periodically as the interpreter allocates more and more memory during execution. The exact behavior can be fine-tuned and controlled using functions in the `gc` standard library module. The `gc.collect()` function can be used to immediately invoke the cyclic garbage collector.

In most programs, garbage collection is something that simply happens without you having to think much about it. However, there are certain situations where manually deleting objects might make sense. One such scenario arises when working with gigantic data structures. For example, consider this code:

```
def some_calculation():
    data = create_giant_data_structure()
    # Use data for some part of a calculation
    ...
    # Release the data
    del data

    # Calculation continues
    ...
```

In this code, the use of the del data statement indicates that the data variable is no longer needed. If this causes the reference count to reach 0, the object is garbage-collected at that point. Without the del statement, the object persists for some indeterminate amount of time until the data variable goes out of scope at the end of the function. You might only notice this when trying to figure out why your program is using more memory than it ought to.

4.4 References and Copies

When a program makes an assignment such as b = a, a new reference to a is created. For immutable objects such as numbers and strings, this assignment appears to create a copy of a (even though this is not the case). However, the behavior appears quite different for mutable objects such as lists and dictionaries. Here's an example:

```
>>> a = [1,2,3,4]
>>> b = a                # b is a reference to a
>>> b is a
True
>>> b[2] = -100          # Change an element in b
>>> a                    # Notice how a also changed
[1, 2, -100, 4]
>>>
```

Since a and b refer to the same object in this example, a change made to one of the variables is reflected in the other. To avoid this, you have to create a copy of an object rather than a new reference.

Two types of copy operations are applied to container objects such as lists and dictionaries: a shallow copy and a deep copy. A shallow copy creates a new object, but populates it with references to the items contained in the original object. Here's an example:

```
>>> a = [ 1, 2, [3,4] ]
>>> b = list(a)          # Create a shallow copy of a
>>> b is a
False
```

```
>>> b.append(100)          # Append element to b
>>> b
[1, 2, [3, 4], 100]
>>> a                      # Notice that a is unchanged
[1, 2, [3, 4]]
>>> b[2][0] = -100         # Modify an element inside b
>>> b
[1, 2, [-100, 4], 100]
>>> a                      # Notice the change inside a
[1, 2, [-100, 4]]
>>>
```

In this case, a and b are separate list objects, but the elements they contain are shared. Therefore, a modification to one of the elements of a also modifies an element of b, as shown.

A deep copy creates a new object and recursively copies all the objects it contains. There is no built-in operator to create deep copies of objects, but you can use the copy.deepcopy() function in the standard library:

```
>>> import copy
>>> a = [1, 2, [3, 4]]
>>> b = copy.deepcopy(a)
>>> b[2][0] = -100
>>> b
[1, 2, [-100, 4]]
>>> a                      # Notice that a is unchanged
[1, 2, [3, 4]]
>>>
```

Use of deepcopy() is actively discouraged in most programs. Copying of an object is slow and often unnecessary. Reserve deepcopy() for situations where you actually need a copy because you're about to mutate data and you don't want your changes to affect the original object. Also, be aware that deepcopy() will fail with objects that involve system or runtime state (such as open files, network connections, threads, generators, and so on).

4.5   Object Representation and Printing

Programs often need to display objects—for example, to show data to the user or print it for the purposes of debugging. If you supply an object x to the print(x) function or convert it to a string using str(x), you will generally get a "nice" human-readable representation of the object's value. For example, consider an example involving dates:

```
>>> from datetime import date
>>> d = date(2012, 12, 21)
>>> print(d)
```

```
2012-12-21
>>> str(d)
'2012-12-21'
>>>
```

This "nice" representation of an object may not be sufficient for debugging. For example, in the output of the above code, there is no obvious way to know if the variable d is a `date` instance or a simple string containing the text '2012-12-21'. To get more information, use the `repr(x)` function that creates a string with a representation of the object that you would have to type out in source code to create it. For example:

```
>>> d = date(2012, 12, 21)
>>> repr(d)
'datetime.date(2012, 12, 21)'
>>> print(repr(d))
datetime.date(2012, 12, 21)
>>> print(f'The date is: {d!r}')
The date is: datetime.date(2012, 12, 21)
>>>
```

In string formatting, the `!r` suffix can be added to a value to produce its `repr()` value instead of the normal string conversion.

4.6 First-Class Objects

All objects in Python are said to be *first-class*. This means that all objects that can be assigned to a name can also be treated as data. As data, objects can be stored as variables, passed as arguments, returned from functions, compared against other objects, and more. For example, here is a simple dictionary containing two values:

```
items = {
    'number' : 42
    'text' : "Hello World"
}
```

The first-class nature of objects can be seen by adding some more unusual items to this dictionary:

```
items['func']   = abs           # Add the abs() function
import math
items['mod']    = math          # Add a module
items['error']  = ValueError    # Add an exception type
nums = [1,2,3,4]
items['append'] = nums.append   # Add a method of another object
```

In this example, the `items` dictionary now contains a function, a module, an exception, and a method of another object. If you want, you can use dictionary lookups on `items` in place of the original names and the code will still work. For example:

```
>>> items['func'](-45)          # Executes abs(-45)
45
>>> items['mod'].sqrt(4)        # Executes math.sqrt(4)
2.0
>>> try:
...     x = int('a lot')
... except items['error'] as e:  # Same as: except ValueError as e
...     print("Couldn't convert")
...
Couldn't convert
>>> items['append'](100)        # Executes nums.append(100)
>>> nums
[1, 2, 3, 4, 100]
>>>
```

The fact that everything in Python is first-class is often not fully appreciated by newcomers. However, it can be used to write very compact and flexible code.

For example, suppose you have a line of text such as "ACME,100,490.10" and you want to convert it into a list of values with appropriate type conversions. Here's a clever way to do it by creating a list of types (which are first-class objects) and executing a few common list-processing operations:

```
>>> line = 'ACME,100,490.10'
>>> column_types = [str, int, float]
>>> parts = line.split(',')
>>> row = [ty(val) for ty, val in zip(column_types, parts)]
>>> row
['ACME', 100, 490.1]
>>>
```

Placing functions or classes in a dictionary is a common technique for eliminating complex `if-elif-else` statements. For example, if you have code like this:

```
if format == 'text':
    formatter = TextFormatter()
elif format == 'csv':
    formatter = CSVFormatter()
elif format == 'html':
    formatter = HTMLFormatter()
else:
    raise RuntimeError('Bad format')
```

you could rewrite it using a dictionary:

```
_formats = {
    'text': TextFormatter,
    'csv': CSVFormatter,
    'html': HTMLFormatter
}

if format in _formats:
    formatter = _formats[format]()
else:
    raise RuntimeError('Bad format')
```

This latter form is also more flexible as new cases can be added by inserting more entries into the dictionary without having to modify a large if-elif-else statement block.

4.7 Using None for Optional or Missing Data

Sometimes programs need to represent an optional or missing value. None is a special instance reserved for this purpose. None is returned by functions that don't explicitly return a value. None is also frequently used as the default value of optional arguments, so that the function can detect whether the caller has actually passed a value for that argument. None has no attributes and evaluates to False in Boolean expressions.

Internally, None is stored as a singleton—that is, there is only one None value in the interpreter. Therefore, a common way to test a value against None is to use the is operator like this:

```
if value is None:
    statements
    ...
```

Testing for None using the == operator also works, but it's not recommended and might be flagged as a style error by code-checking tools.

4.8 Object Protocols and Data Abstraction

Most Python language features are defined by *protocols*. Consider the following function:

```
def compute_cost(unit_price, num_units):
    return unit_price * num_units
```

Now, ask yourself the question: What inputs are allowed? The answer is deceptively simple—everything is allowed! At first glance, this function looks like it might apply to numbers:

```
>>> compute_cost(1.25, 50)
62.5
>>>
```

Indeed, it works as expected. However, the function works with much more. You can use specialized numbers such as fractions or decimals:

```
>>> from fractions import Fraction
>>> compute_cost(Fraction(5, 4), 50)
Fraction(125, 2)
>>> from decimal import Decimal
>>> compute_cost(Decimal('1.25'), Decimal('50'))
Decimal('62.50')
>>>
```

Not only that—the function works with arrays and other complex structures from packages such as numpy. For example:

```
>>> import numpy as np
>>> prices = np.array([1.25, 2.10, 3.05])
>>> units = np.array([50, 20, 25])
>>> compute_cost(prices, quantities)
array([62.5 , 42.  , 76.25])
>>>
```

The function might even work in unexpected ways:

```
>>> compute_cost('a lot', 10)
'a lota lota lota lota lota lota lota lota lota lot'
>>>
```

And yet, certain combinations of types fail:

```
>>> compute_cost(Fraction(5, 4), Decimal('50'))
Traceback (most recent call last):
  File "<stdin>", line 1, in <module>
  File "<stdin>", line 2, in compute_cost
TypeError: unsupported operand type(s) for *: 'Fraction' and 'decimal.Decimal'
>>>
```

Unlike a compiler for a static language, Python does not verify correct program behavior in advance. Instead, the behavior of an object is determined by a dynamic process that involves the dispatch of so-called "special" or "magic" methods. The names of these special methods are always preceded and followed by double underscores (__). The methods are automatically triggered by the interpreter as a program executes. For example, the operation x * y is carried out by a method x.__mul__(y). The names of these methods and their corresponding operators are hard-wired. The behavior of any given object depends entirely on the set of special methods that it implements.

The next few sections describe the special methods associated with different categories of core interpreter features. These categories are sometimes called "protocols." An object, including a user-defined class, may define any combination of these features to make the object behave in different ways.

4.9 Object Protocol

The methods in Table 4.1 are related to the overall management of objects. This includes object creation, initialization, destruction, and representation.

Table 4.1 Methods for Object Management

Method	Description
__new__(cls [,*args [,**kwargs]])	A static method called to create a new instance.
__init__(self [,*args [,**kwargs]])	Called to initialize a new instance after it's been created.
__del__(self)	Called when an instance is being destroyed.
__repr__(self)	Create a string representation.

The __new__() and __init__() methods are used together to create and initialize instances. When an object is created by calling SomeClass(args), it is translated into the following steps:

```
x = SomeClass.__new__(SomeClass, args)
if isinstance(x, SomeClass):
    x.__init__(args)
```

Normally, these steps are handled behind the scenes and you don't need to worry about it. The most common method implemented in a class is __init__(). Use of __new__() almost always indicates the presence of advanced magic related to instance creation (for example, it is used in class methods that want to bypass __init__() or in certain creational design patterns such as singletons or caching). The implementation of __new__() doesn't necessarily need to return an instance of the class in question—if not, the subsequent call to __init__() on creation is skipped.

The __del__() method is invoked when an instance is about to be garbage-collected. This method is invoked only when an instance is no longer in use. Note that the statement del x only decrements the instance reference count and doesn't necessarily result in a call to this function. __del__() is almost never defined unless an instance needs to perform additional resource management steps upon destruction.

The __repr__() method, called by the built-in repr() function, creates a string representation of an object that can be useful for debugging and printing. This is also the method responsible for creating the output of values you see when inspecting variables in the interactive interpreter. The convention is for __repr__() to return an expression string that can be evaluated to re-create the object using eval(). For example:

```
a = [2, 3, 4, 5]    # Create a list
s = repr(a)         # s = '[2, 3, 4, 5]'
b = eval(s)         # Turns s back into a list
```

If a string expression cannot be created, the convention is for __repr__() to return a string of the form <...message...>, as shown here:

```
f = open('foo.txt')
a = repr(f)
# a = "<_io.TextIOWrapper name='foo.txt' mode='r' encoding='UTF-8'>
```

4.10 Number Protocol

Table 4.2 lists special methods that objects must implement to provide mathematical operations.

Table 4.2   Methods for Mathematical Operations

Method	Operation
__add__(self, other)	self + other
__sub__(self, other)	self - other
__mul__(self, other)	self * other
__truediv__(self, other)	self / other
__floordiv__(self, other)	self // other
__mod__(self, other)	self % other
__matmul__(self, other)	self @ other
__divmod__(self, other)	divmod(self, other)
__pow__(self, other [, modulo])	self ** other, pow(self, other, modulo)
__lshift__(self, other)	self << other
__rshift__(self, other)	self >> other
__and__(self, other)	self & other
__or__(self, other)	self | other
__xor__(self, other)	self ^ other
__radd__(self, other)	other + self
__rsub__(self, other)	other - self
__rmul__(self, other)	other * self
__rtruediv__(self, other)	other / self
__rfloordiv__(self, other)	other // self
__rmod__(self, other)	other % self
__rmatmul__(self, other)	other @ self
__rdivmod__(self, other)	divmod(other, self)

Method	Operation
__rpow__(self, other)	other ** self
__rlshift__(self, other)	other << self
__rrshift__(self, other)	other >> self
__rand__(self, other)	other & self
__ror__(self, other)	other | self
__rxor__(self, other)	other ^ self
__iadd__(self, other)	self += other
__isub__(self, other)	self -= other
__imul__(self, other)	self *= other
__itruediv__(self, other)	self /= other
__ifloordiv__(self, other)	self //= other
__imod__(self, other)	self %= other
__imatmul__(self, other)	self @= other
__ipow__(self, other)	self **= other
__iand__(self, other)	self &= other
__ior__(self, other)	self |= other
__ixor__(self, other)	self ^= other
__ilshift__(self, other)	self <<= other
__irshift__(self, other)	self >>= other
__neg__(self)	-self
__pos__(self)	+self
__invert__(self)	~self
__abs__(self)	abs(self)
__round__(self, n)	round(self, n)
__floor__(self)	math.floor(self)
__ceil__(self)	math.ceil(self)
__trunc__(self)	math.trunc(self)

When presented with an expression such as x + y, the interpreter invokes a combination of the methods x.__add__(y) or y.__radd__(x) to carry out the operation. The initial choice is to try x.__add__(y) in all cases except for the special case where y happens to be a subtype of x; in that case, y.__radd__(x) executes first. If the initial method fails by returning NotImplemented, an attempt is made to invoke the operation with reversed operands such as y.__radd__(x). If this second attempt fails, the entire operation fails. Here is an example:

```
>>> a = 42       # int
>>> b = 3.7      # float
>>> a.__add__(b)
NotImplemented
```

```
>>> b.__radd__(a)
45.7
>>>
```

This example might seem surprising but it reflects the fact that integers don't actually know anything about floating-point numbers. However, floating-point numbers do know about integers—as integers are, mathematically, a special kind of floating-point numbers. Thus, the reversed operand produces the correct answer.

The methods __iadd__(), __isub__(), and so forth are used to support in-place arithmetic operators such as a += b and a -= b (also known as augmented assignment). A distinction is made between these operators and the standard arithmetic methods because the implementation of the in-place operators might be able to provide certain customizations or performance optimizations. For instance, if the object is not shared, the value of an object could be modified in place without allocating a newly created object for the result. If the in-place operators are left undefined, an operation such as a += b is evaluated using a = a + b instead.

There are no methods that can be used to define the behavior of the logical and, or, or not operators. The and and or operators implement short-circuit evaluation where evaluation stops if the final result can already be determined. For example:

```
>>> True or 1/0    # Does not evaluate 1/0
True
>>>
```

This behavior involving unevaluated subexpressions can't be expressed using the evaluation rules of a normal function or method. Thus, there is no protocol or set of methods for redefining it. Instead, it is handled as a special case deep inside the implementation of Python itself.

4.11 Comparison Protocol

Objects can be compared in various ways. The most basic check is an identity check with the is operator. For example, a is b. Identity does not consider the values stored inside of an object, even if they happen to be the same. For example:

```
>>> a = [1, 2, 3]
>>> b = a
>>> a is b
True
>>> c = [1, 2, 3]
>>> a is c
False
>>>
```

The is operator is an internal part of Python that can't be redefined. All other comparisons on objects are implemented by the methods in Table 4.3.

Table 4.3 Methods for Instance Comparison and Hashing

Method	Description
__bool__(self)	Returns False or True for truth-value testing
__eq__(self, other)	self == other
__ne__(self, other)	self != other
__lt__(self, other)	self < other
__le__(self, other)	self <= other
__gt__(self, other)	self > other
__ge__(self, other)	self >= other
__hash__(self)	Computes an integer hash index

The __bool__() method, if present, is used to determine the truth value when an object is tested as part of a condition or conditional expression. For example:

```
if a:           # Executes a.__bool__()
    ...
else:
    ...
```

If __bool__() is undefined, then __len__() is used as a fallback. If both __bool__() and __len__() are undefined, an object is simply considered to be True.

The __eq__() method is used to determine basic equality for use with the == and != operators. The default implementation of __eq__() compares objects by identity using the is operator. The __ne__() method, if present, can be used to implement special processing for !=, but is usually not required as long as __eq__() is defined.

Ordering is determined by the relational operators (<, >, <=, and >=) using methods such as __lt__() and __gt__(). As with other mathematical operations, the evaluation rules are subtle. To evaluate a < b, the interpreter will first try to execute a.__lt__(b) except where b is a subtype of a. In that one specific case, b.__gt__(a) executes instead. If this initial method is not defined or returns NotImplemented, the interpreter tries a reversed comparison, calling b.__gt__(a). Similar rules apply to operators such as <= and >=. For example, evaluating <= first tries to evaluate a.__le__(b). If not implemented, b.__ge__(a) is tried.

Each of the comparison methods takes two arguments and is allowed to return any kind of value, including a Boolean value, a list, or any other Python type. For instance, a numerical package might use this to perform an element-wise comparison of two matrices, returning a matrix with the results. If comparison is not possible, the methods should return the built-in object NotImplemented. This is not the same as the NotImplementedError exception. For example:

```
>>> a = 42      # int
>>> b = 52.3    # float
>>> a.__lt__(b)
NotImplemented
```

```
>>> b.__gt__(a)
True
>>>
```

It is not necessary for an ordered object to implement all of the comparison operations in Table 4.3. If you want to be able to sort objects or use functions such as `min()` or `max()`, then `__lt__()` must be minimally defined. If you are adding comparison operators to a user-defined class, the `@total_ordering` class decorator in the `functools` module may be of some use. It can generate all of the methods as long as you minimally implement `__eq__()` and one of the other comparisons.

The `__hash__()` method is defined on instances that are to be placed into a set or be used as keys in a mapping (dictionary). The value returned is an integer that should be the same for two instances that compare as equal. Moreover, `__eq__()` should always be defined together with `__hash__()` because the two methods work together. The value returned by `__hash__()` is typically used as an internal implementation detail of various data structures. However, it's possible for two different objects to have the same hash value. Therefore, `__eq__()` is necessary to resolve potential collisions.

4.12 Conversion Protocols

Sometimes, you must convert an object to a built-in type such as a string or a number. The methods in Table 4.4 can be defined for this purpose.

Table 4.4   Methods for Conversions

Method	Description
`__str__(self)`	Conversion to a string
`__bytes__(self)`	Conversion to bytes
`__format__(self, format_spec)`	Creates a formatted representation
`__bool__(self)`	`bool(self)`
`__int__(self)`	`int(self)`
`__float__(self)`	`float(self)`
`__complex__(self)`	`complex(self)`
`__index__(self)`	Conversion to a integer index `[self]`

The `__str__()` method is called by the built-in `str()` function and by functions related to printing. The `__format__()` method is called by the `format()` function or the `format()` method of strings. The `format_spec` argument is a string containing the format specification. This string is the same as the `format_spec` argument to `format()`. For example:

```
f'{x:spec}'                # Calls x.__format__('spec')
format(x, 'spec')          # Calls x.__format__('spec')
'x is {0:spec}'.format(x)  # Calls x.__format__('spec')
```

The syntax of the format specification is arbitrary and can be customized on an object-by-object basis. However, there is a standard set of conventions used for the built-in types. More information about string formatting, including the general format of the specifier, can be found in Chapter 9.

The __bytes__() method is used to create a byte representation if an instance is passed to bytes(). Not all types support byte conversion.

The numeric conversions __bool__(), __int__(), __float__(), and __complex__() are expected to produce a value of the corresponding built-in type.

Python never performs implicit type conversions using these methods. Thus, even if an object x implements an __int__() method, the expression 3 + x will still produce a TypeError. The only way to execute __int__() is through an explicit use of the int() function.

The __index__() method performs an integer conversion of an object when it's used in an operation that requires an integer value. This includes indexing in sequence operations. For example, if items is a list, performing an operation such as items[x] will attempt to execute items[x.__index__()] if x is not an integer. __index__() is also used in various base conversions such as oct(x) and hex(x).

4.13 Container Protocol

The methods in Table 4.5 are used by objects that want to implement containers of various kinds—lists, dicts, sets, and so on.

Table 4.5 Methods for Containers

Method	Description
__len__(self)	Returns the length of self
__getitem__(self, key)	Returns self[key]
__setitem__(self, key, value)	Sets self[key] = value
__delitem__(self, key)	Deletes self[key]
__contains__(self, obj)	obj in self

Here's an example:

```
a = [1, 2, 3, 4, 5, 6]
len(a)                    # a.__len__()
x = a[2]                  # x = a.__getitem__(2)
a[1] = 7                  # a.__setitem__(1,7)
del a[2]                  # a.__delitem__(2)
5 in a                    # a.__contains__(5)
```

The __len__() method is called by the built-in len() function to return a non-negative length. This function also determines truth values unless the __bool__() method has also been defined.

For accessing individual items, the __getitem__() method can return an item by key value. The key can be any Python object, but it is expected to be an integer for ordered sequences such as lists and arrays. The __setitem__() method assigns a value to an element. The __delitem__() method is invoked whenever the del operation is applied to a single element. The __contains__() method is used to implement the in operator.

Slicing operations such as x = s[i:j] are also implemented using __getitem__(), __setitem__(), and __delitem__(). For slices, a special slice instance is passed as the key. This instance has attributes that describe the range of the slice being requested. For example:

```
a = [1,2,3,4,5,6]
x = a[1:5]              # x = a.__getitem__(slice(1, 5, None))
a[1:3] = [10,11,12]    # a.__setitem__(slice(1, 3, None), [10, 11, 12])
del a[1:4]             # a.__delitem__(slice(1, 4, None))
```

The slicing features of Python are more powerful than many programmers realize. For example, the following variations of extended slicing are all supported and may be useful for working with multidimensional data structures such as matrices and arrays:

```
a = m[0:100:10]             # Strided slice (stride=10)
b = m[1:10, 3:20]           # Multidimensional slice
c = m[0:100:10, 50:75:5]    # Multiple dimensions with strides
m[0:5, 5:10] = n            # extended slice assignment
del m[:10, 15:]             # extended slice deletion
```

The general format for each dimension of an extended slice is i:j[:stride], where stride is optional. As with ordinary slices, you can omit the starting or ending values for each part of a slice.

In addition, the Ellipsis (written as ...) is available to denote any number of trailing or leading dimensions in an extended slice:

```
a = m[..., 10:20]      # extended slice access with Ellipsis
m[10:20, ...] = n
```

When using extended slices, the __getitem__(), __setitem__(), and __delitem__() methods implement access, modification, and deletion, respectively. However, instead of an integer, the value passed to these methods is a tuple containing a combination of slice or Ellipsis objects. For example,

```
a = m[0:10, 0:100:5, ...]
```

invokes __getitem__() as follows:

```
a = m.__getitem__((slice(0,10,None), slice(0,100,5), Ellipsis))
```

Python strings, tuples, and lists currently provide some support for extended slices. No part of Python or its standard library make use of multidimensional slicing or the Ellipsis. Those features are reserved purely for third-party libraries and frameworks. Perhaps the most common place you would see them used is in a library such as numpy.

4.14 Iteration Protocol

If an instance, obj, supports iteration, it provides a method, obj.__iter__(), that returns an iterator. An iterator iter, in turn, implements a single method, iter.__next__(), that returns the next object or raises StopIteration to signal the end of iteration. These methods are used by the implementation of the for statement as well as other operations that implicitly perform iteration. For example, the statement for x in s is carried out by performing these steps:

```
_iter = s.__iter__()
while True:
    try:
        x = _iter.__next__()
    except StopIteration:
        break
    # Do statements in body of for loop
    ...
```

An object may optionally provide a reversed iterator if it implements the __reversed__() special method. This method should return an iterator object with the same interface as a normal iterator (that is, a __next__() method that raises StopIteration at the end of iteration). This method is used by the built-in reversed() function. For example:

```
>>> for x in reversed([1,2,3]):
...     print(x)
3
2
1
>>>
```

A common implementation technique for iteration is to use a generator function involving yield. For example:

```
class FRange:
    def __init__(self, start, stop, step):
        self.start = start
        self.stop = stop
        self.step = step

    def __iter__(self):
        x = self.start
        while x < self.stop:
            yield x
            x += self.step

# Example use:
```

```
nums = FRange(0.0, 1.0, 0.1)
for x in nums:
    print(x)        # 0.0, 0.1, 0.2, 0.3, ...
```

This works because generator functions conform to the iteration protocol themselves. It's a bit easier to implement an iterator in this way since you only have to worry about the __iter__() method. The rest of the iteration machinery is already provided by the generator.

4.15   Attribute Protocol

The methods in Table 4.6 read, write, and delete the attributes of an object using the dot (.) operator and the del operator, respectively.

Table 4.6   Methods for Attribute Access

Method	Description
__getattribute__(self, name)	Returns the attribute self.name
__getattr__(self, name)	Returns the attribute self.name if it's not found through __getattribute__()
__setattr__(self, name, value)	Sets the attribute self.name = value
__delattr__(self, name)	Deletes the attribute del self.name

Whenever an attribute is accessed, the __getattribute__() method is invoked. If the attribute is located, its value is returned. Otherwise, the __getattr__() method is invoked. The default behavior of __getattr__() is to raise an AttributeError exception. The __setattr__() method is always invoked when setting an attribute, and the __delattr__() method is always invoked when deleting an attribute.

These methods are fairly blunt—in that they allow a type to completely redefine attribute access for all attributes. User-defined classes can define properties and descriptors which allow for more fine-grained control of attribute access. This is discussed further in Chapter 7.

4.16   Function Protocol

An object can emulate a function by providing the __call__() method. If an object, x, provides this method, it can be invoked like a function. That is, x(arg1, arg2, ...) invokes x.__call__(arg1, arg2, ...).

There are many built-in types that support function calls. For example, types implement __call__() to create new instances. Bound methods implement __call__() to pass the self argument to instance methods. Library functions such as functools.partial() also create objects that emulate functions.

4.17   Context Manager Protocol

The `with` statement allows a sequence of statements to execute under the control of an instance known as a context manager. The general syntax is as follows:

```
with context [ as var]:
    statements
```

A context object shown here is expected to implement the methods listed in Table 4.7.

Table 4.7   Methods for Context Managers

Method	Description
__enter__(self)	Called when entering a new context. The return value is placed in the variable listed with the **as** specifier to the **with** statement.
__exit__(self, type, value, tb)	Called when leaving a context. If an exception occurred, **type**, **value**, and **tb** have the exception type, value, and traceback information.

The __enter__() method is invoked when the `with` statement executes. The value returned by this method is placed into the variable specified with the optional **as var** specifier. The __exit__() method is called as soon as control flow leaves the block of statements associated with the `with` statement. As arguments, __exit__() receives the current exception type, value, and a traceback if an exception has been raised. If no errors are being handled, all three values are set to `None`. The __exit__() method should return `True` or `False` to indicate if a raised exception was handled or not. If `True` is returned, any pending exception is cleared and program execution continues normally with the first statement after the `with` block.

The primary use of the context management interface is to allow for simplified resource control on objects involving system state such as open files, network connections, and locks. By implementing this interface, an object can safely clean up resources when execution leaves a context in which an object is being used. Further details are found in Chapter 3.

4.18   Final Words: On Being Pythonic

A commonly cited design goal is to write code that is "Pythonic." That can mean many things, but basically it encourages you to follow established idioms used by the rest of Python. That means knowing Python's protocols for containers, iterables, resource management, and so forth. Many of Python's most popular frameworks use these protocols to provide good user experience. You should strive for that as well.

Of the different protocols, three deserve special attention because of their widespread use. One is creating a proper object representation using the __repr__() method. Python programs are often debugged and experimented with at the interactive REPL. It is also common to output objects using `print()` or a logging library. If you make it easy to observe the state of your objects, it will make all of these things easier.

Second, iterating over data is one of the most common programming tasks. If you're going to do it, you should make your code work with Python's `for` statement. Many core parts of Python and the standard library are designed to work with iterable objects. By supporting iteration in the usual way, you'll automatically get a significant amount of extra functionality and your code will be intuitive to other programmers.

Finally, use context managers and the `with` statement for the common programming pattern where statements get sandwiched between some kind of startup and teardown steps—for example, opening and closing resources, acquiring and releasing locks, subscribing and unsubscribing, and so on.

5

Functions

Functions are a fundamental building block of most Python programs. This chapter describes function definitions, function application, scoping rules, closures, decorators, and other functional programming features. Particular attention is given to different programming idioms, evaluation models, and patterns associated with functions.

5.1   Function Definitions

Functions are defined with the `def` statement:

```
def add(x, y):
    return x + y
```

The first part of a function definition specifies the function name and parameter names that represent input values. The body of a function is a sequence of statements that execute when the function is called or applied. You apply a function to arguments by writing the function name followed by the arguments enclosed in parentheses: `a = add(3, 4)`. Arguments are fully evaluated left-to-right before executing the function body. For example, `add(1+1, 2+2)` is first reduced to `add(2, 4)` before calling the function. This is known as *applicative evaluation order*. The order and number of arguments must match the parameters given in the function definition. If a mismatch exists, a `TypeError` exception is raised. The structure of calling a function (such as the number of required arguments) is known as the function's call signature.

5.2   Default Arguments

You can attach default values to function parameters by assigning values in the function definition. For example:

```
def split(line, delimiter=','):
    statements
```

When a function defines a parameter with a default value, that parameter and all the parameters that follow it are optional. It is not possible to specify a parameter with no default value after any parameter with a default value.

Default parameter values are evaluated once when the function is first defined, not each time the function is called. This often leads to surprising behavior if mutable objects are used as a default:

```
def func(x, items=[]):
    items.append(x)
    return items
```

```
func(1)        # returns [1]
func(2)        # returns [1, 2]
func(3)        # returns [1, 2, 3]
```

Notice how the default argument retains the modifications made from previous invocations. To prevent this, it is better to use None and add a check as follows:

```
def func(x, items=None):
    if items is None:
        items = []
    items.append(x)
    return items
```

As a general practice, to avoid such surprises, only use immutable objects for default argument values—numbers, strings, Booleans, None, and so on.

5.3   Variadic Arguments

A function can accept a variable number of arguments if an asterisk (*) is used as a prefix on the last parameter name. For example:

```
def product(first, *args):
    result = first
    for x in args:
        result = result * x
    return result
```

```
product(10, 20)        # -> 200
product(2, 3, 4, 5)    # -> 120
```

In this case, all of the extra arguments are placed into the args variable as a tuple. You can then work with the arguments using the standard sequence operations—iteration, slicing, unpacking, and so on.

5.4 Keyword Arguments

Function arguments can be supplied by explicitly naming each parameter and specifying a value. These are known as keyword arguments. Here is an example:

```
def func(w, x, y, z):
    statements


# Keyword argument invocation
func(x=3, y=22, w='hello', z=[1, 2])
```

With keyword arguments, the order of the arguments doesn't matter as long as each required parameter gets a single value. If you omit any of the required arguments or if the name of a keyword doesn't match any of the parameter names in the function definition, a TypeError exception is raised. Keyword arguments are evaluated in the same order as they are specified in the function call.

Positional arguments and keyword arguments can appear in the same function call, provided that all the positional arguments appear first, values are provided for all nonoptional arguments, and no argument receives more than one value. Here's an example:

```
func('hello', 3, z=[1, 2], y=22)
func(3, 22, w='hello', z=[1, 2])    # TypeError. Multiple values for w
```

If desired, it is possible to force the use of keyword arguments. This is done by listing parameters after a * argument or just by including a single * in the definition. For example:

```
def read_data(filename, *, debug=False):
    ...


def product(first, *values, scale=1):
    result = first * scale
    for val in values:
        result = result * val
    return result
```

In this example, the debug argument to read_data() can only be specified by keyword. This restriction often improves code readability:

```
data = read_data('Data.csv', True)       # NO. TypeError
data = read_data('Data.csv', debug=True) # Yes.
```

The product() function takes any number of positional arguments and an optional keyword-only argument. For example:

```
result = product(2,3,4)          # Result = 24
result = product(2,3,4, scale=10) # Result = 240
```

5.5 Variadic Keyword Arguments

If the last argument of a function definition is prefixed with `**`, all the additional keyword arguments (those that don't match any of the other parameter names) are placed in a dictionary and passed to the function. The order of items in this dictionary is guaranteed to match the order in which keyword arguments were provided.

Arbitrary keyword arguments might be useful for defining functions that accept a large number of potentially open-ended configuration options that would be too unwieldy to list as parameters. Here's an example:

```
def make_table(data, **parms):
    # Get configuration parameters from parms (a dict)
    fgcolor = parms.pop('fgcolor', 'black')
    bgcolor = parms.pop('bgcolor', 'white')
    width = parms.pop('width', None)
    ...
    # No more options
    if parms:
        raise TypeError(f'Unsupported configuration options {list(parms)}')

make_table(items, fgcolor='black', bgcolor='white', border=1,
                  borderstyle='grooved', cellpadding=10,
                  width=400)
```

The `pop()` method of a dictionary removes an item from a dictionary, returning a possible default value if it's not defined. The `parms.pop('fgcolor', 'black')` expression used in this code mimics the behavior of a keyword argument specified with a default value.

5.6 Functions Accepting All Inputs

By using both `*` and `**`, you can write a function that accepts any combination of arguments. The positional arguments are passed as a tuple and the keyword arguments are passed as a dictionary. For example:

```
# Accept variable number of positional or keyword arguments
def func(*args, **kwargs):
    # args is a tuple of positional args
    # kwargs is dictionary of keyword args
    ...
```

This combined use of `*args` and `**kwargs` is commonly used to write wrappers, decorators, proxies, and similar functions. For example, suppose you have a function to parse lines of text taken from an iterable:

```
def parse_lines(lines, separator=',', types=(), debug=False):
    for line in lines:
        ...
        statements
        ...
```

Now, suppose you want to make a special-case function that parses data from a file specified by filename instead. To do that, you could write:

```
def parse_file(filename, *args, **kwargs):
    with open(filename, 'rt') as file:
        return parse_lines(file, *args, **kwargs)
```

The benefit of this approach is that the `parse_file()` function doesn't need to know anything about the arguments of `parse_lines()`. It accepts any extra arguments the caller provides and passes them along. This also simplifies the maintenance of the `parse_file()` function. For example, if new arguments are added to `parse_lines()`, those arguments will magically work with the `parse_file()` function too.

5.7 Positional-Only Arguments

Many of Python's built-in functions only accept arguments by position. You'll see this indicated by the presence of a slash (/) in the calling signature of a function shown by various help utilities and IDEs. For example, you might see something like `func(x, y, /)`. This means that all arguments appearing before the slash can only be specified by position. Thus, you could call the function as `func(2, 3)` but not as `func(x=2, y=3)`. For completeness, this syntax may also be used when defining functions. For example, you can write the following:

```
def func(x, y, /):
    pass
```

```
func(1, 2)      # Ok
func(1, y=2)    # Error
```

This definition form is rarely found in code since it was first supported only in Python 3.8. However, it can be a useful way to avoid potential name clashes between argument names. For example, consider the following code:

```
import time

def after(seconds, func, /, *args, **kwargs):
    time.sleep(seconds)
    return func(*args, **kwargs)
```

```
def duration(*, seconds, minutes, hours):
    return seconds + 60 * minutes + 3600 * hours

after(5, duration, seconds=20, minutes=3, hours=2)
```

In this code, `seconds` is being passed as a keyword argument, but it's intended to be used with the `duration` function that's passed to `after()`. The use of positional-only arguments in `after()` prevents a name clash with the `seconds` argument that appears first.

5.8 Names, Documentation Strings, and Type Hints

The standard naming convention for functions is to use lowercase letters with an underscore (_) used as a word separator—for example, `read_data()` and not `readData()`. If a function is not meant to be used directly because it's a helper or some kind of internal implementation detail, its name usually has a single underscore prepended to it—for example, `_helper()`. These are only conventions, however. You are free to name a function whatever you want as long as the name is a valid identifier.

The name of a function can be obtained via the __name__ attribute. This is sometimes useful for debugging.

```
>>> def square(x):
...     return x * x
...
>>> square.__name__
'square'
>>>
```

It is common for the first statement of a function to be a documentation string describing its usage. For example:

```
def factorial(n):
    '''
    Computes n factorial. For example:

    >>> factorial(6)
    120
    >>>
    '''
    if n <= 1:
        return 1
    else:
        return n*factorial(n-1)
```

The documentation string is stored in the __doc__ attribute of the function. It's often accessed by IDEs to provide interactive help.

Functions can also be annotated with type hints. For example:

```
def factorial(n: int) -> int:
    if n <= 1:
        return 1
    else:
        return n * factorial(n - 1)
```

The type hints don't change anything about how the function evaluates. That is, the presence of hints provides no performance benefits or extra runtime error checking. The hints are merely stored in the __annotations__ attribute of the function which is a dictionary mapping argument names to the supplied hints. Third-party tools such as IDEs and code checkers might use the hints for various purposes.

Sometimes you will see type hints attached to local variables within a function. For example:

```
def factorial(n:int) -> int:
    result: int = 1        # Type-hinted local variable
    while n > 1:
        result *= n
        n -= 1
    return result
```

Such hints are completely ignored by the interpreter. They're not checked, stored, or even evaluated. Again, the purpose of the hints is to help third-party code-checking tools. Adding type hints to functions is not advised unless you are actively using code-checking tools that make use of them. It is easy to specify type hints incorrectly—and, unless you're using a tool that checks them, errors will go undiscovered until someone else decides to run a type-checking tool on your code.

5.9 Function Application and Parameter Passing

When a function is called, the function parameters are local names that get bound to the passed input objects. Python passes the supplied objects to the function "as is" without any extra copying. Care is required if mutable objects, such as lists or dictionaries, are passed. If changes are made, those changes are reflected in the original object. Here's an example:

```
def square(items):
    for i, x in enumerate(items):
        items[i] = x * x        # Modify items in-place
```

```
a = [1, 2, 3, 4, 5]
square(a)                # Changes a to [1, 4, 9, 16, 25]
```

Functions that mutate their input values, or change the state of other parts of the program behind the scenes, are said to have "side effects." As a general rule, side effects are best avoided. They can become a source of subtle programming errors as programs grow in size and complexity—it may not be obvious from reading a function call if a function has side effects or not. Such functions also interact poorly with programs involving threads and concurrency since side effects typically need to be protected by locks.

It's important to make a distinction between modifying an object and reassigning a variable name. Consider this function:

```
def sum_squares(items):
    items = [x*x for x in items]     # Reassign "items" name
    return sum(items)

a = [1, 2, 3, 4, 5]
result = sum_squares(a)
print(a)                             # [1, 2, 3, 4, 5]   (Unchanged)
```

In this example, it appears as if the sum_squares() function might be overwriting the passed items variable. Yes, the local items label is reassigned to a new value. But the original input value (a) is not changed by that operation. Instead, the local variable name items is bound to a completely different object—the result of the internal list comprehension. There is a difference between assigning a variable name and modifying an object. When you assign a value to a name, you're not overwriting the object that was already there—you're just reassigning the name to a different object.

Stylistically, it is common for functions with side effects to return None as a result. As an example, consider the sort() method of a list:

```
>>> items = [10, 3, 2, 9, 5]
>>> items.sort()                     # Observe: no return value
>>> items
[2, 3, 5, 9, 10]
>>>
```

The sort() method performs an in-place sort of list items. It returns no result. The lack of a result is a strong indicator of a side effect—in this case, the elements of the list got rearranged.

Sometimes you already have data in a sequence or a mapping that you'd like to pass to a function. To do this, you can use * and ** in function invocations. For example:

```
def func(x, y, z):
    ...

s = (1, 2, 3)
```

```
# Pass a sequence as arguments
result = func(*s)

# Pass a mapping as keyword arguments
d = { 'x':1, 'y':2, 'z':3 }
result = func(**d)
```

You may be taking data from multiple sources or even supplying some of the arguments explicitly, and it will all work as long as the function gets all of its required arguments, there is no duplication, and everything in its calling signature aligns properly. You can even use * and ** more than once in the same function call. If you're missing an argument or specify duplicate values for an argument, you'll get an error. Python will never let you call a function with arguments that don't satisfy its signature.

5.10 Return Values

The return statement returns a value from a function. If no value is specified or you omit the return statement, None is returned. To return multiple values, place them in a tuple:

```
def parse_value(text):
    '''
    Split text of the form name=val into (name, val)
    '''
    parts = text.split('=', 1)
    return (parts[0].strip(), parts[1].strip())
```

Values returned in a tuple can be unpacked to individual variables:

```
name, value = parse_value('url=http://www.python.org')
```

Sometimes named tuples are used as an alternative:

```
from typing import NamedTuple

class ParseResult(NamedTuple):
    name: str
    value: str

def parse_value(text):
    '''
    Split text of the form name=val into (name, val)
    '''
    parts = text.split('=', 1)
    return ParseResult(parts[0].strip(), parts[1].strip())
```

A named tuple works the same way as a normal tuple (you can perform all the same operations and unpacking), but you can also reference the returned values using named attributes:

```
r = parse_value('url=http://www.python.org')
print(r.name, r.value)
```

5.11 Error Handling

One problem with the `parse_value()` function in the previous section is error handling. What course of action should be taken if the input text is malformed and no correct result can be returned?

One approach is to treat the result as optional—that is, the function either works by returning an answer or returns `None` which is commonly used to indicate a missing value. For example, the function could be modified like this:

```
def parse_value(text):
    parts = text.split('=', 1)
    if len(parts) == 2:
        return ParseResult(parts[0].strip(), parts[1].strip())
    else:
        return None
```

With this design, the burden of checking for the optional result is placed on the caller:

```
result = parse_value(text)
if result:
    name, value = result
```

Or, in Python 3.8+, more compactly as follows:

```
if result := parse_value(text):
    name, value = result
```

Instead of returning `None`, you could treat malformed text as an error by raising an exception. For example:

```
def parse_value(text):
    parts = text.split('=', 1)
    if len(parts) == 2:
        return ParseResult(parts[0].strip(), parts[1].strip())
    else:
        raise ValueError('Bad value')
```

In this case, the caller is given the option of handling bad values with `try-except`. For example:

```
try:
    name, value = parse_value(text)
    ...
except ValueError:
    ...
```

The choice of whether or not to use an exception is not always clear-cut. As a general rule, exceptions are the more common way to handle an abnormal result. However, exceptions are also expensive if they frequently occur. If you're writing code where performance matters, returning None, False, -1, or some other special value to indicate failure might be better.

5.12 Scoping Rules

Each time a function executes, a local namespace is created. This namespace is an environment that contains the names and values of the function parameters as well as all variables that are assigned inside the function body. The binding of names is known in advance when a function is defined and all names assigned within the function body are bound to the local environment. All other names that are used but not assigned in the function body (the free variables) are dynamically found in the global namespace which is always the enclosing module where a function was defined.

There are two types of name-related errors that can occur during function execution. Looking up an undefined name of a free variable in the global environment results in a NameError exception. Looking up a local variable that hasn't been assigned a value yet results in an UnboundLocalError exception. This latter error is often a result of control flow bugs. For example:

```
def func(x):
    if x > 0:
        y = 42
    return x + y   # y not assigned if conditional is false

func(10)     # Returns 52
func(-10)    # UnboundLocalError: y referenced before assignment
```

UnboundLocalError is also sometimes caused by a careless use of in-place assignment operators. A statement such as n += 1 is handled as n = n + 1. If used before n is assigned an initial value, it will fail.

```
def func():
    n += 1     # Error: UnboundLocalError
```

It's important to emphasize that variable names never change their scope—they are either global variables or local variables, and this is determined at function definition time. Here is an example that illustrates this:

```
x = 42
def func():
    print(x)      # Fails. UnboundLocalError
    x = 13

func()
```

In this example, it might look as though the `print()` function would output the value of the global variable x. However, the assignment of x that appears later marks x as a local variable. The error is a result of accessing a local variable that hasn't yet been assigned a value.

If you remove the `print()` function, you get code that looks like it might be reassigning the value of a global variable. For example, consider this:

```
x = 42
def func():
    x = 13
func()
# x is still 42
```

When this code executes, x retains its value of 42, despite the appearance that it might be modifying the global variable x from inside the function func. When variables are assigned inside a function, they're always bound as local variables; as a result, the variable x in the function body refers to an entirely new object containing the value 13, not the outer variable. To alter this behavior, use the `global` statement. `global` declares names as belonging to the global namespace, and it's necessary when a global variable needs to be modified. Here's an example:

```
x = 42
y = 37
def func():
    global x      # 'x' is in global namespace
    x = 13
    y = 0
func()
# x is now 13. y is still 37.
```

It should be noted that use of the `global` statement is usually considered poor Python style. If you're writing code where a function needs to mutate state behind the scenes, consider using a class definition and modify state by mutating an instance or class variable instead. For example:

```
class Config:
    x = 42

def func():
    Config.x = 13
```

Python allows nested function definitions. Here's an example:

```
def countdown(start):
    n = start
    def display():                  # Nested function definition
        print('T-minus', n)
    while n > 0:
        display()
        n -= 1
```

Variables in nested functions are bound using lexical scoping. That is, names are resolved first in the local scope and then in successive enclosing scopes from the innermost scope to the outermost scope. Again, this is not a dynamic process—the binding of names is determined once at function definition time based on syntax. As with global variables, inner functions can't reassign the value of a local variable defined in an outer function. For example, this code does not work:

```
def countdown(start):
    n = start
    def display():
        print('T-minus', n)
    def decrement():
        n -= 1                      # Fails: UnboundLocalError
    while n > 0:
        display()
        decrement()
```

To fix this, you can declare n as nonlocal like this:

```
def countdown(start):
    n = start
    def display():
        print('T-minus', n)
    def decrement():
        nonlocal n
        n -= 1                      # Modifies the outer n
    while n > 0:
        display()
        decrement()
```

nonlocal cannot be used to refer to a global variable—it must reference a local variable in an outer scope. Thus, if a function is assigning to a global, you should still use the global declaration as previously described.

Use of nested functions and nonlocal declarations is not a common programming style. For example, inner functions have no outside visibility, which can complicate testing and debugging. Nevertheless, nested functions are sometimes useful for breaking complex calculations into smaller parts and hiding internal implementation details.

5.13   Recursion

Python supports recursive functions. For example:

```
def sumn(n):
    if n == 0:
        return 0
    else:
        return n + sumn(n-1)
```

However, there is a limit on the depth of recursive function calls. The function `sys.getrecursionlimit()` returns the current maximum recursion depth, and the function `sys.setrecursionlimit()` can be used to change the value. The default value is 1000. Although it is possible to increase the value, programs are still limited by the stack size enforced by the host operating system. When the recursion depth limit is exceeded, a `RuntimeError` exception is raised. If the limit is increased too much, Python might crash with a segmentation fault or another operating system error.

In practice, issues with the recursion limit only arise when you work with deeply nested recursive data structures such as trees and graphs. Many algorithms involving trees naturally lend themselves to recursive solutions—and, if your data structure is too large, you might blow the stack limit. However, there are some clever workarounds; see Chapter 6 on generators for an example.

5.14   The `lambda` Expression

An anonymous—unnamed—function can be defined with a `lambda` expression:

```
lambda args: expression
```

args is a comma-separated list of arguments, and `expression` is an expression involving those arguments. Here's an example:

```
a = lambda x, y: x + y
r = a(2, 3)              # r gets 5
```

The code defined with `lambda` must be a valid expression. Multiple statements, or nonexpression statements such as `try` and `while`, cannot appear in a `lambda` expression. `lambda` expressions follow the same scoping rules as functions.

One of the main uses of `lambda` is to define small callback functions. For example, you may see it used with built-in operations such as `sorted()`. For example:

```
# Sort a list of words by the number of unique letters
result = sorted(words, key=lambda word: len(set(word)))
```

Caution is required when a `lambda` expression contains free variables (not specified as parameters). Consider this example:

```
x = 2
f = lambda y: x * y
x = 3
g = lambda y: x * y
print(f(10))              # --> prints 30
print(g(10))              # --> prints 30
```

In this example, you might expect the call f(10) to print 20, reflecting the fact that x was 2 at the time of definition. However, this is not the case. As a free variable, the evaluation of f(10) uses whatever value x happens to have at the time of evaluation. It could be different from the value it had when the lambda function was defined. Sometimes this behavior is referred to as *late binding*.

If it's important to capture the value of a variable at the time of definition, use a default argument:

```
x = 2
f = lambda y, x=x: x * y
x = 3
g = lambda y, x=x: x * y
print(f(10))              # --> prints 20
print(g(10))              # --> prints 30
```

This works because default argument values are only evaluated at the time of function definition and thus would capture the current value of x.

5.15 Higher-Order Functions

Python supports the concept of *higher-order functions*. This means that functions can be passed as arguments to other functions, placed in data structures, and returned by a function as a result. Functions are said to be *first-class objects*, meaning there is no difference between how you might handle a function and any other kind of data. Here is an example of a function that accepts another function as input and calls it after a time delay—for example, to emulate the performance of a microservice in the cloud:

```
import time

def after(seconds, func):
    time.sleep(seconds)
    func()

# Example usage
def greeting():
    print('Hello World')

after(10, greeting)       # Prints 'Hello World' after 10 seconds
```

Here, the `func` argument to `after()` is an example of what's known as a *callback function*. This refers to the fact that the `after()` function "calls back" to the function supplied as an argument.

When a function is passed as data, it implicitly carries information related to the environment in which the function was defined. For example, suppose the `greeting()` function makes use of a variable like this:

```python
def main():
    name = 'Guido'
    def greeting():
        print('Hello', name)
    after(10, greeting)          # Produces: 'Hello Guido'

main()
```

In this example, the variable `name` is used by `greeting()`, but it's a local variable of the outer `main()` function. When `greeting` is passed to `after()`, the function remembers its environment and uses the value of the required `name` variable. This relies on a feature known as a *closure*. A closure is a function along with an environment containing all of the variables needed to execute the function body.

Closures and nested functions are useful when you write code based on the concept of lazy or delayed evaluation. The `after()` function, shown above, is an illustration of this concept. It receives a function that is not evaluated right away — that only happens at some later point in time. This is a common programming pattern that arises in other contexts. For example, a program might have functions that only execute in response to events — key presses, mouse movement, arrival of network packets, and so on. In all of these cases, function evaluation is deferred until something interesting happens. When the function finally executes, a closure ensures that the function gets everything that it needs.

You can also write functions that create and return other functions. For example:

```python
def make_greeting(name):
    def greeting():
        print('Hello', name)
    return greeting

f = make_greeting('Guido')
g = make_greeting('Ada')

f()       # Produces: 'Hello Guido'
g()       # Produces: 'Hello Ada'
```

In this example, the `make_greeting()` function doesn't carry out any interesting computations. Instead, it creates and returns a function `greeting()` that does the actual work. That only happens when that function gets evaluated later.

In this example, the two variables `f` and `g` hold two different versions of the `greeting()` function. Even though the `make_greeting()` function that created those functions is no longer executing, the `greeting()` functions still remember the `name` variable that was defined—it's part of each function's closure.

One caution about closures is that binding to variable names is not a "snapshot" but a dynamic process—meaning the closure points to the `name` variable and the value that it was most recently assigned. This is subtle, but here's an example that illustrates where trouble can arise:

```python
def make_greetings(names):
    funcs = []
    for name in names:
        funcs.append(lambda: print('Hello', name))
    return funcs

# Try it
a, b, c = make_greetings(['Guido', 'Ada', 'Margaret'])
a()     # Prints 'Hello Margaret'
b()     # Prints 'Hello Margaret'
c()     # Prints 'Hello Margaret'
```

In this example, a list of different functions is made (using `lambda`). It may appear as if they are all using a unique value of `name`, as it changes on each iteration of a `for` loop. This is not the case. All functions end up using the same value of `name`—the value it has when the outer `make_greetings()` function returns.

This is probably unexpected and not what you want. If you want to capture a copy of a variable, capture it as a default argument, as previously described:

```python
def make_greetings(names):
    funcs = []
    for name in names:
        funcs.append(lambda name=name: print('Hello', name))
    return funcs

# Try it
a, b, c = make_greetings(['Guido', 'Ada', 'Margaret'])
a()     # Prints 'Hello Guido'
b()     # Prints 'Hello Ada'
c()     # Prints 'Hello Margaret'
```

In the last two examples, functions have been defined using `lambda`. This is often used as a shortcut for creating small callback functions. However, it's not a strict requirement. You could have rewritten it like this:

```python
def make_greetings(names):
    funcs = []
    for name in names:
        def greeting(name=name):
            print('Hello', name)
```

```
        funcs.append(greeting)
    return funcs
```

The choice of when and where to use lambda is one of personal preference and a matter of code clarity. If it makes code harder to read, perhaps it should be avoided.

5.16 Argument Passing in Callback Functions

One challenging problem with callback functions is that of passing arguments to the supplied function. Consider the after() function written earlier:

```
import time

def after(seconds, func):
    time.sleep(seconds)
    func()
```

In this code, func() is hardwired to be called with no arguments. If you want to pass extra arguments, you're out of luck. For example, you might try this:

```
def add(x, y):
    print(f'{x} + {y} -> {x+y}')
    return x + y

after(10, add(2, 3))      # Fails: add() called immediately
```

In this example, the add(2, 3) function runs immediately, returning 5. The after() function then crashes 10 seconds later as it tries to execute 5(). That is definitely not what you intended. Yet there seems to be no obvious way to make it work if add() is called with its desired arguments.

This problem hints towards a greater design issue concerning the use of functions and functional programming in general—function composition. When functions are mixed together in various ways, you need to think about how function inputs and outputs connect together. It is not always simple.

In this case, one solution is to package up computation into a zero-argument function using lambda. For example:

```
after(10, lambda: add(2, 3))
```

A small zero-argument function like this is sometimes known as a *thunk*. Basically, it's an expression that will be evaluated later when it's eventually called as a zero-argument function. This can be a general-purpose way to delay the evaluation of any expression to a later point in time: put the expression in a lambda and call the function when you actually need the value.

As an alternative to using `lambda`, you could use `functools.partial()` to create a partially evaluated function like this:

```
from functools import partial

after(10, partial(add, 2, 3))
```

`partial()` creates a callable where one or more of the arguments have already been specified and are cached. It can be a useful way to make nonconforming functions match expected calling signatures in callbacks and other applications. Here are a few more examples of using `partial()`:

```
def func(a, b, c, d):
    print(a, b, c, d)

f = partial(func, 1, 2)        # Fix a=1, b=2
f(3, 4)                        # func(1, 2, 3, 4)
f(10, 20)                      # func(1, 2, 10, 20)

g = partial(func, 1, 2, d=4)   # Fix a=1, b=2, d=4
g(3)                           # func(1, 2, 3, 4)
g(10)                          # func(1, 2, 10, 4)
```

`partial()` and `lambda` can be used for similar purposes, but there is an important semantic distinction between the two techniques. With `partial()`, the arguments are evaluated and bound at the time the partial function is first defined. With a zero-argument `lambda`, the arguments are evaluated and bound when the `lambda` function actually executes later (the evaluation of everything is delayed). To illustrate:

```
>>> def func(x, y):
...         return x + y
...
>>> a = 2
>>> b = 3
>>> f = lambda: func(a, b)
>>> g = partial(func, a, b)
>>> a = 10
>>> b = 20
>>> f()       # Uses current values of a, b
30
>>> g()       # Uses initial values of a, b
5
>>>
```

Since partials are fully evaluated, the callables created by `partial()` are objects that can be serialized into bytes, saved in files, and even transmitted across network connections (for example, using the `pickle` standard library module). This is not possible with a `lambda` function. Thus, in applications where functions are passed around, possibly to Python interpreters running in different processes or on different machines, you'll find `partial()` to be a bit more adaptable.

As an aside, partial function application is closely related to a concept known as *currying*. Currying is a functional programming technique where a multiple-argument function is expressed as a chain of nested single-argument functions. Here is an example:

```
# Three-argument function
def f(x, y, z):
    return x + y + z

# Curried version
def fc(x):
    return lambda y: (lambda z: x + y + z)

# Example use
a = f(2, 3, 4)      # Three-argument function
b = fc(2)(3)(4)     # Curried version
```

This is not a common Python programming style and there are few practical reasons for doing it. However, sometimes you'll hear the word "currying" thrown about in conversations with coders who've spent too much time warping their brains with things like `lambda` calculus. This technique of handling multiple arguments is named in honor of the famous logician Haskell Curry. Knowing what it is might be useful—should you stumble into a group of functional programmers having a heated flamewar at a social event.

Getting back to the original problem of argument passing, another option for passing arguments to a callback function is to accept them separately as arguments to the outer calling function. Consider this version of the `after()` function:

```
def after(seconds, func, *args):
    time.sleep(seconds)
    func(*args)

after(10, add, 2, 3)    # Calls add(2, 3) after 10 seconds
```

You will notice that passing keyword arguments to `func()` is not supported. This is by design. One issue with keyword arguments is that the argument names of the given function might clash with argument names already in use (that is, `seconds` and `func`). Keyword arguments might also be reserved for specifying options to the `after()` function itself. For example:

```
def after(seconds, func, *args, debug=False):
    time.sleep(seconds)
    if debug:
        print('About to call', func, args)
    func(*args)
```

All is not lost, however. If you need to specify keyword arguments to `func()`, you can still do it using `partial()`. For example:

```
after(10, partial(add, y=3), 2)
```

If you wanted the `after()` function to accept keyword arguments, a safe way to do it might be to use positional-only arguments. For example:

```
def after(seconds, func, debug=False, /, *args, **kwargs):
    time.sleep(seconds)
    if debug:
        print('About to call', func, args, kwargs)
    func(*args, **kwargs)
```

```
after(10, add, 2, y=3)
```

Another possibly unsettling insight is that `after()` actually represents two different function calls merged together. Perhaps the problem of passing arguments can be decomposed into two functions like this:

```
def after(seconds, func, debug=False):
    def call(*args, **kwargs):
        time.sleep(seconds)
        if debug:
            print('About to call', func, args, kwargs)
        func(*args, **kwargs)
    return call
```

```
after(10, add)(2, y=3)
```

Now, there are no conflicts whatsoever between the arguments to `after()` and the arguments to `func`. However, there is a chance that doing this will introduce a conflict between you and your coworkers.

5.17 Returning Results from Callbacks

Another problem not addressed in the previous section is that of returning the results of the calculation. Consider this modified `after()` function:

```
def after(seconds, func, *args):
    time.sleep(seconds)
    return func(*args)
```

This works, but there are some subtle corner cases that arise from the fact that two separate functions are involved—the `after()` function itself and the supplied callback `func`.

One issue concerns exception handling. For example, try these two examples:

```
after("1", add, 2, 3)   # Fails: TypeError (integer is expected)
after(1, add, "2", 3)   # Fails: TypeError (can't concatenate int to str)
```

A TypeError is raised in both cases, but it's for very different reasons and in different functions. The first error is due to a problem in the after() function itself: A bad argument is being given to time.sleep(). The second error is due to a problem with the execution of the callback function func(*args).

If it's important to distinguish between these two cases, there are a few options for that. One option is to rely on chained exceptions. The idea is to package errors from the callback in a different way that allows them to be handled separately from other kinds of errors. For example:

```
class CallbackError(Exception):
    pass

def after(seconds, func, *args):
    time.sleep(seconds)
    try:
        return func(*args)
    except Exception as err:
        raise CallbackError('Callback function failed') from err
```

This modified code isolates errors from the supplied callback into its own exception category. Use it like this:

```
try:
    r = after(delay, add, x, y)
except CallbackError as err:
    print("It failed. Reason", err.__cause__)
```

If there was a problem with the execution of after() itself, that exception would propagate out, uncaught. On the other hand, problems related to the execution of the supplied callback function would be caught and reported as a CallbackError. All of this is quite subtle, but in practice, managing errors is hard. This approach makes the attribution of blame more precise and the behavior of after() easier to document. Specifically, if there is a problem in the callback, it's always reported as a CallbackError.

Another option is to package the result of the callback function into some kind of result instance that holds both a value and an error. For example, define a class like this:

```
class Result:
    def __init__(self, value=None, exc=None):
        self._value = value
        self._exc = exc
    def result(self):
        if self._exc:
            raise self._exc
```

```
    else:
        return self._value
```

Then, use this class to return results from the `after()` function:

```
def after(seconds, func, *args):
    time.sleep(seconds)
    try:
        return Result(value=func(*args))
    except Exception as err:
        return Result(exc=err)

# Example use:

r = after(1, add, 2, 3)
print(r.result())            # Prints 5

s = after("1", add, 2, 3)    # Immediately raises TypeError. Bad sleep() arg.

t = after(1, add, "2", 3)    # Returns a "Result"
print(t.result())            # Raises TypeError
```

This second approach works by deferring the result reporting of the callback function to a separate step. If there is a problem with `after()`, it gets reported immediately. If there is a problem with the callback `func()`, that gets reported when a user tries to obtain the result by calling the `result()` method.

This style of boxing a result into a special instance to be unwrapped later is an increasingly common pattern found in modern programming languages. One reason for its use is that it facilitates type checking. For example, if you were to put a type hint on `after()`, its behavior is fully defined—it always returns a `Result` and nothing else:

```
def after(seconds, func, *args) -> Result:
    ...
```

Although it's not so common to see this kind of pattern in Python code, it does arise with some regularity when working with concurrency primitives such as threads and processes. For example, instances of a so-called `Future` behave like this when working with thread pools. For example:

```
from concurrent.futures import ThreadPoolExecutor

pool = ThreadPoolExecutor(16)
r = pool.submit(add, 2, 3)     # Returns a Future
print(r.result())              # Unwrap the Future result
```

5.18   Decorators

A decorator is a function that creates a wrapper around another function. The primary purpose of this wrapping is to alter or enhance the behavior of the object being wrapped. Syntactically, decorators are denoted using the special @ symbol as follows:

```
@decorate
def func(x):
    ...
```

The preceding code is shorthand for the following:

```
def func(x):
    ...
func = decorate(func)
```

In the example, a function `func()` is defined. However, immediately after its definition, the function object itself is passed to the function `decorate()`, which returns an object that replaces the original `func`.

As an example of a concrete implementation, here is a decorator `@trace` that adds debugging messages to a function:

```
def trace(func):
    def call(*args, **kwargs):
        print('Calling', func.__name__)
        return func(*args, **kwargs)
    return call


# Example use
@trace
def square(x):
    return x * x
```

In this code, `trace()` creates a wrapper function that writes some debugging output and then calls the original function object. Thus, if you call `square()`, you will see the output of the `print()` function in the wrapper.

If only it were so easy! In practice, functions also contain metadata such as the function name, doc string, and type hints. If you put a wrapper around a function, this information gets hidden. When writing a decorator, it's considered best practice to use the `@wraps()` decorator as shown in this example:

```
from functools import wraps

def trace(func):
    @wraps(func)
    def call(*args, **kwargs):
        print('Calling', func.__name__)
```

```
        return func(*args, **kwargs)
    return call
```

The @wraps() decorator copies various function metadata to the replacement function. In this case, metadata from the given function func() is copied to the returned wrapper function call().

When decorators are applied, they must appear on their own line immediately prior to the function. More than one decorator can be applied. Here's an example:

```
@decorator1
@decorator2
def func(x):
    pass
```

In this case, the decorators are applied as follows:

```
def func(x):
    pass


func = decorator1(decorator2(func))
```

The order in which decorators appear might matter. For example, in class definitions, decorators such as @classmethod and @staticmethod often have to be placed at the outermost level. For example:

```
class SomeClass(object):
    @classmethod          # Yes
    @trace
    def a(cls):
        pass


    @trace                # No. Fails.
    @classmethod
    def b(cls):
        pass
```

The reason for this placement restriction has to do with the values returned by @classmethod. Sometimes a decorator returns an object that's different than a normal function. If the outermost decorator isn't expecting this, things can break. In this case, @classmethod creates a classmethod descriptor object (see Chapter 7). Unless the @trace decorator was written to account for this, it will fail if decorators are listed in the wrong order.

A decorator can also accept arguments. Suppose you want to change the @trace decorator to allow for a custom message like this:

```
@trace("You called {func.__name__}")
def func():
    pass
```

If arguments are supplied, the semantics of the decoration process is as follows:

```
def func():
    pass


# Create the decoration function
temp = trace("You called {func.__name__}")


# Apply it to func
func = temp(func)
```

In this case, the outermost function that accepts the arguments is responsible for creating a decoration function. That function is then called with the function to be decorated to obtain the final result. Here's what the decorator implementation might look like:

```
from functools import wraps

def trace(message):
    def decorate(func):
        @wraps(func)
        def wrapper(*args, **kwargs):
            print(message.format(func=func))
            return func(*args, **kwargs)
        return wrapper
    return decorate
```

One interesting feature of this implementation is that the outer function is actually a kind of a "decorator factory." Suppose you found yourself writing code like this:

```
@trace('You called {func.__name__}')
def func1():
    pass


@trace('You called {func.__name__}')
def func2():
    pass
```

That would quickly get tedious. You could simplify it by calling the outer decorator function once and reusing the result like this:

```
logged = trace('You called {func.__name__}')

@logged
def func1():
    pass
```

```
@logged
def func2():
    pass
```

Decorators don't necessarily have to replace the original function. Sometimes a decorator merely performs an action such as registration. For example, if you are building a registry of event handlers, you could define a decorator that works like this:

```
@eventhandler('BUTTON')
def handle_button(msg):
    . . .

@eventhandler('RESET')
def handle_reset(msg):
    . . .
```

Here's a decorator that manages it:

```
# Event handler decorator
_event_handlers = { }
def eventhandler(event):
    def register_function(func):
        _event_handlers[event] = func
        return func
    return register_function
```

5.19 Map, Filter, and Reduce

Programmers familiar with functional languages often inquire about common list operations such as map, filter, and reduce. Much of this functionality is provided by list comprehensions and generator expressions. For example:

```
def square(x):
    return x * x

nums = [1, 2, 3, 4, 5]
squares = [ square(x) for x in nums ]   # [1, 4, 9, 16, 25]
```

Technically, you don't even need the short one-line function. You could write:

```
squares = [ x * x for x in nums ]
```

Filtering can also be performed with a list comprehension:

```
a = [ x for x in nums if x > 2 ]    # [3, 4, 5]
```

If you use a generator expression, you'll get a generator that produces the results incrementally through iteration. For example:

```
squares = (x*x for x in nums)      # Creates a generator
for n in squares:
    print(n)
```

Python provides a built-in `map()` function that is the same as mapping a function with a generator expression. For example, the above example could be written:

```
squares = map(lambda x: x*x, nums)
for n in squares:
    print(n)
```

The built-in `filter()` function creates a generator that filters values:

```
for n in filter(lambda x: x > 2, nums):
    print(n)
```

If you want to accumulate or reduce values, you can use `functools.reduce()`. For example:

```
from functools import reduce
total = reduce(lambda x, y: x + y, nums)
```

In its general form, `reduce()` accepts a two-argument function, an iterable, and an initial value. Here are a few examples:

```
nums = [1, 2, 3, 4, 5]
total = reduce(lambda x, y: x + y, nums)        # 15
product = reduce(lambda x, y: x * y, nums, 1)    # 120

pairs = reduce(lambda x, y: (x, y), nums, None)
# (((((None, 1), 2), 3), 4), 5)
```

`reduce()` accumulates values left-to-right on the supplied iterable. This is known as a left-fold operation. Here is pseudocode for `reduce(func, items, initial)`:

```
def reduce(func, items, initial):
    result = initial
    for item in items:
        result = func(result, item)
    return result
```

Using `reduce()` in practice may be confusing. Moreover, common reduction operations such as `sum()`, `min()`, and `max()` are already built-in. Your code will be easier to follow (and likely run faster) if you use one of those instead of trying to implement common operations with `reduce()`.

5.20 Function Introspection, Attributes, and Signatures

As you have seen, functions are objects—which means they can be assigned to variables, placed in data structures, and used in the same way as any other kind of data in a program. They can also be inspected in various ways. Table 5.1 shows some common attributes of functions. Many of these attributes are useful in debugging, logging, and other operations involving functions.

Table 5.1   Function Attributes

Attribute	Description
f.__name__	Function name
f.__qualname__	Fully qualified name (if nested)
f.__module__	Name of module in which defined
f.__doc__	Documentation string
f.__annotations__	Type hints
f.__globals__	Dictionary that is the global namespace
f.__closure__	Closure variables (if any)
f.__code__	Underlying code object

The f.__name__ attribute contains the name that was used when defining a function. f.__qualname__ is a longer name that includes additional information about the surrounding definition environment.

The f.__module__ attribute is a string that holds the module name in which the function was defined. The f.__globals__ attribute is a dictionary that serves as the global namespace for the function. It is normally the same dictionary that's attached to the associated module object.

f.__doc__ holds the function documentation string. The f.__annotations__ attribute is a dictionary that holds type hints, if any.

f.__closure__ holds references to the values of closure variables for nested functions. These are a bit buried, but the following example shows how to view them:

```
def add(x, y):
    def do_add():
        return x + y
    return do_add
```

```
>>> a = add(2, 3)
>>> a.__closure__
(<cell at 0x10edf1e20: int object at 0x10ecc1950>,
 <cell at 0x10edf1d90: int object at 0x10ecc1970>)
>>> a.__closure__[0].cell_contents
```

```
2
>>>
```

The `f.__code__` object represents the compiled interpreter bytecode for the function body.

Functions can have arbitrary attributes attached to them. Here's an example:

```
def func():
    statements

func.secure = 1
func.private = 1
```

Attributes are not visible within the function body—they are not local variables and do not appear as names in the execution environment. The main use of function attributes is to store extra metadata. Sometimes frameworks or various metaprogramming techniques utilize function tagging—that is, attaching attributes to functions. One example is the `@abstractmethod` decorator that's used on methods within abstract base classes. All that decorator does is attach an attribute:

```
def abstractmethod(func):
    func.__isabstractmethod__ = True
    return func
```

Some other bit of code (in this case, a metaclass) looks for this attribute and uses it to add extra checks to instance creation.

If you want to know more about a function's parameters, you can obtain its signature using the `inspect.signature()` function:

```
import inspect

def func(x: int, y:float, debug=False) -> float:
    pass

sig = inspect.signature(func)
```

Signature objects provide many convenient features for printing and obtaining detailed information about the parameters. For example:

```
# Print out the signature in a nice form
print(sig)  # Produces (x: int, y: float, debug=False) -> float

# Get a list of argument names
print(list(sig.parameters))   # Produces [ 'x', 'y', 'debug']

# Iterate over the parameters and print various metadata
for p in sig.parameters.values():
    print('name', p.name)
```

```
print('annotation', p.annotation)
print('kind', p.kind)
print('default', p.default)
```

A signature is metadata that describes the nature of a function—how you would call it, type hints, and so on. There are various things that you might do with a signature. One useful operation on signatures is comparison. For example, here's how you check to see if two functions have the same signature:

```
def func1(x, y):
    pass

def func2(x, y):
    pass


assert inspect.signature(func1) == inspect.signature(func2)
```

This kind of comparison might be useful in frameworks. For example, a framework could use signature comparison to see if you're writing functions or methods that conform to an expected prototype.

If stored in the __signature__ attribute of a function, a signature will be shown in help messages and returned on further uses of inspect.signature(). For example:

```
def func(x, y, z=None):
    ...


func.__signature__ = inspect.signature(lambda x,y: None)
```

In this example, the optional argument z would be hidden in further inspection of func. Instead, the attached signature would be returned by inspect.signature().

5.21 Environment Inspection

Functions can inspect their execution environment using the built-in functions globals() and locals(). globals() returns the dictionary that's serving as the global namespace. This is the same as the func.__globals__ attribute. This is usually the same dictionary that's holding the contents of the enclosing module. locals() returns a dictionary containing the values of all local and closure variables. This dictionary is not the actual data structure used to hold these variables. Local variables can come from outer functions (via a closure) or be defined internally. locals() collects all of these variables and puts them into a dictionary for you. Changing an item in the locals() dictionary has no effect on the underlying variable. For example:

```
def func():
    y = 20
    locs = locals()
```

```
    locs['y'] = 30          # Try to change y
    print(locs['y'])        # Prints 30
    print(y)                # Prints 20
```

If you wanted a change to take effect, you'd have to copy it back into the local variable using normal assignment.

```
def func():
    y = 20
    locs = locals()
    locs['y'] = 30
    y = locs['y']
```

A function can obtain its own stack frame using `inspect.currentframe()`. A function can obtain the stack frame of its caller by following the stack trace through `f.f_back` attributes on the frame. Here is an example:

```
import inspect

def spam(x, y):
    z = x + y
    grok(z)

def grok(a):
    b = a * 10

    # outputs: {'a':5, 'b':50 }
    print(inspect.currentframe().f_locals)

    # outputs: {'x':2, 'y':3, 'z':5 }
    print(inspect.currentframe().f_back.f_locals)

spam(2, 3)
```

Sometimes you will see stack frames obtained using the `sys._getframe()` function instead. For example:

```
import sys
def grok(a):
    b = a * 10
    print(sys._getframe(0).f_locals)   # myself
    print(sys._getframe(1).f_locals)   # my caller
```

The attributes in Table 5.2 can be useful for inspecting frames.

Table 5.2 Frame Attributes

Attribute	Description
f.f_back	Previous stack frame (toward the caller)
f.f_code	Code object being executed
f.f_locals	Dictionary of local variables (locals())
f.f_globals	Dictionary used for global variables (globals())
f.f_builtins	Dictionary used for built-in names
f.f_lineno	Line number
f.f_lasti	Current instruction. This is an index into the bytecode string of f_code.
f.f_trace	Function called at start of each source code line

Looking at stack frames is useful for debugging and code inspection. For example, here's an interesting debug function that lets you view the values of the selected variables of the caller:

```
import inspect
from collections import ChainMap

def debug(*varnames):
    f = inspect.currentframe().f_back
    vars = ChainMap(f.f_locals, f.f_globals)
    print(f'{f.f_code.co_filename}:{f.f_lineno}')
    for name in varnames:
        print(f'    {name} = {vars[name]!r}')

# Example use
def func(x, y):
    z = x + y
    debug('x','y')  # Shows x and y along with file/line
    return z
```

5.22 Dynamic Code Execution and Creation

The exec(str [, globals [, locals]]) function executes a string containing arbitrary Python code. The code supplied to exec() is executed as if the code actually appeared in place of the exec operation. Here's an example:

```
a = [3, 5, 10, 13]
exec('for i in a: print(i)')
```

The code given to `exec()` executes within the local and global namespace of the caller. However, be aware that changes to local variables have no effect. For example:

```
def func():
    x = 10
    exec("x = 20")
    print(x)            # Prints 10
```

The reasons for this have to do with the locals being a dictionary of collected local variables, not the actual local variables (see the previous section for more detail).

Optionally, `exec()` can accept one or two dictionary objects that serve as the global and local namespaces for the code to be executed, respectively. Here's an example:

```
globs = {'x': 7,
         'y': 10,
         'birds': ['Parrot', 'Swallow', 'Albatross']
        }

locs = { }

# Execute using the above dictionaries as the global and local namespace
exec('z = 3 * x + 4 * y', globs, locs)
exec('for b in birds: print(b)', globs, locs)
```

If you omit one or both namespaces, the current values of the global and local namespaces are used. If you only provide a dictionary for `globals`, it's used for both the globals and locals.

A common use of dynamic code execution is for creating functions and methods. For example, here's a function that creates an `__init__()` method for a class given a list of names:

```
def make_init(*names):
    parms = ','.join(names)
    code = f'def __init__(self, {parms}):\n'
    for name in names:
        code += f'    self.{name} = {name}\n'
    d = { }
    exec(code, d)
    return d['__init__']

# Example use
class Vector:
    __init__ = make_init('x','y','z')
```

This technique is used in various parts of the standard library. For example, `namedtuple()`, `@dataclass`, and similar features all rely on dynamic code creation with `exec()`.

5.23 Asynchronous Functions and await

Python provides a number of language features related to the asynchronous execution of code. These include so-called *async functions* (or coroutines) and *awaitables*. They are mostly used by programs involving concurrency and the `asyncio` module. However, other libraries may also build upon these.

An asynchronous function, or coroutine function, is defined by prefacing a normal function definition with the extra keyword `async`. For example:

```
async def greeting(name):
    print(f'Hello {name}')
```

If you call such a function, you'll find that it doesn't execute in the usual way—in fact, it doesn't execute at all. Instead, you get an instance of a coroutine object in return. For example:

```
>>> greeting('Guido')
<coroutine object greeting at 0x104176dc8>
>>>
```

To make the function run, it must execute under the supervision of other code. A common option is `asyncio`. For example:

```
>>> import asyncio
>>> asyncio.run(greeting('Guido'))
Hello Guido
>>>
```

This example brings up the most important feature of asynchronous functions—that they never execute on their own. Some kind of manager or library code is always required for their execution. It's not necessarily `asyncio` as shown, but something is always involved in making async functions run.

Aside from being managed, an asynchronous function evaluates in the same manner as any other Python function. Statements run in order and all of the usual control-flow features work. If you want to return a result, use the usual `return` statement. For example:

```
async def make_greeting(name):
    return f'Hello {name}'
```

The value given to `return` is returned by the outer `run()` function used to execute the async function. For example:

```
>>> import asyncio
>>> a = asyncio.run(make_greeting('Paula'))
>>> a
'Hello Paula'
>>>
```

Async functions can call other async functions using an `await` expression like this:

```
async def make_greeting(name):
    return f'Hello {name}'

async def main():
    for name in ['Paula', 'Thomas', 'Lewis']:
        a = await make_greeting(name)
        print(a)

# Run it.  Will see greetings for Paula, Thomas, and Lewis
asyncio.run(main())
```

Use of await is only valid within an enclosing async function definition. It's also a required part of making async functions execute. If you leave off the await, you'll find that the code breaks.

The requirement of using await hints at a general usage issue with asynchronous functions. Namely, their different evaluation model prevents them from being used in combination with other parts of Python. Specifically, it is never possible to write code that calls an async function from a non-async function:

```
async def twice(x):
    return 2 * x

def main():
    print(twice(2))        # Error. Doesn't execute the function.
    print(await twice(2))  # Error. Can't use await here.
```

Combining async and non-async functionality in the same application is a complex topic, especially if you consider some of the programming techniques involving higher-order functions, callbacks, and decorators. In most cases, support for asynchronous functions has to be built as a special case.

Python does precisely this for the iterator and context manager protocols. For example, an asynchronous context manager can be defined using __aenter__() and __aexit__() methods on a class like this:

```
class AsyncManager(object):
    def __init__(self, x):
        self.x = x

    async def yow(self):
        pass

    async def __aenter__(self):
        return self

    async def __aexit__(self, ty, val, tb):
        pass
```

Note that these methods are async functions and can thus execute other async functions using `await`. To use such a manager, you must use the special `async with` syntax that is only legal within an async function:

```
# Example use
async def main():
    async with AsyncManager(42) as m:
        await m.yow()


asyncio.run(main())
```

A class can similarly define an async iterator by defining methods __aiter__() and __anext__(). These are used by the `async for` statement which also may only appear inside an async function.

From a practical point of view, an async function behaves exactly the same as a normal function—it's just that it has to execute within a managed environment such as `asyncio`. Unless you've made a conscious decision to work in such an environment, you should move along and ignore async functions. You'll be a lot happier.

5.24　Final Words: Thoughts on Functions and Composition

Any system is built as a composition of components. In Python, these components include various sorts of libraries and objects. However, underlying everything are functions. Functions are the glue by which a system is put together and the basic mechanism of moving data around.

Much of the discussion in this chapter focused on the nature of functions and their interfaces. How are the inputs presented to a function? How are the outputs handled? How are errors reported? How can all of these things be more tightly controlled and better understood?

The interaction of functions as a potential source of complexity is worth thinking about when working on larger projects. It can often mean the difference between an intuitive easy-to-use API and a mess.

6

Generators

Generator functions are one of Python's most interesting and powerful features. Generators are often presented as a convenient way to define new kinds of iteration patterns. However, there is much more to them: Generators can also fundamentally change the whole execution model of functions. This chapter discusses generators, generator delegation, generator-based coroutines, and common applications of generators.

6.1 Generators and `yield`

If a function uses the `yield` keyword, it defines an object known as a generator. The primary use of a generator is to produce values for use in iteration. Here's an example:

```python
def countdown(n):
    print('Counting down from', n)
    while n > 0:
        yield n
        n -= 1

# Example use
for x in countdown(10):
    print('T-minus', x)
```

If you call this function, you will find that none of its code starts executing. For example:

```python
>>> c = countdown(10)
>>> c
<generator object countdown at 0x105f73740>
>>>
```

Instead, a generator object is created. The generator object, in turn, only executes the function when you start iterating on it. One way to do that is to call `next()` on it:

```python
>>> next(c)
Counting down from 10
```

```
10
>>> next(c)
9
```

When `next()` is called, the generator function executes statements until it reaches a `yield` statement. The `yield` statement returns a result, at which point execution of the function is suspended until `next()` is invoked again. While it's suspended, the function retains all of its local variables and execution environment. When resumed, execution continues with the statement following the `yield`.

`next()` is a shorthand for invoking the `__next__()` method on a generator. For example, you could also do this:

```
>>> c.__next__()
8
>>> c.__next__()
7
>>>
```

You normally don't call `next()` on a generator directly, but use the `for` statement or some other operation that consumes the items. For example:

```
for n in countdown(10):
    statements


a = sum(countdown(10))
```

A generator function produces items until it returns—by reaching the end of the function or by using a `return` statement. This raises a `StopIteration` exception that terminates a `for` loop. If a generator function returns a non-None value, it is attached to the `StopIteration` exception. For example, this generator function uses both `yield` and `return`:

```
def func():
    yield 37
    return 42
```

Here's how the code would execute:

```
>>> f = func()
>>> f
<generator object func at 0x10b7cd480>
>>> next(f)
37
>>> next(f)
Traceback (most recent call last):
  File "<stdin>", line 1, in <module>
StopIteration: 42
>>>
```

Observe that the return value is attached to `StopIteration`. To collect this value, you need to explicitly catch `StopIteration` and extract the value:

```
try:
    next(f)
except StopIteration as e:
    value = e.value
```

Normally, generator functions don't return a value. Generators are almost always consumed by a `for` loop where there is no way to obtain the exception value. This means the only practical way to get the value is to drive the generator manually with explicit `next()` calls. Most code involving generators just doesn't do that.

A subtle issue with generators is where a generator function is only partially consumed. For example, consider this code that abandons a loop early:

```
for n in countdown(10):
    if n == 2:
        break
    statements
```

In this example, the `for` loop aborts by calling `break` and the associated generator never runs to full completion. If it's important for your generator function to perform some kind of cleanup action, make sure you use `try-finally` or a context manager. For example:

```
def countdown(n):
    print('Counting down from', n)
    try:
        while n > 0:
            yield n
            n = n - 1
    finally:
        print('Only made it to', n)
```

Generators are guaranteed to execute the `finally` block code even if the generator is not fully consumed—it will execute when the abandoned generator is garbage-collected. Similarly, any cleanup code involving a context manager is also guaranteed to execute when a generator terminates:

```
def func(filename):
    with open(filename) as file:
        ...
        yield data
        ...
    # file closed here even if generator is abandoned
```

Proper cleanup of resources is a tricky problem. As long as you use constructs such as `try-finally` or context managers, generators are guaranteed to do the right thing even if they are terminated early.

6.2 Restartable Generators

Normally a generator function executes only once. For example:

```
>>> c = countdown(3)
>>> for n in c:
...     print('T-minus', n)
...
T-minus 3
T-minus 2
T-minus 1
>>> for n in c:
...     print('T-minus', n)
...
>>>
```

If you want an object that allows repeated iteration, define it as a class and make the __iter__() method a generator:

```
class countdown:
    def __init__(self, start):
        self.start = start

    def __iter__(self):
        n = self.start
        while n > 0:
            yield n
            n -= 1
```

This works because each time you iterate, a fresh generator is created by __iter__().

6.3 Generator Delegation

An essential feature of generators is that a function involving yield never executes by itself—it always has to be driven by some other code using a for loop or explicit next() calls. This makes it somewhat difficult to write library functions involving yield because calling a generator function is not enough to make it execute. To address this, the yield from statement can be used. For example:

```
def countup(stop):
    n = 1
    while n <= stop:
        yield n
        n += 1
```

```
def countdown(start):
    n = start
    while n > 0:
        yield n
        n -= 1

def up_and_down(n):
    yield from countup(n)
    yield from countdown(n)
```

`yield from` effectively delegates the iteration process to an outer iteration. For example, you would write code like this to drive the iteration:

```
>>> for x in up_and_down(5):
...     print(x, end=' ')
1 2 3 4 5 5 4 3 2 1
>>>
```

`yield from` mainly saves you from having to drive iteration yourself. Without this feature, you would have to write up_and_down(n) as follows:

```
def up_and_down(n):
    for x in countup(n):
        yield x
    for x in countdown(n):
        yield x
```

`yield from` is especially useful when writing code that must recursively iterate through nested iterables. For example, this code flattens nested lists:

```
def flatten(items):
    for i in items:
        if isinstance(i, list):
            yield from flatten(i)
        else:
            yield i
```

Here is an example of how this works:

```
>>> a = [1, 2, [3, [4, 5], 6, 7], 8]
>>> for x in flatten(a):
...     print(x, end=' ')
...
1 2 3 4 5 6 7 8
>>>
```

One limitation of this implementation is that it is still subject to Python's recursion limit, so it would not be able to handle deeply nested structures. This will be addressed in the next section.

6.4   Using Generators in Practice

At first glance, it might not be obvious how to use generators for practical problems beyond defining simple iterators. However, generators are particularly effective at structuring various data handling problems related to pipelines and workflows.

One useful application of generators is as a tool for restructuring code that consists of deeply nested `for` loops and conditionals. Consider this script that searches a directory of Python files for all comments containing the word "spam":

```python
import pathlib
import re

for path in pathlib.Path('.').rglob('*.py'):
    if path.exists():
        with path.open('rt', encoding='latin-1') as file:
            for line in file:
                m = re.match('.*(#.*)$', line)
                if m:
                    comment = m.group(1)
                    if 'spam' in comment:
                        print(comment)
```

Notice the number of levels of nested control flow. Your eyes are already starting to hurt as you look at the code. Now, consider this version using generators:

```python
import pathlib
import re

def get_paths(topdir, pattern):
    for path in pathlib.Path(topdir).rglob(pattern)
        if path.exists():
            yield path

def get_files(paths):
    for path in paths:
        with path.open('rt', encoding='latin-1') as file:
            yield file

def get_lines(files):
    for file in files:
        yield from file
```

```
def get_comments(lines):
    for line in lines:
        m = re.match('.*(#.*)$', line)
        if m:
            yield m.group(1)

def print_matching(lines, substring):
    for line in lines:
        if substring in lines:
            print(substring)

paths = get_paths('.', '*.py')
files = get_files(paths)
lines = get_lines(files)
comments = get_comments(lines)
print_matching(comments, 'spam')
```

In this section, the problem is broken down into smaller self-contained components. Each component only concerns itself with a specific task. For example, the get_paths() generator is only concerned with path names, the get_files() generator is only concerned with opening files, and so forth. It is only at the end that these generators are hooked together into a workflow to solve a problem.

Making each component small and isolated is a good abstraction technique. For example, consider the get_comments() generator. As input, it takes any iterable producing lines of text. This text could come from almost anywhere—a file, a list, a generator, and so on. As a result, this functionality is much more powerful and adaptable than it was when it was embedded into a deeply nested for loop involving files. Generators thus encourage code reuse by breaking problems into small well-defined computational tasks. Smaller tasks are also easier to reason about, debug, and test.

Generators are also useful for altering the normal evaluation rules of function application. Normally, when you apply a function, it executes immediately, producing a result. Generators don't do that. When a generator function is applied, its execution is delayed until some other bit of code invokes next() on it (either explicitly or by a for loop).

As an example, consider again the generator function for flattening nested lists:

```
def flatten(items):
    for i in items:
        if isinstance(i, list):
            yield from flatten(i)
        else:
            yield i
```

One problem with this implementation is that, due to Python's recursion limit, it won't work with deeply nested structures. This can be fixed by driving iteration in a different way using a stack. Consider this version:

```
def flatten(items):
    stack = [ iter(items) ]
    while stack:
        try:
            item = next(stack[-1])
            if isinstance(item, list):
                stack.append(iter(item))
            else:
                yield item
        except StopIteration:
            stack.pop()
```

This implementation builds an internal stack of iterators. It is not subject to Python's recursion limit because it's putting data on an internal list as opposed to building frames on the internal interpreter stack. Thus, if you find yourself in need of flattening a few million layers of some uncommonly deep data structure, you'll find that this version works fine.

Do these examples mean that you should rewrite all of your code using wild generator patterns? No. The main point is that the delayed evaluation of generators allows you to alter the spacetime dimensions of normal function evaluation. There are various real-world scenarios where these techniques can be useful and applied in unexpected ways.

6.5 Enhanced Generators and `yield` Expressions

Inside a generator function, the `yield` statement can also be used as an expression that appears on the right-hand side of an assignment operator. For example:

```
def receiver():
    print('Ready to receive')
    while True:
        n = yield
        print('Got', n)
```

A function that uses `yield` in this manner is sometimes known as an "enhanced generator" or "generator-based coroutine." Sadly, this terminology is a bit imprecise and made even more confusing since "coroutines" are more recently associated with async functions. To avoid this confusion, we'll use the term "enhanced generator" to make it clear that we're still talking about standard functions that use `yield`.

A function that uses `yield` as an expression is still a generator, but its usage is different. Instead of producing values, it executes in response to values sent to it. For example:

```
>>> r = receiver()
>>> r.send(None)        # Advances to the first yield
Ready to receive
```

```
>>> r.send(1)
Got 1
>>> r.send(2)
Got 2
>>> r.send('Hello')
Got Hello
>>>
```

In this example, the initial call to `r.send(None)` is necessary so that the generator executes statements leading to the first `yield` expression. At this point, the generator suspends, waiting for a value to be sent to it using the `send()` method of the associated generator object r. The value passed to `send()` is returned by the `yield` expression in the generator. Upon receiving a value, a generator executes statements until the next `yield` is encountered.

As written, the function runs indefinitely. The `close()` method can be used to shut down the generator as follows:

```
>>> r.close()
>>> r.send(4)
Traceback (most recent call last):
  File "<stdin>", line 1, in <module>
StopIteration
>>>
```

The `close()` operation raises a `GeneratorExit` exception inside the generator at the current `yield`. Normally, this causes the generator to terminate silently; if you're so inclined, you can catch it to perform cleanup actions. Once closed, a `StopIteration` exception will be raised if further values are sent to a generator.

Exceptions can be raised inside a generator using the `throw(ty [,val [,tb]])` method where `ty` is the exception type, `val` is the exception argument (or tuple of arguments), and `tb` is an optional traceback. For example:

```
>>> r = receiver()
Ready to receive
>>> r.throw(RuntimeError, "Dead")
Traceback (most recent call last):
  File "<stdin>", line 1, in <module>
  File "receiver.py", line 14, in receiver
    n = yield
RuntimeError: Dead
>>>
```

Exceptions raised in either manner will propagate from the currently executing `yield` statement in the generator. A generator can elect to catch the exception and handle it as is appropriate. If a generator doesn't handle the exception, it propagates out of the generator to be handled at a higher level.

6.6   Applications of Enhanced Generators

Enhanced generators are an odd programming construct. Unlike a simple generator which naturally feeds a for loop, there is no core language feature that drives an enhanced generator. Why, then, would you ever want a function that needs values to be sent to it? Is it purely academic?

Historically, enhanced generators have been used in the context of concurrency libraries—especially those based on asynchronous I/O. In that context, they're usually referred to as "coroutines" or "generator-based coroutines." However, much of that functionality has been folded into the async and await features of Python. There is little practical reason to use yield for that specific use case. That said, there are still some practical applications.

Like generators, an enhanced generator can be used to implement different kinds of evaluation and control flow. One example is the @contextmanager decorator found in the contextlib module. For example:

```
from contextlib import contextmanager

@contextmanager
def manager():
    print("Entering")
    try:
        yield 'somevalue'
    except Exception as e:
        print("An error occurred", e)
    finally:
        print("Leaving")
```

Here, a generator is being used to glue together the two halves of a context manager. Recall that context managers are defined by objects implementing the following protocol:

```
class Manager:
    def __enter__(self):
        return somevalue

    def __exit__(self, ty, val, tb):
        if ty:
            # An exception occurred.
            ...
            # Return True if handled, False otherwise
```

With the @contextmanager generator, everything prior to the yield statement executes when the manager enters (via the __enter__() method). Everything after the yield executes when the manager exits (via the __exit__() method). If an error took place, it is reported as an exception on the yield statement. Here is an example:

```
>>> with manager() as val:
...       print(val)
...
Entering
somevalue
Leaving
>>> with manager() as val:
...       print(int(val))
...
Entering
An error occurred invalid literal for int() with base 10: 'somevalue'
Leaving
>>>
```

To implement this, a wrapper class is used. This is a simplified implementation that illustrates the basic idea:

```
class Manager:
    def __init__(self, gen):
        self.gen = gen

    def __enter__(self):
        # Run to the yield
        return self.gen.send(None)

    def __exit__(self, ty, val, tb):
        # Propagate an exception (if any)
        try:
            if ty:
                try:
                    self.gen.throw(ty, val, tb)
                except ty:
                    return False
            else:
                self.gen.send(None)
        except StopIteration:
            return True
```

Another application of extended generators is using functions to encapsulate a "worker" task. One of the central features of a function call is that it sets up an environment of local variables. Access to those variables is highly optimized—it's much faster than accessing attributes of classes and instances. Since generators stay alive until explicitly closed or destroyed, one might use a generator to set up a long-lived task. Here is an example of a generator that receives byte fragments and assembles them into lines:

```
def line_receiver():
    data = bytearray()
    line = None
    linecount = 0
    while True:
        part = yield line
        linecount += part.count(b'\n')
        data.extend(part)
        if linecount > 0:
            index = data.index(b'\n')
            line = bytes(data[:index+1])
            data = data[index+1:]
            linecount -= 1
        else:
            line = None
```

In this example, a generator receives byte fragments that are collected into a byte array. If the array contains a newline, a line is extracted and returned. Otherwise, **None** is returned. Here's an example illustrating how it works:

```
>>> r = line_receiver()
>>> r.send(None)        # Prime the generator
>>> r.send(b'hello')
>>> r.send(b'world\nit ')
b'hello world\n'
>>> r.send(b'works!')
>>> r.send(b'\n')
b'it works!\n''
>>>
```

Similar code could be written as a class such as this:

```
class LineReceiver:
    def __init__(self):
        self.data = bytearray()
        self.linecount = 0
    def send(self, part):
        self.linecount += part.count(b'\n')
        self.data.extend(part)
        if self.linecount > 0:
            index = self.data.index(b'\n')
            line = bytes(self.data[:index+1])
            self.data = self.data[index+1:]
            self.linecount -= 1
            return line
```

```
    else:
        return None
```

Although writing a class might be more familiar, the code is more complex and runs slower. Tested on the author's machine, feeding a large collection of chunks into a receiver is about 40–50% faster with a generator than with this class code. Most of those savings are due to the elimination of instance attribute lookup—local variables are faster.

Although there are many other potential applications, the important thing to keep in mind is that if you see `yield` being used in a context that is not involving iteration, it is probably using the enhanced features such as `send()` or `throw()`.

6.7 Generators and the Bridge to Awaiting

A classic use of generator functions is in libraries related to asynchronous I/O such as in the standard `asyncio` module. However, since Python 3.5 much of this functionality has been moved into a different language feature related to `async` functions and the `await` statement (see the last part of Chapter 5).

The `await` statement involves interacting with a generator in disguise. Here is an example that illustrates the underlying protocol used by `await`:

```
class Awaitable:
    def __await__(self):
        print('About to await')
        yield    # Must be a generator
        print('Resuming')


# Function compatible with "await". Returns an "awaitable".
def function():
    return Awaitable()


async def main():
    await function()
```

Here is how you might try the code using `asyncio`:

```
>>> import asyncio
>>> asyncio.run(main())
About to await
Resuming
>>>
```

Is it absolutely essential to know how this works? Probably not. All of this machinery is normally hidden from view. However, if you ever find yourself using async functions, just know that there is a generator function buried somewhere inside. You'll eventually find it if you just keep on digging the hole of technical debt deep enough.

6.8   Final Words: A Brief History of Generators and Looking Forward

Generators are one of Python's more interesting success stories. They are also part of a greater story concerning iteration. Iteration is one of the most common programming tasks of all. In early versions of Python, iteration was implemented via sequence indexing and the __getitem__() method. This later evolved into the current iteration protocol based on __iter__() and __next__() methods. Generators appeared shortly thereafter as a more convenient way to implement an iterator. In modern Python, there is almost no reason to ever implement an iterator using anything other than a generator. Even on iterable objects that you might define yourself, the __iter__() method itself is conveniently implemented in this way.

In later versions of Python, generators took on a new role as they evolved enhanced features related to coroutines—the send() and throw() methods. These were no longer limited to iteration but opened up possibilities for using generators in other contexts. Most notably, this formed the basis of many so-called "async" frameworks used for network programming and concurrency. However, as asynchronous programming has evolved, most of this has transformed into later features that use the async/await syntax. Thus, it's not so common to see generator functions used outside of the context of iteration—their original purpose. In fact, if you find yourself defining a generator function and you're *not* performing iteration, you should probably reconsider your approach. There may be a better or more modern way to accomplish what you're doing.

7

Classes and Object-Oriented Programming

Classes are used to create new kinds of objects. This chapter covers the details of classes—but is not intended to be an in-depth reference on object-oriented programming and design. Some programming patterns common in Python are discussed, as well as ways that you can customize classes to behave in interesting ways. The overall structure of this chapter is top-down. High-level concepts and techniques for using classes are described first. In later parts of the chapter, the material gets more technical and focused on internal implementation.

7.1 Objects

Almost all code in Python involves creating and performing actions on *objects*. For example, you might make a string object and manipulate it as follows:

```
>>> s = "Hello World"
>>> s.upper()
'HELLO WORLD'
>>> s.replace('Hello', 'Hello Cruel')
'Hello Cruel World'
>>> s.split()
['Hello', 'World']
>>>
```

or a list object:

```
>>> names = ['Paula', 'Thomas']
>>> names.append('Lewis')
>>> names
['Paula', 'Thomas', 'Lewis']
>>> names[1] = 'Tom'
>>>
```

An essential feature of each object is that it usually has some kind of state—the characters of a string, the elements of a list, and so on, as well as methods that operate on that state. The methods are invoked through the object itself—as if they are functions attached to the object via the dot (.) operator.

Objects always have an associated type. You can view it using `type()`:

```
>>> type(names)
<class 'list'>
>>>
```

An object is said to be an *instance* of its type. For example, `names` is an instance of `list`.

7.2 The `class` **Statement**

New objects are defined using the `class` statement. A class typically consists of a collection of functions that make up the methods. Here's an example:

```
class Account:
    def __init__(self, owner, balance):
        self.owner = owner
        self.balance = balance

    def __repr__(self):
        return f'Account({self.owner!r}, {self.balance!r})'

    def deposit(self, amount):
        self.balance += amount

    def withdraw(self, amount):
        self.balance -= amount

    def inquiry(self):
        return self.balance
```

It's important to note that a `class` statement by itself doesn't create any instances of the class. For example, no accounts are actually created in the preceding example. Rather, a class merely holds the methods that will be available on the instances created later. You might think of it as a blueprint.

The functions defined inside a class are known as methods. An instance method is a function that operates on an instance of the class, which is passed as the first argument. By convention, this argument is called `self`. In the preceding example, `deposit()`, `withdraw()`, and `inquiry()` are examples of instance methods.

The `__init__()` and `__repr__()` methods of the class are examples of so-called *special* or *magic* methods. These methods have special meaning to the interpreter runtime. The `__init__()` method is used to initialize state when a new instance is created. The __repr__() method returns a string for viewing an object. Defining this method is optional, but doing so simplifies debugging and makes it easier to view objects from the interactive prompt.

A class definition may optionally include a documentation string and type hints. For example:

```python
class Account:
    '''
    A simple bank account
    '''
    owner: str
    balance: float

    def __init__(self, owner, balance):
        self.owner = owner
        self.balance = balance

    def __repr__(self):
        return f'Account({self.owner!r}, {self.balance!r})'

    def deposit(self, amount):
        self.balance += amount

    def withdraw(self, amount):
        self.balance -= amount

    def inquiry(self):
        return self.balance
```

Type hints do not change any aspect of how a class works—that is, they do not introduce any extra checking or validation. It is purely metadata that might be useful for third-party tools or IDEs, or used by certain advanced programming techniques. They are not used in most examples that follow.

7.3 Instances

Instances of a class are created by calling a class object as a function. This creates a new instance that is then passed to the __init__() method. The arguments to __init__() consist of the newly created instance self along with the arguments supplied in calling the class object. For example:

```python
# Create a few accounts

a = Account('Guido', 1000.0)
# Calls Account.__init__(a, 'Guido', 1000.0)
```

```
b = Account('Eva', 10.0)
# Calls Account.__init__(b, 'Eva', 10.0)
```

Inside __init__(), attributes are saved on the instance by assigning to self. For example, self.owner = owner is saving an attribute on the instance. Once the newly created instance has been returned, these attributes, as well as methods of the class, are accessed using the dot (.) operator:

```
a.deposit(100.0)       # Calls Account.deposit(a, 100.0)
b.withdraw(50.00       # Calls Account.withdraw(b, 50.0)
owner = a.owner        # Get account owner
```

It's important to emphasize that each instance has its own state. You can view instance variables using the vars() function. For example:

```
>>> a = Account('Guido', 1000.0)
>>> b = Account('Eva', 10.0)
>>> vars(a)
{'owner': 'Guido', 'balance': 1000.0}
>>> vars(b)
{'owner': 'Eva', 'balance': 10.0}
>>>
```

Notice that the methods do not appear here. The methods are found on the class instead. Every instance keeps a link to its class via its associated type. For example:

```
>>> type(a)
<class 'Account'>
>>> type(b)
<class 'Account'>
>>> type(a).deposit
<function Account.deposit at 0x10a032158>
>>> type(a).inquiry
<function Account.inquiry at 0x10a032268>
>>>
```

A later section discusses the implementation details of attribute binding and the relationship between instances and classes.

7.4 Attribute Access

There are only three basic operations that can be performed on an instance: getting, setting, and deleting an attribute. For example:

```
>>> a = Account('Guido', 1000.0)
>>> a.owner                # get
```

```
'Guido'
>>> a.balance = 750.0      # set
>>> del a.balance          # delete
>>> a.balance
Traceback (most recent call last):
  File "<stdin>", line 1, in <module>
AttributeError: 'Account' object has no attribute 'balance'
>>>
```

Everything in Python is a dynamic process with very few restrictions. If you want to add a new attribute to an object after it's been created, you're free to do that. For example:

```
>>> a = Account('Guido', 1000.0)
>>> a.creation_date = '2019-02-14'
>>> a.nickname = 'Former BDFL'
>>> a.creation_date
'2019-02-14'
>>>
```

Instead of using dot (.) to perform these operations, you can supply an attribute name as a string to the getattr(), setattr(), and delattr() functions. The hasattr() function tests for the existence of an attribute. For example:

```
>>> a = Account('Guido', 1000.0)
>>> getattr(a, 'owner')
'Guido'
>>> setattr(a, 'balance', 750.0)
>>> delattr(a, 'balance')
>>> hasattr(a, 'balance')
False
>>> getattr(a, 'withdraw')(100)      # Method call
>>> a
Account('Guido', 650.0)
>>>
```

a.attr and getattr(a, 'attr') are interchangeable, so getattr(a, 'withdraw')(100) is the same as a.withdraw(100). It matters not that withdraw() is a method.

The getattr() function is notable for taking an optional default value. If you wanted to look up an attribute that may or may not exist, you could do this:

```
>>> a = Account('Guido', 1000.0)
>>> getattr(s, 'balance', 'unknown')
1000.0
>>> getattr(s, 'creation_date', 'unknown')
'unknown'
>>>
```

When you access a method as an attribute, you get an object known as a *bound method*. For example:

```
>>> a = Account('Guido', 1000.0)
>>> w = a.withdraw
>>> w
<bound method Account.withdraw of Account('Guido', 1000.0)>
>>> w(100)
>>> a
Account('Guido', 900.0)
>>>
```

A bound method is an object that contains both an instance (the `self`) and the function that implements the method. When you call a bound method by adding parentheses and arguments, it executes the method, passing the attached instance as the first argument. For example, calling `w(100)` above turns into a call to `Account.withdraw(a, 100)`.

7.5   Scoping Rules

Although classes define an isolated namespace for the methods, that namespace does not serve as a scope for resolving names used inside methods. Therefore, when you're implementing a class, references to attributes and methods must be fully qualified. For example, in methods you always reference attributes of the instance through `self`. Thus, you use `self.balance`, not `balance`. This also applies if you want to call a method from another method. For example, suppose you want to implement `withdraw()` in terms of depositing a negative amount:

```
class Account:
    def __init__(self, owner, balance):
        self.owner = owner
        self.balance = balance

    def __repr__(self):
        return f'Account({self.owner!r}, {self.balance!r})'

    def deposit(self, amount):
        self.balance += amount

    def withdraw(self, amount):
        self.deposit(-amount)     # Must use self.deposit()

    def inquiry(self):
        return self.balance
```

The lack of a class-level scope is one area where Python differs from C++ or Java. If you have used those languages, the `self` parameter in Python is the same as the so-called "this" pointer, except that in Python you always have to use it explicitly.

7.6 Operator Overloading and Protocols

In Chapter 4, we discussed Python's data model. Particular attention was given to the so-called special methods that implement Python operators and protocols. For example, the `len(obj)` function calls `obj.__len__()` and `obj[n]` calls `obj.__getitem__(n)`.

When defining new classes, it is common to define some of these methods. The `__repr__()` method in the Account class was one such method for improving debugging output. You might define more of these methods if you're creating something more complicated, such as a custom container. For example, suppose you wanted to make a portfolio of accounts:

```python
class AccountPortfolio:
    def __init__(self):
        self.accounts = []

    def add_account(self, account):
        self.accounts.append(account)

    def total_funds(self):
        return sum(account.inquiry() for account in self)

    def __len__(self):
        return len(self.accounts)

    def __getitem__(self, index):
        return self.accounts[index]

    def __iter__(self):
        return iter(self.accounts)

# Example
port = AccountPortfolio()
port.add_account(Account('Guido', 1000.0))
port.add_account(Account('Eva', 50.0))

print(port.total_funds())    # -> 1050.0
len(port)                    # -> 2

# Print the accounts
```

```
for account in port:
    print(account)

# Access an individual account by index
port[1].inquiry()            # -> 50.0
```

The special methods that appear at the end, such as __len__(), __getitem__(), and __iter__(), make an AccountPortfolio work with Python operators such as indexing and iteration.

Sometimes you'll hear the word "Pythonic," as in "this code is Pythonic." The term is informal, but it usually refers to whether or not an object plays nicely with the rest of the Python environment. This implies supporting—to the extent that it makes sense—core Python features such as iteration, indexing, and other operations. You almost always do this by having your class implement predefined special methods as described in Chapter 4.

7.7 Inheritance

Inheritance is a mechanism for creating a new class that specializes or modifies the behavior of an existing class. The original class is called a base class, superclass, or parent class. The new class is called a derived class, child class, subclass, or subtype. When a class is created via inheritance, it inherits the attributes defined by its base classes. However, a derived class may redefine any of these attributes and add new attributes of its own.

Inheritance is specified with a comma-separated list of base-class names in the class statement. If there is no specified base class, a class implicitly inherits from object. object is a class that is the root of all Python objects; it provides the default implementation of some common methods such as __str__() and __repr__().

One use of inheritance is to extend an existing class with new methods. For example, suppose you want to add a panic() method to Account that would withdraw all funds. Here's how:

```
class MyAcount(Account):
    def panic(self):
        self.withdraw(self.balance)

# Example
a = MyAccount('Guido', 1000.0)
a.withdraw(23.0)             # a.balance = 977.0
a.panic()                    # a.balance = 0
```

Inheritance can also be used to redefine the already existing methods. For example, here's a specialized version of Account that redefines the inquiry() method to periodically overstate the balance with the hope that someone not paying close attention will overdraw their account and incur a big penalty when making a payment on their subprime mortgage:

```
import random

class EvilAccount(Account):
    def inquiry(self):
        if random.randint(0,4) == 1:
            return self.balance * 1.10
        else:
            return self.balance

a = EvilAccount('Guido', 1000.0)
a.deposit(10.0)                    # Calls Account.deposit(a, 10.0)
available = a.inquiry()            # Calls EvilAccount.inquiry(a)
```

In this example, instances of EvilAccount are identical to instances of Account except for the redefined inquiry() method.

Occasionally, a derived class would reimplement a method but also need to call the original implementation. A method can explicitly call the original method using super():

```
class EvilAccount(Account):
    def inquiry(self):
        if random.randint(0,4) == 1:
            return 1.10 * super().inquiry()
        else:
            return super().inquiry()
```

In this example, super() allows you to access a method as it was previously defined. The super().inquiry() call is using the original definition of inquiry() before it got redefined by EvilAccount.

It's less common, but inheritance might also be used to add additional attributes to instances. Here's how you could make the 1.10 factor in the above example an instance-level attribute that could be adjusted:

```
class EvilAccount(Account):
    def __init__(self, owner, balance, factor):
        super().__init__(owner, balance)
        self.factor = factor

    def inquiry(self):
        if random.randint(0,4) == 1:
            return self.factor * super().inquiry()
        else:
            return super().inquiry()
```

A tricky issue with adding attributes is dealing with the existing __init__() method. In this example, we define a new version of __init__() that includes our additional instance variable factor. However, when __init__() is redefined, it is the responsibility of the child to initialize its parent using super().__init__() as shown. If you forget to do this, you'll end up with a half-initialized object and everything will break. Since initialization of the parent requires additional arguments, those still must be passed to the child __init__() method.

Inheritance can break code in subtle ways. Consider the __repr__() method of the Account class:

```
class Account:
    def __init__(self, owner, balance):
        self.owner = owner
        self.balance = balance

    def __repr__(self):
        return f'Account({self.owner!r}, {self.balance!r})'
```

The purpose of this method is to assist in debugging by making nice output. However, the method is hardcoded to use the name Account. If you start using inheritance, you'll find that the output is wrong:

```
>>> class EvilAccount(Account):
...     pass
...
>>> a = EvilAccount('Eva', 10.0)
>>> a
Account('Eva', 10.0)      # Notice misleading output
>>> type(a)
<class 'EvilAccount'>
>>>
```

To fix this, you need to modify the __repr__() method to use the proper type name. For example:

```
class Account:
    ...
    def __repr__(self):
        return f'{type(self).__name__}({self.owner!r}, {self.balance!r})'
```

Now you'll see more accurate output. Inheritance is not used with every class, but if it's an anticipated use case of the class you're writing, you need to pay attention to details like this. As a general rule, avoid the hardcoding of class names.

Inheritance establishes a relationship in the type system where any child class will type-check as the parent class. For example:

```
>>> a = EvilAccount('Eva', 10)
>>> type(a)
<class 'EvilAccount'>
>>> isinstance(a, Account)
```

```
True
>>>
```

This is the so-called "is a" relationship: `EvilAccount` is an `Account`. Sometimes, the "is a" inheritance relationship is used to define object type ontologies or taxonomies. For example:

```
class Food:
    pass

class Sandwich(Food):
    pass

class RoastBeef(Sandwich):
    pass

class GrilledCheese(Sandwich):
    pass

class Taco(Food):
    pass
```

In practice, organizing objects in this manner can be quite difficult and fraught with peril. Suppose you wanted to add a `HotDog` class to the above hierarchy. Where does it go? Given that a hot dog has a bun, you might be inclined to make it a subclass of `Sandwich`. However, based on the overall curved shape of the bun with a tasty filling inside, perhaps a hot dog is really more like a `Taco`. Maybe you decide to make it a subclass of both:

```
class HotDog(Sandwich, Taco):
    pass
```

At this point, everyone's head is exploding and the office is embroiled in a heated argument. This might as well be a good time to mention that Python supports multiple inheritance. To do that, list more than one class as a parent. The resulting child class will inherit all of the combined features of the parents. See Section 7.19 for more about multiple inheritance.

7.8 Avoiding Inheritance via Composition

One concern with inheritance is what's known as implementation inheritance. To illustrate, suppose you wanted to make a stack data structure with push and pop operations. A quick way to do that would be to inherit from a list and add a new method to it:

```
class Stack(list):
    def push(self, item):
        self.append(item)
```

```
# Example
s = Stack()
s.push(1)
s.push(2)
s.push(3)
s.pop()        # -> 3
s.pop()        # -> 2
```

Sure enough, this data structure works like a stack, but it also has every other feature of lists—insertion, sorting, slice reassignment, and so forth. This is implementation inheritance—you used inheritance to reuse some code upon which you built something else, but you also got a lot of features that aren't pertinent to the problem actually being solved. Users will probably find the object strange. Why does a stack have methods for sorting?

A better approach is composition. Instead of building a stack by inheriting from a list, you should build a stack as an independent class that happens to have a list contained in it. The fact that there's a list inside is an implementation detail. For example:

```
class Stack:
    def __init__(self):
        self._items = list()

    def push(self, item):
        self._items.append(item)

    def pop(self):
        return self._items.pop()

    def __len__(self):
        return len(self._items)

# Example use
s = Stack()
s.push(1)
s.push(2)
s.push(3)
s.pop()        # -> 3
s.pop()        # -> 2
```

This object works exactly the same as before, but it's focused exclusively on just being a stack. There are no extraneous list methods or nonstack features. There is much more clarity of purpose.

A slight extension of this implementation might accept the internal list class as an optional argument:

```
class Stack:
    def __init__(self, *, container=None):
        if container is None:
            container = list()
        self._items = container

    def push(self, item):
        self._items.append(item)

    def pop(self):
        return self._items.pop()

    def __len__(self):
        return len(self._items)
```

One benefit of this approach is that it promotes loose coupling of components. For example, you might want to make a stack that stores its elements in a typed array instead of a list. Here's how you could do it:

```
import array

s = Stack(container=array.array('i'))
s.push(42)
s.push(23)
s.push('a lot')        # TypeError
```

This is also an example of what's known as *dependency injection*. Instead of hardwiring Stack to depend on list, you can make it depend on any container a user decides to pass in, provided it implements the required interface.

More broadly, making the internal list a hidden implementation detail is related to the problem of data abstraction. Perhaps you later decide that you don't even want to use a list. The above design makes that easy to change. For example, if you change the implementation to use linked tuples as follows, the users of Stack won't even notice:

```
class Stack:
    def __init__(self):
        self._items = None
        self._size = 0

    def push(self, item):
        self._items = (item, self._items)
        self._size += 1

    def pop(self):
        (item, self._items) = self._items
        self._size -= 1
```

```
        return item

    def __len__(self):
        return self._size
```

To decide whether to use inheritance or not, you should step back and ask yourself if the object you're building is a specialized version of the parent class or if you are merely using it as a component in building something else. If it's the latter, don't use inheritance.

7.9   Avoiding Inheritance via Functions

Sometimes you might find yourself writing classes with just a single method that needs to be customized. For example, maybe you wrote a data parsing class like this:

```
class DataParser:
    def parse(self, lines):
        records = []
        for line in lines:
            row = line.split(',')
            record = self.make_record(row)
            records.append(row)
        return records

    def make_record(self, row):
        raise NotImplementedError()

class PortfolioDataParser(DataParser):
    def make_record(self, row):
        return {
            'name': row[0],
            'shares': int(row[1]),
            'price': float(row[2])
        }

parser = PortfolioDataParser()
data = parser.parse(open('portfolio.csv'))
```

There is too much plumbing going on here. If you're writing a lot of single-method classes, consider using functions instead. For example:

```
def parse_data(lines, make_record):
    records = []
    for line in lines:
        row = line.split(',')
        record = make_record(row)
```

```
        records.append(row)
    return records

def make_dict(row):
    return {
        'name': row[0],
        'shares': int(row[1]),
        'price': float(row[2])
    }


data = parse_data(open('portfolio.csv'), make_dict)
```

This code is much simpler and just as flexible, plus simple functions are easier to test. If there's a need to expand it into classes, you can always do it later. Premature abstraction is often not a good thing.

7.10   Dynamic Binding and Duck Typing

Dynamic binding is the runtime mechanism that Python uses to find the attributes of objects. This is what allows Python to work with instances without regard for their type. In Python, variable names do not have an associated type. Thus, the attribute binding process is independent of what kind of object obj is. If you make a lookup, such as obj.name, it will work on any obj whatsoever that happens to have a name attribute. This behavior is sometimes referred to as duck typing—in reference to the adage "if it looks like a duck, quacks like a duck, and walks like a duck, then it's a duck."

Python programmers often write programs that rely on this behavior. For example, if you want to make a customized version of an existing object, you can either inherit from it, or you can create a completely new object that looks and acts like it but is otherwise unrelated. This latter approach is often used to maintain loose coupling of program components. For example, code may be written to work with any kind of object whatsoever as long as it has a certain set of methods. One of the most common examples is with various iterable objects defined in the standard library. There are all sorts of objects that work with the for loop to produce values—lists, files, generators, strings, and so on. However, none of these inherit from any kind of special Iterable base class. They merely implement the methods required to perform iteration—and it all works.

7.11   The Danger of Inheriting from Built-in Types

Python allows inheritance from built-in types. However, doing so invites danger. As an example, if you decide to subclass dict in order to force all keys to be uppercase, you might redefine the __setitem__() method like this:

```
class udict(dict):
    def __setitem__(self, key, value):
        super().__setitem__(key.upper(), value)
```

Indeed, it initially even seems to work:

```
>>> u = udict()
>>> u['name'] = 'Guido'
>>> u['number'] = 37
>>> u
{ 'NAME': 'Guido', 'NUMBER': 37 }
>>>
```

Further use, however, reveals that it only seems to work. In fact, it doesn't really seem to work at all:

```
>>> u = udict(name='Guido', number=37)
>>> u
{ 'name': 'Guido', 'number': 37 }
>>> u.update(color='blue')
>>> u
{ 'name': 'Guido', 'number': 37, 'color': 'blue' }
>>>
```

At issue here is the fact that Python's built-in types aren't implemented like normal Python classes—they're implemented in C. Most of the methods operate in the world of C. For example, the dict.update() method directly manipulates the dictionary data without ever routing through the redefined __setitem__() method in your custom udict class above.

The collections module has special classes UserDict, UserList, and UserString that can be used to make safe subclasses of dict, list, and str types. For example, you'll find that this solution works a lot better:

```
from collections import UserDict

class udict(UserDict):
    def __setitem__(self, key, value):
        super().__setitem__(key.upper(), value)
```

Here's an example of this new version in action:

```
>>> u = udict(name='Guido', num=37)
>>> u.update(color='Blue')
>>> u
{'NAME': 'Guido', 'NUM': 37, 'COLOR': 'Blue'}
>>> v = udict(u)
>>> v['title'] = 'BDFL'
>>> v
```

```
{'NAME': 'Guido', 'NUM': 37, 'COLOR': 'Blue', 'TITLE': 'BDFL'}
>>>
```

Most of the time, subclassing a built-in type can be avoided. For example, when building new containers, it is probably better to make a new class, as was shown for the Stack class in Section 7.8. If you really do need to subclass a built-in, it might be a lot more work than you think.

7.12   Class Variables and Methods

In a class definition, all functions are assumed to operate on an instance, which is always passed as the first parameter self. However, the class itself is also an object that can carry state and be manipulated as well. As an example, you could track how many instances have been created using a class variable num_accounts:

```
class Account:
    num_accounts = 0

    def __init__(self, owner, balance):
        self.owner = owner
        self.balance = balance
        Account.num_accounts += 1

    def __repr__(self):
        return f'{type(self).__name__}({self.owner!r}, {self.balance!r})'

    def deposit(self, amount):
        self.balance += amount

    def withdraw(self, amount):
        self.deposit(-amount)      # Must use self.deposit()

    def inquiry(self):
        return self.balance
```

Class variables are defined outside the normal __init__() method. To modify them, use the class, not self. For example:

```
>>> a = Account('Guido', 1000.0)
>>> b = Account('Eva', 10.0)
>>> Account.num_accounts
2
>>>
```

It's a bit unusual, but class variables can also be accessed via instances. For example:

```
>>> a.num_accounts
2
>>> c = Account('Ben', 50.0)
>>> Account.num_accounts
3
>>> a.num_accounts
3
>>>
```

This works because attribute lookup on instances checks the associated class if there's no matching attribute on the instance itself. This is the same mechanism by which Python normally finds methods.

It is also possible to define what's known as a *class method*. A class method is a method applied to the class itself, not to instances. A common use of class methods is to define alternate instance constructors. For example, suppose there was a requirement to create Account instances from a legacy enterprise-grade input format:

```
data = '''
<account>
    <owner>Guido</owner>
    <amount>1000.0</amount>
</account>
'''
```

To do that, you can write a @classmethod like this:

```
class Account:
    def __init__(self, owner, balance):
        self.owner = owner
        self.balance = balance

    @classmethod
    def from_xml(cls, data):
        from xml.etree.ElementTree import XML
        doc = XML(data)
        return cls(doc.findtext('owner'), float(doc.findtext('amount')))

# Example use
data = '''
<account>
    <owner>Guido</owner>
    <amount>1000.0</amount>
</account>
'''

a = Account.from_xml(data)
```

The first argument of a class method is always the class itself. By convention, this argument is often named `cls`. In this example, `cls` is set to `Account`. If the purpose of a class method is to create a new instance, explicit steps must be taken to do so. In the final line of the example, the call `cls(..., ...)` is the same as calling `Account(..., ...)` on the two arguments.

The fact that the class is passed as argument solves an important problem related to inheritance. Suppose you define a subclass of `Account` and now want to create an instance of that class. You'll find that it still works:

```
class EvilAccount(Account):
    pass


e = EvilAccount.from_xml(data)    # Creates an 'EvilAccount'
```

The reason this code works is that `EvilAccount` is now passed as `cls`. Thus, the last statement of the `from_xml()` classmethod now creates an `EvilAccount` instance.

Class variables and class methods are sometimes used together to configure and control how instances operate. As another example, consider the following `Date` class:

```
import time


class Date:
    datefmt = '{year}-{month:02d}-{day:02d}'
    def __init__(self, year, month, day):
        self.year = year
        self.month = month
        self.day = day

    def __str__(self):
        return self.datefmt.format(year=self.year,
                                   month=self.month,
                                   day=self.day)

    @classmethod
    def from_timestamp(cls, ts):
        tm = time.localtime(ts)
        return cls(tm.tm_year, tm.tm_mon, tm.tm_mday)

    @classmethod
    def today(cls):
        return cls.from_timestamp(time.time())
```

This class features a class variable `datefmt` that adjusts output from the `__str__()` method. This is something that can be customized via inheritance:

```
class MDYDate(Date):
    datefmt = '{month}/{day}/{year}'

class DMYDate(Date):
    datefmt = '{day}/{month}/{year}'

# Example
a = Date(1967, 4, 9)
print(a)        # 1967-04-09

b = MDYDate(1967, 4, 9)
print(b)        # 4/9/1967

c = DMYDate(1967, 4, 9)
print(c)        # 9/4/1967
```

Configuration via class variables and inheritance like this is a common tool for adjusting the behavior of instances. The use of class methods is critical to making it work since they ensure that the proper kind of object gets created. For example:

```
a = MDYDate.today()
b = DMYDate.today()
print(a)        # 2/13/2019
print(b)        # 13/2/2019
```

Alternate construction of instances is, by far, the most common use of class methods. A common naming convention for such methods is to include the word from_ as a prefix, such as from_timestamp(). You will see this naming convention used in class methods throughout the standard library and in third-party packages. For example, dictionaries have a class method for creating a preinitialized dictionary from a set of keys:

```
>>> dict.from_keys(['a','b','c'], 0)
{'a': 0, 'b': 0, 'c': 0}
>>>
```

One caution about class methods is that Python does not manage them in a namespace separate from the instance methods. As a result, they can still be invoked on an instance. For example:

```
d = Date(1967,4,9)
b = d.today()           # Calls Date.now(Date)
```

This is potentially quite confusing because a call to d.today() doesn't really have anything to do with the instance d. Yet, you might see today() listed as a valid method on Date instances in your IDE and in documentation.

7.13   Static Methods

Sometimes a class is merely used as a namespace for functions declared as static methods using @staticmethod. Unlike a normal method or class method, a static method does not take an extra self or cls argument. A static method is just a ordinary function that happens to be defined inside a class. For example:

```
class Ops:
    @staticmethod
    def add(x, y):
        return x + y

    @staticmethod
    def sub(x, y):
        return x - y
```

You don't normally create instances of such a class. Instead, call the functions directly through the class:

```
a = Ops.add(2, 3)       # a = 5
b = Ops.sub(4, 5)       # a = -1
```

Sometimes other classes will use a collection of static methods like this to implement "swappable" or "configurable" behavior, or as something that loosely mimics the behavior of an import module. Consider the use of inheritance in the earlier Account example:

```
class Account:
    def __init__(self, owner, balance):
        self.owner = owner
        self.balance = balance

    def __repr__(self):
        return f'{type(self).__name__}({self.owner!r}, {self.balance!r})'

    def deposit(self, amount):
        self.balance += amount

    def withdraw(self, amount):
        self.balance -= amount

    def inquiry(self):
        return self.balance

# A special "Evil" account
class EvilAccount(Account):
    def deposit(self, amount):
        self.balance += 0.95 * amount
```

```
def inquiry(self):
    if random.randint(0,4) == 1:
        return 1.10 * self.balance
    else:
        return self.balance
```

The use of inheritance here is a little strange. It introduces two different kinds of objects, `Account` and `EvilAccount`. There is also no obvious way to change an existing `Account` instance into an `EvilAccount` or back, because this involves changing the instance type. Perhaps it's better to have evil manifest as a kind of an account policy instead. Here is an alternate formulation of `Account` that does that with static methods:

```
class StandardPolicy:
    @staticmethod
    def deposit(account, amount):
        account.balance += amount

    @staticmethod
    def withdraw(account, amount):
        account.balance -= amount

    @staticmethod
    def inquiry(account):
        return account.balance

class EvilPolicy(StandardPolicy):
    @staticmethod
    def deposit(account, amount):
        account.balance += 0.95*amount

    @staticmethod
    def inquiry(account):
        if random.randint(0,4) == 1:
            return 1.10 * account.balance
        else:
            return account.balance

class Account:
    def __init__(self, owner, balance, *, policy=StandardPolicy):
        self.owner = owner
        self.balance = balance
        self.policy = policy

    def __repr__(self):
        return f'Account({self.policy}, {self.owner!r}, {self.balance!r})'
```

```
    def deposit(self, amount):
        self.policy.deposit(self, amount)

    def withdraw(self, amount):
        self.policy.withdraw(self, amount)

    def inquiry(self):
        return self.policy.inquiry(self)
```

In this reformulation, there is only one type of instance that gets created, `Account`. However, it has a special `policy` attribute that provides the implementation of various methods. If needed, the policy can be dynamically changed on an existing `Account` instance:

```
>>> a = Account('Guido', 1000.0)
>>> a.policy
<class 'StandardPolicy'>
>>> a.deposit(500)
>>> a.inquiry()
1500.0
>>> a.policy = EvilPolicy
>>> a.deposit(500)
>>> a.inquiry()        # Could randomly be 1.10x more
1975.0
>>>
```

One reason why `@staticmethod` makes sense here is that there is no need to create instances of `StandardPolicy` or `EvilPolicy`. The main purpose of these classes is to organize a bundle of methods, not to store additional instance data that's related to `Account`. Still, the loosely coupled nature of Python could certainly allow a policy to be upgraded to hold its own data. Change the static methods to normal instance methods like this:

```
class EvilPolicy(StandardPolicy):
    def __init__(self, deposit_factor, inquiry_factor):
        self.deposit_factor = deposit_factor
        self.inquiry_factor = inquiry_factor

    def deposit(self, account, amount):
        account.balance += self.deposit_factor * amount

    def inquiry(self, account):
        if random.randint(0,4) == 1:
            return self.inquiry_factor * account.balance
        else:
            return account.balance
```

```
# Example use
a = Account('Guido', 1000.0, policy=EvilPolicy(0.95, 1.10))
```

This approach of delegating methods to supporting classes is a common implementation strategy for state machines and similar objects. Each operational state can be encapsulated into its own class of methods (often static). A mutable instance variable, such as the `policy` attribute in this example, can then be used to hold implementation-specific details related to the current operational state.

7.14   A Word about Design Patterns

In writing object-oriented programs, programmers sometimes get fixated on implementing named design patterns—such as the "strategy pattern," the "flyweight pattern," the "singleton pattern," and so forth. Many of these originate from the famous *Design Patterns* book by Erich Gamma, Richard Helm, Ralph Johnson, and John Vlissides.

If you are familiar with such patterns, the general design principles used in other languages can certainly be applied to Python. However, many of these documented patterns are aimed at working around specific issues that arise from the strict static type system of C++ or Java. The dynamic nature of Python renders a lot of these patterns obsolete, an overkill, or simply unnecessary.

That said, there are a few overarching principles of writing good software—such as striving to write code that is debuggable, testable, and extensible. Basic strategies such as writing classes with useful `__repr__()` methods, preferring composition over inheritance, and allowing dependency injection can go a long way towards these goals. Python programmers also like to work with code that can be said to be "Pythonic." Usually, that means that objects obey various built-in protocols, such as iteration, containers, or context management. For example, instead of trying to implement some exotic data traversal pattern from a Java programming book, a Python programmer would probably implement it with a generator function feeding a `for` loop, or just replace the entire pattern with a few dictionary lookups.

7.15   Data Encapsulation and Private Attributes

In Python, all attributes and methods of a class are *public*, that is, accessible without any restrictions. This is often undesirable in object-oriented applications that have reasons to hide or encapsulate internal implementation details.

To address this problem, Python relies on naming conventions as a means of signaling intended usage. One such convention is that names starting with a single leading underscore (_) indicate internal implementation. For example, here's a version of the `Account` class where the balance has been turned into a "private" attribute:

```
class Account:
    def __init__(self, owner, balance):
        self.owner = owner
        self._balance = balance

    def __repr__(self):
        return f'Account({self.owner!r}, {self._balance!r})'

    def deposit(self, amount):
        self._balance += amount

    def withdraw(self, amount):
        self._balance -= amount

    def inquiry(self):
        return self._balance
```

In this code, the _balance attribute is meant to be an internal detail. There's nothing that prevents a user from accessing it directly, but the leading underscore is a strong indicator that a user should look for a more public-facing interface—such as the Account.inquiry() method.

A grey area is whether or not internal attributes are available for use in a subclass. For example, is the previous inheritance example allowed to directly access the _balance attribute of its parent?

```
class EvilAccount(Account):
    def inquiry(self):
        if random.randint(0,4) == 1:
            return 1.10 * self._balance
        else:
            return self._balance
```

As a general rule, this is considered acceptable in Python. IDEs and other tools are likely to expose such attributes. If you come from C++, Java, or another similar object-oriented language, consider _balance similar to a "protected" attribute.

If you wish to have an even more private attribute, prefix the name with two leading underscores (__). All names such as __name are automatically renamed into a new name of the form _Classname__name. This ensures that private names used in a superclass won't be overwritten by identical names in a child class. Here's an example that illustrates this behavior:

```
class A:
    def __init__(self):
        self.__x = 3          # Mangled to self._A__x

    def __spam(self):         # Mangled to _A__spam()
```

```
        print('A.__spam', self.__x)

    def bar(self):
        self.__spam()          # Only calls A.__spam()

class B(A):
    def __init__(self):
        A.__init__(self)
        self.__x = 37          # Mangled to self._B__x

    def __spam(self):          # Mangled to _B__spam()
        print('B.__spam', self.__x)

    def grok(self):
        self.__spam()          # Calls B.__spam()
```

In this example, there are two different assignments to an __x attribute. In addition, it appears that class B is trying to override the __spam() method via inheritance. Yet this is not the case. Name mangling causes unique names to be used for each definition. Try the following example:

```
>>> b = B()
>>> b.bar()
A.__spam 3
>>> b.grok()
B.__spam 37
>>>
```

You can see the mangled names more directly if you look at the underlying instance variables:

```
>>> vars(b)
{ '_A__x': 3, '_B__x': 37 }
>>> b._A__spam()
A.__spam 3
>>> b._B__spam
B.__spam 37
>>>
```

Although this scheme provides the illusion of data hiding, there's no mechanism in place to actually prevent access to the "private" attributes of a class. In particular, if the names of the class and the corresponding private attribute are known, they can still be accessed using the mangled name. If such access to private attributes is still a concern, you might consider a more painful code review process.

At first glance, name mangling might look like an extra processing step. However, the mangling process actually only occurs once when the class is defined. It does not occur during execution of the methods, nor does it add extra overhead to program execution.

Be aware that name mangling does not occur in functions such as getattr(), hasattr(), setattr(), or delattr() where the attribute name is specified as a string. For these functions, you would need to explicitly use the mangled name such as '_Classname__name' to access the attribute.

In practice, it's probably best to not overthink the privacy of names. The single-underscore names are quite common; double-underscore names less so. Although you can take further steps to try and truly hide attributes, the extra effort and added complexity is hardly worth the benefits gained. Perhaps the most useful thing is to remember that if you see leading underscores on a name, it's almost certainly some kind of internal detail best left alone.

7.16 Type Hinting

Attributes of user-defined classes have no constraints on their type or value. In fact, you can set an attribute to anything that you want. For example:

```
>>> a = Account('Guido', 1000.0)
>>> a.owner
'Guido'
>>> a.owner = 37
>>> a.owner
37
>>> b = Account('Eva', 'a lot')
>>> b.deposit(' more')
>>> b.inquiry()
'a lot more'
>>>
```

If this is a practical concern, there are a few possible solutions. One is easy—don't do that! Another is to rely upon external tooling such as linters and type checkers. For this, classes allow optional type hints to be specified for selected attributes. For example:

```
class Account:
    owner: str          # Type hint
    _balance: float     # Type hint

    def __init__(self, owner, balance):
        self.owner = owner
        self._balance = balance
    ...
```

The inclusion of type hints changes nothing about the actual runtime behavior of a class—that is, no extra checking takes place and nothing prevents a user from setting bad values in their code. However, the hints might give users more useful information in their editor, thus preventing careless usage errors before they happen.

In practice, accurate type hinting can be difficult. For example, does the `Account` class allow someone to use an `int` instead of a `float`? Or what about a `Decimal`? You'll find that all of these work even though the hint might seem to suggest otherwise.

```
from decimal import Decimal

a = Account('Guido', Decimal('1000.0'))
a.withdraw(Decimal('50.0'))
print(a.inquiry())              # -> 950.0
```

Knowing how to properly organize types in such situations is beyond the scope of this book. When in doubt, it's probably better not to guess unless you are actively using tools that type-check your code.

7.17 Properties

As noted in the previous section, Python places no runtime restrictions on attribute values or types. However, such enforcement is possible if you put an attribute under the management of a so-called *property*. A property is a special kind of attribute that intercepts attribute access and handles it via user-defined methods. These methods have complete freedom to manage the attribute as they see fit. Here is an example:

```
import string

class Account:
    def __init__(self, owner, balance):
        self.owner = owner
        self._balance = balance

    @property
    def owner(self):
        return self._owner

    @owner.setter
    def owner(self, value):
        if not isinstance(value, str):
            raise TypeError('Expected str')
        if not all(c in string.ascii_uppercase for c in value):
            raise ValueError('Must be uppercase ASCII')
        if len(value) > 10:
            raise ValueError('Must be 10 characters or less')
        self._owner = value
```

Here, the `owner` attribute is being constrained to a very enterprise-grade 10-character uppercase ASCII string. Here is how it works when you try to use the class:

```
>>> a = Account('GUIDO', 1000.0)
>>> a.owner = 'EVA'
>>> a.owner = 42
Traceback (most recent call last):
...
TypeError: Expected str
>>> a.owner = 'Carol'
Traceback (most recent call last):
...
ValueError: Must be uppercase ASCII
>>> a.owner = 'RENÉE'
Traceback (most recent call last):
...
ValueError: Must be uppercase ASCII
>>> a.owner = 'RAMAKRISHNAN'
Traceback (most recent call last):
...
ValueError: Must be 10 characters or less
>>>
```

The @property decorator is used to establish an attribute as a property. In this example, it's being applied to the owner attribute. This decorator is always first applied to a method that gets the attribute value. In this case, the method is returning the actual value which is being stored in the private attribute _owner. The @owner.setter decorator that follows is used to optionally implement a method for setting the attribute value. This method performs the various type and value checks before storing the value in the private _owner attribute.

A critical feature of properties is that the associated name, such as owner in the example, becomes "magical." That is, any use of that attribute automatically routes through the getter/setter methods that you implemented. You don't have to change any preexisting code to make this work. For example, no changes need to be made to the Account.__init__() method. This may surprise you because __init__() makes the assignment self.owner = owner instead of using the private attribute self._owner. This is by design—the whole point of the owner property was to validate attribute values. You'd definitely want to do that when instances are created. You'll find that it works exactly as intended:

```
>>> a = Account('Guido', 1000.0)
Traceback (most recent call last):
  File "account.py", line 5, in __init__
    self.owner = owner
  File "account.py", line 15, in owner
    raise ValueError('Must be uppercase ASCII')
ValueError: Must be uppercase ASCII
>>>
```

Since each access to a property attribute automatically invokes a method, the actual value needs to be stored under a different name. This is why _owner is used inside the getter and setter methods. You can't use owner as the storage location because doing so would cause infinite recursion.

In general, properties allow for the interception of any specific attribute name. You can implement methods for getting, setting, or deleting the attribute value. For example:

```
class SomeClass:
    @property
    def attr(self):
        print('Getting')

    @attr.setter
    def attr(self, value):
        print('Setting', value)

    @attr.deleter
    def attr(self):
        print('Deleting')


# Example
s = SomeClass()
s.attr          # Getting
s.attr = 13     # Setting
del s.attr      # Deleting
```

It is not necessary to implement all parts of a property. In fact, it's common to use properties for implementing read-only computed data attributes. For example:

```
class Box(object):
    def __init__(self, width, height):
        self.width = width
        self.height = height

    @property
    def area(self):
        return self.width * self.height

    @property
    def perimeter(self):
        return 2*self.width + 2*self.height

# Example use
b = Box(4, 5)
```

```
print(b.area)        # -> 20
print(b.perimeter)   # -> 18
b.area = 5           # Error: can't set attribute
```

One thing to think about when defining a class is making the programming interface to it as uniform as possible. Without properties, some values would be accessed as simple attributes such as b.width or b.height whereas other values would be accessed as methods such as b.area() and b.perimeter(). Keeping track of when to add the extra () creates unnecessary confusion. A property can help fix this.

Python programmers don't often realize that methods themselves are implicitly handled as a kind of property. Consider this class:

```
class SomeClass:
    def yow(self):
        print('Yow!')
```

When a user creates an instance such as s = SomeClass() and then accesses s.yow, the original function object yow is not returned. Instead, you get a bound method like this:

```
>>> s = SomeClass()
>>> s.yow
<bound method SomeClass.yow of <__main__.SomeClass object at 0x10e2572b0>>
>>>
```

How did this happen? It turns out that functions behave a lot like properties when they're placed in a class. Specifically, functions magically intercept attribute access and create the bound method behind the scenes. When you define static and class methods using @staticmethod and @classmethod, you are actually altering this process. @staticmethod returns the method function back "as is" without any special wrapping or processing. More information about this process is covered later in Section 7.28.

7.18 Types, Interfaces, and Abstract Base Classes

When you create an instance of a class, the type of that instance is the class itself. To test for membership in a class, use the built-in function isinstance(obj, cls). This function returns True if an object, obj, belongs to the class cls or any class derived from cls. Here's an example:

```
class A:
    pass


class B(A):
    pass
```

```
class C:
    pass

a = A()              # Instance of 'A'
b = B()              # Instance of 'B'
c = C()              # Instance of 'C'

type(a)              # Returns the class object A
isinstance(a, A)     # Returns True
isinstance(b, A)     # Returns True, B derives from A
isinstance(b, C)     # Returns False, B not derived from C
```

Similarly, the built-in function issubclass(A, B) returns True if the class A is a subclass of class B. Here's an example:

```
issubclass(B, A)     # Returns True
issubclass(C, A)     # Returns False
```

A common use of class typing relations is the specification of programming interfaces. As an example, a top-level base class might be implemented to specify the requirements of a programming interface. That base class might then be used for type hinting or for defensive type enforcement via isinstance():

```
class Stream:
    def receive(self):
        raise NotImplementedError()

    def send(self, msg):
        raise NotImplementedError()

    def close(self):
        raise NotImplementedError()

# Example.
def send_request(stream, request):
    if not isinstance(stream, Stream):
        raise TypeError('Expected a Stream')
    stream.send(request)
    return stream.receive()
```

The anticipation with such code is not that Stream be used directly. Instead, different classes would inherit from Stream and implement the required functionality. A user would instantiate one of those classes instead. For example:

```
class SocketStream(Stream):
    def receive(self):
        ...
```

```
    def send(self, msg):
        ...

    def close(self):
        ...

class PipeStream(Stream):
    def receive(self):
        ...

    def send(self, msg):
        ...

    def close(self):
        ...

# Example
s = SocketStream()
send_request(s, request)
```

Worth discussing in this example is the runtime enforcement of the interface in `send_request()`. Should one use a type hint instead?

```
# Specifying an interface as a type hint
def send_request(stream:Stream, request):
    stream.send(request)
    return stream.receive()
```

Given that type hints aren't enforced, the decision of how to validate an argument against an interface really depends on when you want it to happen—at runtime, as a code checking step, or not at all.

This use of interface classes is more common in the organization of large frameworks and applications. However, with this approach you need to make sure that subclasses actually implement the required interface. For example, if a subclass chose not to implement one of the required methods or had a simple misspelling, the effects might go unnoticed at first as the code might still work in the common case. However, later on, the program will crash if the unimplemented method is invoked. Naturally, this would only take place at 3:30 AM in production.

To prevent this problem, it is common for interfaces to be defined as *abstract base classes* using the abc module. This module defines a base class (**ABC**) and a decorator (@abstractmethod) that are used together to describe an interface. Here is an example:

```
from abc import ABC, abstractmethod

class Stream(ABC):
    @abstractmethod
```

```
def receive(self):
    pass

@abstractmethod
def send(self, msg):
    pass

@abstractmethod
def close(self):
    pass
```

An abstract class is not meant to be instantiated directly. In fact, if you try to create a
`Stream` instance, you'll get an error:

```
>>> s = Stream()
Traceback (most recent call last):
  File "<stdin>", line 1, in <module>
TypeError: Can't instantiate abstract class Stream with abstract methods
close, receive, send
>>>
```

The error message tells you exactly what methods need to be implemented by a
`Stream`. This serves as a guide for writing subclasses. Suppose you write a subclass but
make a mistake:

```
class SocketStream(Stream):
    def read(self):          # Misnamed
        ...

    def send(self, msg):
        ...

    def close(self):
        ...
```

An abstract base class will catch the mistake upon instantiation. This is useful because
errors are caught early.

```
>>> s = SocketStream()
Traceback (most recent call last):
  File "<stdin>", line 1, in <module>
  TypeError: Can't instantiate abstract class SocketStream with abstract
methods receive
>>>
```

Although an abstract class cannot be instantiated, it can define methods and properties for use in subclasses. Moreover, an abstract method in the base can still be called from a subclass. For example, calling `super().receive()` from a subclass is allowed.

7.19 Multiple Inheritance, Interfaces, and Mixins

Python supports multiple inheritance. If a child class lists more than one parent, the child inherits all of the features of the parents. For example:

```python
class Duck:
    def walk(self):
        print('Waddle')

class Trombonist:
    def noise(self):
        print('Blat!')

class DuckBonist(Duck, Trombonist):
    pass


d = DuckBonist()
d.walk()          # -> Waddle
d.noise()         # -> Blat!
```

Conceptually, it's a neat idea, but then practical realities start to set in. For example, what happens if `Duck` and `Trombonist` each define an `__init__()` method? Or if they both define a `noise()` method? Suddenly, you start to realize that multiple inheritance is fraught with peril.

To better understand the actual usage of multiple inheritance, step back and view it as a highly specialized tool for organization and code reuse—as opposed to a general-purpose programming technique. Specifically, taking a collection of arbitrary unrelated classes and combining them together with multiple inheritance to create weird mutant duck-musicians isn't standard practice. Don't ever do that.

A more common use of multiple inheritance is organizing type and interface relations. For example, the last section introduced the concept of an abstract base class. The purpose of an abstract base is to specify a programming interface. For example, you might have various abstract classes like this:

```python
from abc import ABC, abstractmethod

class Stream(ABC):
    @abstractmethod
```

```python
    def receive(self):
        pass

    @abstractmethod
    def send(self, msg):
        pass

    @abstractmethod
    def close(self):
        pass

class Iterable(ABC):
    @abstractmethod
    def __iter__(self):
        pass
```

With these classes, multiple inheritance might be used to specify which interfaces have been implemented by a child class:

```python
class MessageStream(Stream, Iterable):
    def receive(self):
        ...
    def send(self):
        ...
    def close(self):
        ...
    def __iter__(self):
        ...
```

Again, this use of multiple inheritance is not about implementation, but type relations. For example, none of the inherited methods even do anything in this example. There is no code reuse. Mainly, the inheritance relationship allows you to perform type checks like this:

```python
m = MessageStream()

isinstance(m, Stream)      # -> True
isinstance(m, Iterable)    # -> True
```

The other use of multiple inheritance is to define *mixin classes*. A mixin class is a class that modifies or extends the functionality of other classes. Consider the following class definitions:

```python
class Duck:
    def noise(self):
        return 'Quack'

    def waddle(self):
```

```
          return 'Waddle'

class Trombonist:
    def noise(self):
        return 'Blat!'

    def march(self):
        return 'Clomp'

class Cyclist:
    def noise(self):
        return 'On your left!'

    def pedal(self):
        return 'Pedaling'
```

These classes are completely unrelated to each other. There is no inheritance relationship and they implement different methods. However, there is a shared commonality in that they each define a `noise()` method. Using that as a guide, you could define the following classes:

```
class LoudMixin:
    def noise(self):
        return super().noise().upper()

class AnnoyingMixin:
    def noise(self):
        return 3*super().noise()
```

At first glance, these classes look wrong. There's just a single isolated method and it uses `super()` to delegate to a nonexistent parent class. The classes don't even work:

```
>>> a = AnnoyingMixin()
>>> a.noise()
Traceback (most recent call last):
...
AttributeError: 'super' object has no attribute 'noise'
>>>
```

These are mixin classes. The only way that they work is in combination with other classes that implement the missing functionality. For example:

```
class LoudDuck(LoudMixin, Duck):
    pass


class AnnoyingTrombonist(AnnoyingMixin, Trombonist):
    pass
```

```
class AnnoyingLoudCyclist(AnnoyingMixin, LoudMixin, Cyclist):
    pass

d = LoudDuck()
d.noise() # -> 'QUACK'

t = AnnoyingTrombonist()
t.noise() # -> 'Blat!Blat!Blat!'

c = AnnoyingLoudCyclist()
c.noise() # -> 'ON YOUR LEFT!ON YOUR LEFT!ON YOUR LEFT!'
```

Since mixin classes are defined in the same way as normal classes, it is best to include the word "Mixin" as part of the class name. This naming convention provides a greater clarity of purpose.

To fully understand mixins, you need to know a bit more about how inheritance and the super() function work.

First, whenever you use inheritance, Python builds a linear chain of classes known as the *Method Resolution Order*, or MRO for short. This is available as the __mro__ attribute on a class. Here are some examples for single inheritance:

```
class Base:
    pass

class A(Base):
    pass

class B(A):
    pass

Base.__mro__   # -> (<class 'Base'>, <class 'object'>)
A.__mro__      # -> (<class 'A'>, <class 'Base'>, <class 'object'>)
B.__mro__      # -> (<class 'B'>, <class 'A'>, <class 'Base'>, <class 'object'>)
```

The MRO specifies the search order for attribute lookup. Specifically, whenever you search for an attribute on an instance or class, each class on the MRO is checked in the order listed. The search stops when the first match is made. The object class is listed in the MRO because all classes inherit from object, whether or not it's listed as a parent.

To support multiple inheritance, Python implements what's known as "cooperative multiple inheritance." With cooperative inheritance, all of the classes are placed on the MRO list according to two primary ordering rules. The first rule states that a child class must always be checked before any of its parents. The second rule states that if a class has multiple parents, those parents must be checked in the same order as they're written in the inheritance list of the child. For the most part, these rules produce an MRO that makes sense. However, the precise algorithm that orders the classes is actually quite complex and not based on any simple approach such as depth-first or breadth-first search. Instead, the ordering is determined according to the C3 linearization algorithm, which is described in the paper "A Monotonic Superclass Linearization for Dylan" (K. Barrett, et al., presented at OOPSLA'96). A subtle aspect of this algorithm is that certain class hierarchies will be rejected by Python with a `TypeError`. Here's an example:

```
class X: pass
class Y(X): pass
class Z(X,Y): pass   # TypeError.
                     # Can't create consistent MRO
```

In this case, the method resolution algorithm rejects class Z because it can't determine an ordering of the base classes that makes sense. Here, the class X appears before class Y in the inheritance list, so it must be checked first. However, class Y inherits from X, so if X is checked first, it violates the rule about children being checked first. In practice, these issues rarely arise—and if they do, it usually indicates a more serious design problem.

As an example of an MRO in practice, here's the MRO for the `AnnoyingLoudCyclist` class shown earlier:

```
class AnnoyingLoudCyclist(AnnoyingMixin, LoudMixin, Cyclist):
    pass


AnnoyingLoudCyclist.__mro__
# (<class 'AnnoyingLoudCyclist'>, <class 'AnnoyingMixin'>,
#  <class 'LoudMixin'>, <class 'Cyclist'>, <class 'object'>)
```

In this MRO, you see how both rules are satisfied. Specifically, any child class is always listed before its parents. The `object` class is listed last because it is the parent of all other classes. The multiple parents are listed in the order they appeared in the code.

The behavior of the `super()` function is tied to the underlying MRO. Specifically, its role is to delegate attributes to the next class on the MRO. This is based upon the class where `super()` is used. For example, when the `AnnoyingMixin` class uses `super()`, it looks at the MRO of the instance to find its own position. From there, it delegates attribute lookup to the next class. In this example, using `super().noise()` in the `AnnoyingMixin` class invokes `LoudMixin.noise()`. This is because `LoudMixin` is the next class listed on the MRO for `AnnoyingLoudCyclist`. The `super().noise()` operation in the `LoudMixin` class then delegates to the `Cyclist` class. For any use of `super()`, the choice of the next class varies according to the type of the instance. For example, if you make an instance of `AnnoyingTrombonist`, then `super().noise()` will invoke `Trombonist.noise()` instead.

Designing for cooperative multiple inheritance and mixins is a challenge. Here are some design guidelines. First, child classes are always checked before any base class in the MRO. Thus, it is common for mixins to share a common parent, and for that parent to provide an empty implementation of methods. If multiple mixin classes are used at the same time, they'll line up after each other. The common parent will appear last where it can provide a default implementation or an error check. For example:

```
class NoiseMixin:
    def noise(self):
```

```
        raise NotImplementedError('noise() not implemented')

class LoudMixin(NoiseMixin):
    def noise(self):
        return super().noise().upper()

class AnnoyingMixin(NoiseMixin):
    def noise(self):
        return 3 * super().noise()
```

The second guideline is that all implementations of a mixin method should have an identical function signature. One issue with mixins is that they are optional and often mixed together in unpredictable order. For this to work, you must guarantee that operations involving super() succeed regardless of what class comes next. To do that, all methods in the call chain need to have a compatible calling signature.

Finally, you need to make sure that you use super() everywhere. Sometimes you'll encounter a class that makes a direct call to its parent:

```
class Base:
    def yow(self):
        print('Base.yow')

class A(Base):
    def yow(self):
        print('A.yow')
        Base.yow(self)        # Direct call to parent

class B(Base):
    def yow(self):
        print('B.yow')
        super().yow(self)

class C(A, B):
    pass

c = C()
c.yow()
# Outputs:
#    A.yow
#    Base.yow
```

Such classes are not safe to use with multiple inheritance. Doing so breaks the proper chain of method calls and causes confusion. For instance, in the above example, no output ever appears from B.yow() even though it's part of the inheritance hierarchy. If you're doing anything with multiple inheritance, you should be using super() instead of making direct calls to methods in superclasses.

7.20 Type-Based Dispatch

Sometimes you need to write code that dispatches based on a specific type. For example:

```
if isinstance(obj, Duck):
    handle_duck(obj)
elif isinstance(obj, Trombonist):
    handle_trombonist(obj)
elif isinstance(obj, Cyclist):
    handle_cyclist(obj)
else:
    raise RuntimeError('Unknown object')
```

Such a large if-elif-else block is inelegant and fragile. An often used solution is to dispatch through a dictionary:

```
handlers = {
    Duck: handle_duck,
    Trombonist: handle_trombonist,
    Cyclist: handle_cyclist
}


# Dispatch
def dispatch(obj):
    func = handlers.get(type(obj))
    if func:
        return func(obj)
    else:
        raise RuntimeError(f'No handler for {obj}')
```

This solution assumes an exact type match. If inheritance is also to be supported in such dispatch, you would need to walk the MRO:

```
def dispatch(obj):
    for ty in type(obj).__mro__:
        func = handlers.get(ty)
        if func:
            return func(obj)
    raise RuntimeError(f'No handler for {obj}')
```

Sometimes dispatching is implemented through a class-based interface using `getattr()` like this:

```
class Dispatcher:
    def handle(self, obj):
        for ty in type(obj).__mro__:
            meth = getattr(self, f'handle_{ty.__name__}', None)
```

```
        if meth:
            return meth(obj)
        raise RuntimeError(f'No handler for {obj}')

    def handle_Duck(self, obj):
        ...

    def handle_Trombonist(self, obj):
        ...

    def handle_Cyclist(self, obj):
        ...


# Example
dispatcher = Dispatcher()
dispatcher.handle(Duck())      # -> handle_Duck()
dispatcher.handle(Cyclist())   # -> handle_Cyclist()
```

This last example of using `getattr()` to dispatch onto methods of a class is a fairly common programming pattern.

7.21 Class Decorators

Sometimes you want to perform extra processing steps after a class has been defined—such as adding the class to a registry or generating extra support code. One approach is to use a class decorator. A class decorator is a function that takes a class as input and returns a class as output. For example, here's how you can maintain a registry:

```
_registry = { }
def register_decoder(cls):
    for mt in cls.mimetypes:
        _registry[mt.mimetype] = cls
    return cls

# Factory function that uses the registry
def create_decoder(mimetype):
    return _registry[mimetype]()
```

In this example, the `register_decoder()` function looks inside a class for a `mimetypes` attribute. If found, it's used to add the class to a dictionary mapping MIME types to class objects. To use this function, you apply it as a decorator right before the class definition:

```
@register_decoder
class TextDecoder:
    mimetypes = [ 'text/plain' ]
```

```
    def decode(self, data):
        ...

@register_decoder
class HTMLDecoder:
    mimetypes = [ 'text/html' ]
    def decode(self, data):
        ...

@register_decoder
class ImageDecoder:
    mimetypes = [ 'image/png', 'image/jpg', 'image/gif' ]
    def decode(self, data):
        ...

# Example usage
decoder = create_decoder('image/jpg')
```

A class decorator is free to modify the contents of the class it's given. For example, it might even rewrite existing methods. This is a common alternative to mixin classes or multiple inheritance. For example, consider these decorators:

```
def loud(cls):
    orig_noise = cls.noise
    def noise(self):
        return orig_noise(self).upper()
    cls.noise = noise
    return cls

def annoying(cls):
    orig_noise = cls.noise
    def noise(self):
        return 3 * orig_noise(self)
    cls.noise = noise
    return cls

@annoying
@loud
class Cyclist(object):
    def noise(self):
        return 'On your left!'

    def pedal(self):
        return 'Pedaling'
```

This example produces the same result as the mixin example from the previous section. However, there is no multiple inheritance and no use of super(). Within each decorator, the lookup of cls.noise performs the same action as super(). But, since this only happens once when the decorator is applied (at definition time), the resulting calls to noise() will run a bit faster.

Class decorators can also be used to create entirely new code. For example, a common task when writing a class is to write a useful __repr__() method for improved debugging:

```python
class Point:
    def __init__(self, x, y):
        self.x = x
        self.y = y

    def __repr__(self):
        return f'{type(self).__name__}({self.x!r}, {self.y!r})'
```

Writing such methods is often annoying. Perhaps a class decorator could create the method for you?

```python
import inspect
def with_repr(cls):
    args = list(inspect.signature(cls).parameters)
    argvals = ', '.join('{self.%s!r}' % arg for arg in args)
    code = 'def __repr__(self):\n'
    code += f'    return f"{cls.__name__}({argvals})"\n'
    locs = { }
    exec(code, locs)
    cls.__repr__ = locs['__repr__']
    return cls

# Example
@with_repr
class Point:
    def __init__(self, x, y):
        self.x = x
        self.y = y
```

In this example, a __repr__() method is generated from the calling signature of the __init__() method. The method is created as a text string and passed to exec() to create a function. That function is attached to the class.

Similar code generation techniques are used in parts of the standard library. For example, a convenient way to define data structures is to use a dataclass:

```python
from dataclasses import dataclass

@dataclass
class Point:
```

```
x: int
y: int
```

A dataclass automatically creates methods such as __init__() and __repr__() from class type hints. The methods are created using exec(), similarly to the prior example. Here's how the resulting Point class works:

```
>>> p = Point(2, 3)
>>> p
Point(x=2, y=3)
>>>
```

One downside of such an approach is poor startup performance. Dynamically creating code with exec() bypasses the compilation optimizations that Python normally applies to modules. Defining a large number of classes in this way may therefore significantly slow down the importing of your code.

The examples shown in this section illustrate common uses of class decorators—registration, code rewriting, code generation, validation, and so on. One issue with class decorators is that they must be explicitly applied to each class where they are used. This is not always desired. The next section describes a feature that allows for implicit manipulation of classes.

7.22 Supervised Inheritance

As you saw in the previous section, sometimes you want to define a class and perform additional actions. A class decorator is one mechanism for doing this. However, a parent class can also perform extra actions on behalf of its subclasses. This is accomplished by implementing an __init_subclass__(cls) class method. For example:

```
class Base:
    @classmethod
    def __init_subclass__(cls):
        print('Initializing', cls)

# Example (should see 'Initializing' message for each class)
class A(Base):
    pass

class B(A):
    pass
```

If an __init_subclass__() method is present, it is triggered automatically upon the definition of any child class. This happens even if the child is buried deeply in an inheritance hierarchy.

Many of the tasks commonly performed with class decorators can be performed with __init_subclass__() instead. For example, class registration:

```
class DecoderBase:
    _registry = { }
    @classmethod
    def __init_subclass__(cls):
        for mt in cls.mimetypes:
            DecoderBase._registry[mt.mimetype] = cls

# Factory function that uses the registry
def create_decoder(mimetype):
    return DecoderBase._registry[mimetype]()

class TextDecoder(DecoderBase):
    mimetypes = [ 'text/plain' ]
    def decode(self, data):
        ...

class HTMLDecoder(DecoderBase):
    mimetypes = [ 'text/html' ]
    def decode(self, data):
        ...

class ImageDecoder(DecoderBase):
    mimetypes = [ 'image/png', 'image/jpg', 'image/gif' ]
    def decode(self, data):
        ...

# Example usage
decoder = create_decoder('image/jpg')
```

Here is an example of a class that automatically creates a __repr__() method from the signature of the class __init__() method:

```
import inspect

class Base:
    @classmethod
    def __init_subclass__(cls):
        # Create a __repr__ method
        args = list(inspect.signature(cls).parameters)
        argvals = ', '.join('{self.%s!r}' % arg for arg in args)
        code = 'def __repr__(self):\n'
        code += f'    return f"{cls.__name__}({argvals})"\n'
        locs = { }
        exec(code, locs)
        cls.__repr__ = locs['__repr__']
```

```
class Point(Base):
    def __init__(self, x, y):
        self.x = x
        self.y = y
```

If multiple inheritance is being used, you should use `super()` to make sure all classes that implement __init_subclass__() get called. For example:

```
class A:
    @classmethod
    def __init_subclass__(cls):
        print('A.init_subclass')
        super().__init_subclass__()

class B:
    @classmethod
    def __init_subclass__(cls):
        print('B.init_subclass')
        super().__init_subclass__()

# Should see output from both classes here
class C(A, B):
    pass
```

Supervising inheritance with __init_subclass__() is one of Python's most powerful customization features. Much of its power comes from its implicit nature. A top-level base class can use this to quietly supervise an entire hierarchy of child classes. Such supervision can register classes, rewrite methods, perform validation, and more.

7.23 The Object Life Cycle and Memory Management

When a class is defined, the resulting class is a factory for creating new instances. For example:

```
class Account:
    def __init__(self, owner, balance):
        self.owner = owner
        self.balance = balance

# Create some Account instances
a = Account('Guido', 1000.0)
b = Account('Eva', 25.0)
```

The creation of an instance is carried out in two steps using the special method __new__() that creates a new instance and __init__() that initializes it. For example, the operation a = Account('Guido', 1000.0) performs these steps:

```
a = Account.__new__(Account, 'Guido', 1000.0)
if isinstance(a, Account):
    Account.__init__('Guido', 1000.0)
```

Except for the first argument which is the class instead of an instance, __new__() normally receives the same arguments as __init__(). However, the default implementation of __new__() just ignores them. You'll sometimes see __new__() invoked with just a single argument. For example, this code also works:

```
a = Account.__new__(Account)
Account.__init__('Guido', 1000.0)
```

Direct use of the __new__() method is uncommon, but sometimes it's used to create instances while bypassing the invocation of the __init__() method. One such use is in class methods. For example:

```
import time

class Date:
    def __init__(self, year, month, day):
        self.year = year
        self.month = month
        self.day = day

    @classmethod
    def today(cls):
        t = time.localtime()
        self = cls.__new__(cls)    # Make instance
        self.year = t.tm_year
        self.month = t.tm_month
        self.day = t.tm_day
        return self
```

Modules that perform object serialization such as pickle also utilize __new__() to recreate instances when objects are deserialized. This is done without ever invoking __init__().

Sometimes a class will define __new__() if it wants to alter some aspect of instance creation. Typical applications include instance caching, singletons, and immutability. As an example, you might want Date class to perform date interning—that is, caching and reusing Date instances that have an identical year, month, and day. Here is one way that might be implemented:

```
class Date:
    _cache = { }

    @staticmethod
    def __new__(cls, year, month, day):
        self = Date._cache.get((year,month,day))
        if not self:
            self = super().__new__(cls)
            self.year = year
            self.month = month
            self.day = day
            Date._cache[year,month,day] = self
        return self

    def __init__(self, year, month, day):
        pass

# Example
d = Date(2012, 12, 21)
e = Date(2012, 12, 21)
assert d is e                   # Same object
```

In this example, the class keeps an internal dictionary of previously created `Date` instances. When creating a new `Date`, the cache is consulted first. If a match is found, that instance is returned. Otherwise, a new instance is created and initialized.

A subtle detail of this solution is the empty `__init__()` method. Even though instances are cached, every call to `Date()` still invokes `__init__()`. To avoid duplicated effort, the method simply does nothing—instance creation actually takes place in `__new__()` when an instance is created the first time.

There are ways to avoid the extra call to `__init__()` but it requires sneaky tricks. One way to avoid it is to have `__new__()` return an entirely different type instance—for example, one belonging to a different class. Another solution, described later, is to use a metaclass.

Once created, instances are managed by reference counting. If the reference count reaches zero, the instance is immediately destroyed. When the instance is about to be destroyed, the interpreter first looks for a `__del__()` method associated with the object and calls it. For example:

```
class Account(object):
    def __init__(self, owner, balance):
        self.owner = owner
        self.balance = balance

    def __del__(self):
        print('Deleting Account')
```

```
>>> a = Account('Guido', 1000.0)
>>> del a
Deleting Account
>>>
```

Occasionally, a program will use the `del` statement to delete a reference to an object as shown. If this causes the reference count of the object to reach zero, the `__del__()` method is called. However, in general, the `del` statement doesn't directly call `__del__()` because there may be other object references living elsewhere. There are many other ways that an object might be deleted—for example, reassignment of a variable name or a variable going out of scope in a function:

```
>>> a = Account('Guido', 1000.0)
>>> a = 42
Deleting Account
>>> def func():
...     a = Account('Guido', 1000.0)
...
>>> func()
Deleting Account
>>>
```

In practice, it's rarely necessary for a class to define a `__del__()` method. The only exception is when the destruction of an object requires an extra cleanup action—such as closing a file, shutting down a network connection, or releasing other system resources. Even in these cases, it's dangerous to rely on `__del__()` for a proper shutdown because there's no guarantee that this method will be called when you think it would. For clean shutdown of resources, you should give the object an explicit `close()` method. You should also make your class support the context manager protocol so it can be used with the `with` statement. Here is an example that covers all of the cases:

```
class SomeClass:
    def __init__(self):
        self.resource = open_resource()

    def __del__(self):
        self.close()

    def close(self):
        self.resource.close()

    def __enter__(self):
        return self

    def __exit__(self, ty, val, tb):
        self.close()
```

```
# Closed via __del__()
s = SomeClass()
del s

# Explicit close
s = SomeClass()
s.close()

# Closed at the end of a context block
with SomeClass() as s:
    ...
```

Again, it should be emphasized that writing a __del__() in a class is almost never necessary. Python already has garbage collection and there is simply no need to do it unless there is some extra action that needs to take place upon object destruction. Even then, you still might not need __del__() as it's possible that the object is already programmed to clean itself up properly even if you do nothing.

As if there weren't enough dangers with reference counting and object destruction, there are certain kinds of programming patterns—especially those involving parent–child relationships, graphs, or caching—where objects can create a so-called *reference cycle*. Here is an example:

```
class SomeClass:
    def __del__(self):
        print('Deleting')

parent = SomeClass()
child = SomeClass()

# Create a child-parent reference cycle
parent.child = child
child.parent = parent

# Try deletion (no output from __del__ appears)
del parent
del child
```

In this example, the variable names are destroyed but you never see execution of the __del__() method. The two objects each hold internal references to each other, so there's no way for the reference count to ever drop to 0. To handle this, a special cycle-detecting garbage collector runs every so often. Eventually the objects will be reclaimed, but it's hard to predict when this might happen. If you want to force garbage collection, you can call gc.collect(). The gc module has a variety of other functions related to the cyclic garbage collector and monitoring memory.

Because of the unpredictable timing of garbage collection, the __del__() method has a few restrictions placed on it. First, any exception that propagates out of __del__() is printed to `sys.stderr`, but otherwise ignored. Second, the `__del__()` method should avoid operations such as acquiring locks or other resources. Doing so could result in a deadlock when `__del__()` is unexpectedly fired in the middle of executing an unrelated function within the seventh inner callback circle of signal handling and threads. If you must define `__del__()`, keep it simple.

7.24   Weak References

Sometimes objects are kept alive when you'd much rather see them die. In an earlier example, a `Date` class was shown with internal caching of instances. One problem with this implementation is that there is no way for an instance to ever be removed from the cache. As such, the cache will grow larger and larger over time.

One way to fix this problem is to create a weak reference using the `weakref` module. A weak reference is a way of creating a reference to an object without increasing its reference count. To work with a weak reference, you have to add an extra bit of code to check if the object being referred to still exists. Here's an example of how you create a weakref:

```
>>> a = Account('Guido', 1000.0)
>>> import weakref
>>> a_ref = weakref.ref(a)
>>> a_ref
<weakref at 0x104617188; to 'Account' at 0x1046105c0>
>>>
```

Unlike a normal reference, a weak reference allows the original object to die. For example:

```
>>> del a
>>> a_ref
<weakref at 0x104617188; dead>
>>>
```

A weak reference contains an optional reference to an object. To get the actual object, you need to call the weak reference as a function with no arguments. This will either return the object being pointed at or `None`. For example:

```
acct = a_ref()
if acct is not None:
    acct.withdraw(10)

# Alternative
if acct := a_ref():
    acct.withdraw(10)
```

Weak references are commonly used in conjunction with caching and other advanced memory management. Here is a modified version of the Date class that automatically removes objects from the cache when no more references exist:

```
import weakref

class Date:
    _cache = { }

    @staticmethod
    def __new__(cls, year, month, day):
        selfref = Date._cache.get((year,month,day))
        if not selfref:
            self = super().__new__(cls)
            self.year = year
            self.month = month
            self.day = day
            Date._cache[year,month,day] = weakref.ref(self)
        else:
            self = selfref()
        return self

    def __init__(self, year, month, day):
        pass

    def __del__(self):
        del Date._cache[self.year,self.month,self.day]
```

This might require a bit of study, but here is an interactive session that shows how it works. Notice how an entry is removed from the cache once no more references to it exist:

```
>>> Date._cache
{}
>>> a = Date(2012, 12, 21)
>>> Date._cache
{(2012, 12, 21): <weakref at 0x10c7ee2c8; to 'Date' at 0x10c805518>}
>>> b = Date(2012, 12, 21)
>>> a is b
True
>>> del a
>>> Date._cache
{(2012, 12, 21): <weakref at 0x10c7ee2c8; to 'Date' at 0x10c805518>}
>>> del b
>>> Date._cache
{}
>>>
```

As previously noted, the `__del__()` method of a class is only invoked when the reference count of an object reaches zero. In this example, the first `del a` statement decreases the reference count. However, since there's still another reference to the same object, the object remains in `Date._cache`. When the second object is deleted, `__del__()` is invoked and the cache is cleared.

Support for weak references requires instances to have a mutable `__weakref__` attribute. Instances of user-defined classes normally have such an attribute by default. However, built-in types and certain kinds of special data structures—named tuples, classes with slots—do not. If you want to construct weak references to these types, you can do it by defining variants with a `__weakref__` attribute added:

```
class wdict(dict):
    __slots__ = ('__weakref__',)


w = wdict()
w_ref = weakref.ref(w)        # Now works
```

The use of slots here is to avoid unnecessary memory overhead, as explained shortly.

7.25   Internal Object Representation and Attribute Binding

The state associated with an instance is stored in a dictionary that's accessible as the instance's `__dict__` attribute. This dictionary contains the data that's unique to each instance. Here's an example:

```
>>> a = Account('Guido', 1100.0)
>>> a.__dict__
{'owner': 'Guido', 'balance': 1100.0}
```

New attributes can be added to an instance at any time:

```
a.number = 123456  # Add attribute 'number' to a.__dict__
a.__dict__['number'] = 654321
```

Modifications to an instance are always reflected in the local `__dict__` attribute unless the attribute is being managed by a property. Likewise, if you make modifications to `__dict__` directly, those modifications are reflected in the attributes.

Instances are linked back to their class by a special attribute `__class__`. The class itself is also just a thin layer over a dictionary that can be found in its own `__dict__` attribute. The class dictionary is where you find the methods. For example:

```
>>> a.__class__
<class '__main__.Account'>
>>> Account.__dict__.keys()
```

```
dict_keys(['__module__', '__init__', '__repr__', 'deposit', 'withdraw',
'inquiry', '__dict__', '__weakref__', '__doc__'])
>>> Account.__dict__['withdraw']
<function Account.withdraw at 0x108204158>
>>>
```

Classes are linked to their base classes by a special attribute __bases__, which is a tuple of the base classes. The __bases__ attribute is only informational. The actual runtime implementation of inheritance uses the __mro__ attribute which is a tuple of all parent classes listed in search order. This underlying structure is the basis for all operations that get, set, or delete the attributes of instances.

Whenever an attribute is set using obj.name = value, the special method obj.__setattr__('name', value) is invoked. If an attribute is deleted using del obj.name, the special method obj.__delattr__('name') is invoked. The default behavior of these methods is to modify or remove values from the local __dict__ of obj unless the requested attribute happens to correspond to a property or descriptor. In that case, the set and delete operations will be carried out by the set and delete functions associated with the property.

For attribute lookup such as obj.name, the special method obj.__getattribute__('name') is invoked. This method carries out the search for the attribute, which normally includes checking the properties, looking in the local __dict__, checking the class dictionary, and searching the MRO. If this search fails, a final attempt to find the attribute is made by invoking the obj.__getattr__('name') method of the class (if defined). If this fails, an AttributeError exception is raised.

User-defined classes can implement their own versions of the attribute access functions, if desired. For example, here's a class that restricts the attribute names that can be set:

```
class Account:
    def __init__(self, owner, balance):
        self.owner = owner
        self.balance = balance

    def __setattr__(self, name, value):
        if name not in {'owner', 'balance'}:
            raise AttributeError(f'No attribute {name}')
        super().__setattr__(name, value)

# Example
a = Account('Guido', 1000.0)
a.balance = 940.25            # Ok
a.amount = 540.2              # AttributeError. No attribute amount
```

A class that reimplements these methods should rely upon the default implementation provided by super() to carry out the actual work of manipulating an attribute. This is because the default implementation takes care of the more advanced features of classes such as descriptors and properties. If you don't use `super()`, you will have to take care of these details yourself.

7.26   Proxies, Wrappers, and Delegation

Sometimes classes implement a wrapper layer around another object to create a kind of proxy object. A proxy is an object exposes the same interface as another object but, for some reason, isn't related to the original object via inheritance. This is different from composition where an entirely new object is created from other objects but with its own unique set of methods and attributes.

There are many real-world scenarios where this might arise. For example, in distributed computing, the actual implementation of an object might live on a remote server in the cloud. Clients that interact with that server might use a proxy that looks like the object on the server but, behind the scenes, delegates all of its method calls via network messages.

A common implementation technique for proxies involves the __getattr__() method. Here is a simple example:

```
class A:
    def spam(self):
        print('A.spam')

    def grok(self):
        print('A.grok')

    def yow(self):
        print('A.yow')

class LoggedA:
    def __init__(self):
        self._a = A()

    def __getattr__(self, name):
        print("Accessing", name)
        # Delegate to internal A instance
        return getattr(self._a, name)

# Example use
a = LoggedA()
a.spam()        # prints "Accessing spam" and "A.spam"
a.yow()         # prints "Accessing yow" and "A.yow"
```

Delegation is sometimes used as an alternative to inheritance. Here is an example:

```
class A:
    def spam(self):
```

```
            print('A.spam')

        def grok(self):
            print('A.grok')

        def yow(self):
            print('A.yow')

class B:
    def __init__(self):
        self._a = A()

    def grok(self):
        print('B.grok')

    def __getattr__(self, name):
        return getattr(self._a, name)

# Example use
b = B()
b.spam()        # -> A.spam
b.grok()        # -> B.grok    (redefined method)
b.yow()         # -> A.yow
```

In this example, it appears as if class B might be inheriting from class A and redefining a single method. This is the observed behavior—but inheritance is not being used. Instead, B holds an internal reference to an A inside. Certain methods of A can be redefined. However, all of the other methods are delegated via the __getattr__() method.

The technique of forwarding attribute lookup via __getattr__() is a common technique. However, be aware that it does not apply to operations mapped to special methods. For example, consider this class:

```
class ListLike:
    def __init__(self):
        self._items = list()

    def __getattr__(self, name):
        return getattr(self._items, name)

# Example
a = ListLike()
a.append(1)         # Works
a.insert(0, 2)      # Works
a.sort()            # Works
```

```
len(a)                  # Fails. No __len__() method
a[0]                    # Fails. No __getitem__() method
```

Here, the class successfully forwards all of the standard list methods (`list.sort()`, `list.append()`, and so on) to an inner list. However, none of Python's standard operators work. To make those work, you would have to explicitly implement the required special methods. For example:

```
class ListLike:
    def __init__(self):
        self._items = list()

    def __getattr__(self, name):
        return getattr(self._items, name)

    def __len__(self):
        return len(self._items)

    def __getitem__(self, index):
        return self._items[index]

    def __setitem__(self, index, value):
        self._items[index] = value
```

7.27 Reducing Memory Use with __slots__

As we've seen, an instance stores its data in a dictionary. If you are creating a large number of instances, this can introduce a lot of memory overhead. If you know that the attribute names are fixed, you can specify the names in a special class variable called __slots__. Here's an example:

```
class Account(object):
    __slots__ = ('owner', 'balance')
    ...
```

Slots is a definition hint that allows Python to make performance optimizations for both memory use and execution speed. Instances of a class with __slots__ no longer use a dictionary for storing instance data. Instead, a much more compact data structure based on an array is used. In programs that create a large number of objects, using __slots__ can result in a substantial reduction in memory use and a modest improvement in execution time.

The only entries in __slots__ are instance attributes. You do not list methods, properties, class variables, or any other class-level attributes. Basically, it's the same names that would ordinarily appear as dictionary keys in the instance's __dict__.

Be aware that __slots__ has a tricky interaction with inheritance. If a class inherits from a base class that uses __slots__, it also needs to define __slots__ for storing its own attributes (even if it doesn't add any) to take advantage of the benefits __slots__ provides. If you forget this, the derived class will run slower—and use even more memory than if __slots__ had not been used on any of the classes!

__slots__ is incompatible with multiple inheritance. If multiple base classes are specified, each with nonempty slots, you will get a TypeError.

The use of __slots__ can also break code that expects instances to have an underlying __dict__ attribute. Although this often does not apply to user code, utility libraries and other tools for supporting objects may be programmed to look at __dict__ for debugging, serializing objects, and other operations.

The presence of __slots__ has no effect on the invocation of methods such as __getattribute__(), __getattr__(), and __setattr__() should they be redefined in a class. However, if you're implementing such methods, be aware that there is no longer any instance __dict__ attribute. Your implementation will need to take that into account.

7.28 Descriptors

Normally, attribute access corresponds to dictionary operations. If more control is needed, attribute access can be routed through user-defined get, set, and delete functions. The use of properties was already described. However, a property is actually implemented using a lower-level construct known as a descriptor. A descriptor is a class-level object that manages access to an attribute. By implementing one or more of the special methods __get__(), __set__(), and __delete__(), you can hook directly into the attribute access mechanism and customize those operations. Here is an example:

```
class Typed:
    expected_type = object

    def __set_name__(self, cls, name):
        self.key = name

    def __get__(self, instance, cls):
        if instance:
            return instance.__dict__[self.key]
        else:
            return self

    def __set__(self, instance, value):
        if not isinstance(value, self.expected_type):
            raise TypeError(f'Expected {self.expected_type}')
        instance.__dict__[self.key] = value
```

```
    def __delete__(self,instance):
        raise AttributeError("Can't delete attribute")

class Integer(Typed):
    expected_type = int

class Float(Typed):
    expected_type = float

class String(Typed):
    expected_type = str

# Example use:
class Account:
    owner = String()
    balance = Float()

    def __init__(self, owner, balance):
        self.owner = owner
        self.balance = balance
```

In this example, the class `Typed` defines a descriptor where type checking is performed when an attribute is assigned and an error is produced if an attempt is made to delete the attribute. The `Integer`, `Float`, and `String` subclasses specialize `Type` to match a specific type. The use of these classes in another class (such as `Account`) makes those attributes automatically call the appropriate __get__(), __set__(), or __delete__() methods on access. For example:

```
a = Account('Guido', 1000.0)
b = a.owner              # Calls Account.owner.__get__(a, Account)
a.owner = 'Eva'          # Calls Account.owner.__set__(a, 'Eva')
del f.owner              # Calls Account.owner.__delete__(a)
```

Descriptors can only be instantiated at the class level. It is not legal to create descriptors on a per-instance basis by creating descriptor objects inside __init__() and other methods. The __set_name__() method of a descriptor is invoked after a class has been defined, but before any instances have been created, to inform a descriptor about the name that has been used within the class. For instance, the `balance = Float()` definition calls `Float.__set_name__(Account, 'balance')` to inform the descriptor of the class and name being used.

Descriptors with a __set__() method always take precedence over items in the instance dictionary. For example, if a descriptor happens to have the same name as a key in the instance dictionary, the descriptor takes priority. In the above `Account` example, you'll see the descriptor applying type checking even though the instance dictionary has a matching entry:

```
>>> a = Account('Guido', 1000.0)
>>> a.__dict__
{'owner': 'Guido', 'balance': 1000.0 }
>>> a.balance = 'a lot'
Traceback (most recent call last):
  File "<stdin>", line 1, in <module>
  File "descrip.py", line 63, in __set__
    raise TypeError(f'Expected {self.expected_type}')
TypeError: Expected <class 'float'>
>>>
```

The __get__(instance, cls) method of a descriptor takes arguments for both the instance and the class. It's possible that __get__() is invoked at the class level, in which case the instance argument is None. In most cases, the __get__() returns the descriptor back if no instance is provided. For example:

```
>>> Account.balance
<__main__.Float object at 0x110606710>
>>>
```

A descriptor that only implements __get__() is known as a method descriptor. It has a weaker binding than a descriptor with both get/set capabilities. Specifically, the __get__() method of a method descriptor only gets invoked if there is no matching entry in the instance dictionary. The reason it's called a method descriptor is that this kind of descriptor is mainly used to implement Python's various types of methods—including instance methods, class methods, and static methods.

For example, here's a skeleton implementation that shows how @classmethod and @staticmethod could be implemented from scratch (the real implementation is more efficient):

```
import types
class classmethod:
    def __init__(self, func):
        self.__func__ = func

    # Return a bound method with cls as first argument
    def __get__(self, instance, cls):
        return types.MethodType(self.__func__, cls)

class staticmethod:
    def __init__(self, func):
        self.__func__ = func

    # Return the bare function
    def __get__(self, instance, cls):
        return self.__func__
```

Since method descriptors only act if there is no matching entry in the instance dictionary, they can also be used to implement various forms of lazy evaluation of attributes. For example:

```python
class Lazy:
    def __init__(self, func):
        self.func = func

    def __set_name__(self, cls, name):
        self.key = name

    def __get__(self, instance, cls):
        if instance:
            value = self.func(instance)
            instance.__dict__[self.key] = value
            return value
        else:
            return self

class Rectangle:
    def __init__(self, width, height):
        self.width = width
        self.height = height

    area = Lazy(lambda self: self.width * self.height)
    perimeter = Lazy(lambda self: 2*self.width + 2*self.height)
```

In this example, `area` and `perimeter` are attributes that are computed on demand and stored in the instance dictionary. Once computed, values are just returned directly from the instance dictionary.

```python
>>> r = Rectangle(3, 4)
>>> r.__dict__
{'width': 3, 'height': 4 }
>>> r.area
12
>>> r.perimeter
14
>>> r.__dict__
{'width': 3, 'height': 4, 'area': 12, 'perimeter': 14 }
>>>
```

7.29 Class Definition Process

The definition of a class is a dynamic process. When you define a class using the `class` statement, a new dictionary is created that serves as the local class namespace. The body of the class then executes as a script within this namespace. Eventually, the namespace becomes the `__dict__` attribute of the resulting class object.

Any legal Python statement is allowed in the body of a class. Normally, you just define functions and variables, but control flow, imports, nested classes, and everything else is allowed. For example, here is a class that conditionally defines methods:

```python
debug = True


class Account:
    def __init__(self, owner, balance):
        self.owner = owner
        self.balance = balance

    if debug:
        import logging
        log = logging.getLogger(f'{__module__}.{__qualname__}')
        def deposit(self, amount):
            Account.log.debug('Depositing %f', amount)
            self.balance += amount

        def withdraw(self, amount):
            Account.log.debug('Withdrawing %f', amount)
            self.balance -= amount
    else:
        def deposit(self, amount):
            self.balance += amount

        def withdraw(self, amount):
            self.balance -= amount
```

In this example, a global variable `debug` is being used to conditionally define methods. The `__qualname__` and `__module__` variables are predefined strings that hold information about the class name and enclosing module. These can be used by statements in the class body. In this example, they're being used to configure the logging system. There are probably cleaner ways of organizing the above code, but the key point is that you can put anything you want in a class.

One critical point about class definition is that the namespace used to hold the contents of the class body is not a scope of variables. Any name that gets used within a method (such as `Account.log` in the above example) needs to be fully qualified.

If a function like `locals()` is used in a class body (but not inside a method), it returns the dictionary being used for the class namespace.

7.30 Dynamic Class Creation

Normally, classes are created using the `class` statement, but this is not a requirement. As noted in the previous section, classes are defined by executing the body of a class to populate a namespace. If you're able to populate a dictionary with your own definitions, you can make a class without ever using the `class` statement. To do that, use `types.new_class()`:

```python
import types

# Some methods (not in a class)
def __init__(self, owner, balance):
    self.owner = owner
    self.balance = balance

def deposit(self, amount):
    self.balance -= amount

def withdraw(self, amount):
    self.balance += amount

methods = {
    '__init__': __init__,
    'deposit': deposit,
    'withdraw': withdraw,
}

Account = types.new_class('Account', (),
                    exec_body=lambda ns: ns.update(methods))

# You now have a class
a = Account('Guido', 1000.0)
a.deposit(50)
a.withdraw(25)
```

The `new_class()` function requires a class name, a tuple of base classes, and a callback function responsible for populating the class namespace. This callback receives the class namespace dictionary as an argument. It should update this dictionary in place. The return value of the callback is ignored.

Dynamic class creation may be useful if you want to create classes from data structures. For example, in the section on descriptors, the following classes were defined:

```python
class Integer(Typed):
    expected_type = int
```

```
class Float(Typed):
    expected_type = float

class String(Typed):
    expected_type = str
```

This code is highly repetitive. Perhaps a data-driven approach would be better:

```
typed_classes = [
    ('Integer', int),
    ('Float', float),
    ('String', str),
    ('Bool', bool),
    ('Tuple', tuple),
]

globals().update(
    (name, types.new_class(name, (Typed,),
        exec_body=lambda ns: ns.update(expected_type=ty)))
    for name, ty in typed_classes)
```

In this example, the global module namespace is being updated with dynamically created classes using `types.new_class()`. If you want to make more classes, put an appropriate entry in the `typed_classes` list.

Sometimes you will see `type()` being used to dynamically create a class instead. For example:

```
Account = type('Account', (), methods)
```

This works, but it doesn't take into account some of the more advanced class machinery such as metaclasses (to be discussed shortly). In modern code, try to use `types.new_class()` instead.

7.31 Metaclasses

When you define a class in Python, the class definition itself becomes an object. Here's an example:

```
class Account:
    def __init__(self, owner, balance):
        self.owner = owner
        self.balance = balance

    def deposit(self, amount):
        self.balance += amount
```

```
    def withdraw(self, amount):
        self.balance -= amount

isinstance(Account, object)          # -> True
```

If you think about this long enough, you will realize that if `Account` is an object, then something had to create it. This creation of the class object is controlled by a special kind of class called a *metaclass*. Simply put, a metaclass is a class that creates instances of classes.

In the preceding example, the metaclass that created `Account` is a built-in class called `type`. In fact, if you check the type of `Account`, you will see that it is an instance of `type`:

```
>>> Account.__class__
<type 'type'>
>>>
```

It's a bit brain-bending, but it's similar to integers. For example, if you write `x = 42` and then look at `x.__class__`, you'll get `int`, which is the class that creates integers. Similarly, `type` makes instances of types or classes.

When a new class is defined with the `class` statement, a number of things happen. First, a new namespace for the class is created. Next, the body of the class is executed in this namespace. Finally, the class name, base classes, and populated namespace are used to create the class instance. The following code illustrates the low-level steps that take place:

```
# Step 1: Create the class namespace
namespace = type.__prepare__('Account', ())

# Step 2: Execute the class body
exec('''
def __init__(self, owner, balance):
    self.owner = owner
    self.balance = balance

def deposit(self, amount):
    self.balance += amount

def withdraw(self, amount):
    self.balance -= amount
''', globals(), namespace)

# Step 3: Create the final class object
Account = type('Account', (), namespace)
```

In the definition process, there is interaction with the `type` class to create the class namespace and to create the final class object. The choice of using `type` can be customized—a class can choose to be processed by a different type class by specifying a different metaclass. This is done by using the `metaclass` keyword argument in inheritance:

```
class Account(metaclass=type):
    ...
```

If no `metaclass` is given, the `class` statement examines the type of the first entry in the tuple of base classes (if any) and uses that as the metaclass. Therefore, if you write `class Account(object)`, the resulting `Account` class will have the same type as `object` (which is `type`). Note that classes that don't specify any parent at all always inherit from `object`, so this still applies.

To create a new metaclass, define a class that inherits from `type`. Within this class, you can redefine one or more methods that are used during the class creation process. Typically, this includes the `__prepare__()` method used to create the class namespace, the `__new__()` method used to create the class instance, the `__init__()` method called after a class has already been created, and the `__call__()` method used to create new instances. The following example implements a metaclass that merely prints the input arguments to each method so you can experiment:

```
class mytype(type):

    # Creates the class namespace
    @classmethod
    def __prepare__(meta, clsname, bases):
        print("Preparing:", clsname, bases)
        return super().__prepare__(clsname, bases)

    # Creates the class instance after body has executed
    @staticmethod
    def __new__(meta, clsname, bases, namespace):
        print("Creating:", clsname, bases, namespace)
        return super().__new__(meta, clsname, bases, namespace)

    # Initializes the class instance
    def __init__(cls, clsname, bases, namespace):
        print("Initializing:", clsname, bases, namespace)
        super().__init__(clsname, bases, namespace)

    # Creates new instances of the class
    def __call__(cls, *args, **kwargs):
        print("Creating instance:", args, kwargs)
        return super().__call__(*args, **kwargs)

# Example
class Base(metaclass=mytype):
    pass

# Definition of the Base produces the following output
```

```
# Preparing: Base ()
# Creating: Base () {'__module__': '__main__', '__qualname__': 'Base'}
# Initializing: Base () {'__module__': '__main__', '__qualname__': 'Base'}


b = Base()
# Creating instance: () {}
```

One tricky facet of working with metaclasses is the naming of variables and keeping track of the various entities involved. In the above code, the meta name refers to the metaclass itself. The cls name refers to a class instance created by the metaclass. Although not used here, the self name refers to a normal instance created by a class.

Metaclasses propagate via inheritance. So, if you've defined a base class to use a different metaclass, all child classes will also use that metaclass. Try this example to see your custom metaclass at work:

```
class Account(Base):
    def __init__(self, owner, balance):
        self.owner = owner
        self.balance = balance

    def deposit(self, amount):
        self.balance += amount

    def withdraw(self, amount):
        self.balance -= amount

print(type(Account))    # -> <class 'mytype'>
```

The primary use of metaclasses is in situations where you want to exert extreme low-level control over the class definition environment and creation process. Before proceeding, however, remember that Python already provides a lot of functionality for monitoring and altering class definitions (such as the __init_subclass__() method, class decorators, descriptors, mixins, and so on). Most of the time, you probably don't need a metaclass. That said, the next few examples show situations where a metaclass provides the only sensible solution.

One use of a metaclass is in rewriting the contents of the class namespace prior to the creation of the class object. Certain features of classes are established at definition time and can't be modified later. One such feature is __slots__. As noted earlier, __slots__ is a performance optimization related to the memory layout of instances. Here's a metaclass that automatically sets the __slots__ attribute based on the calling signature of the __init__() method.

```
import inspect

class SlotMeta(type):
    @staticmethod
```

```
    def __new__(meta, clsname, bases, methods):
        if '__init__' in methods:
            sig = inspect.signature(methods['__init__'])
            __slots__ = tuple(sig.parameters)[1:]
        else:
            __slots__ = ()
        methods['__slots__'] = __slots__
        return super().__new__(meta, clsname, bases, methods)

class Base(metaclass=SlotMeta):
    pass


# Example
class Point(Base):
    def __init__(self, x, y):
        self.x = x
        self.y = y
```

In this example, the `Point` class that's created is automatically created with `__slots__` of
(`'x'`, `'y'`). The resulting instances of `Point` now get memory savings without knowing
that slots are being used. It doesn't have to be specified directly. This kind of trick is not
possible with class decorators or with `__init_subclass__()` because those features only
operate on a class after it's been created. By then, it's too late to apply the `__slots__`
optimization.

Another use of metaclasses is for altering the class definition environment. For example,
duplicate definitions of a name during class definition normally result in a silent error—the
second definition overwrites the first. Suppose you wanted to catch that. Here's a metaclass
that does that by defining a different kind of dictionary for the class namespace:

```
class NoDupeDict(dict):
    def __setitem__(self, key, value):
        if key in self:
            raise AttributeError(f'{key} already defined')
        super().__setitem__(key, value)

class NoDupeMeta(type):
    @classmethod
    def __prepare__(meta, clsname, bases):
        return NoDupeDict()

class Base(metaclass=NoDupeMeta):
    pass


# Example
class SomeClass(Base):
```

```
def yow(self):
    print('Yow!')

def yow(self, x):              # Fails. Already defined
    print('Different Yow!')
```

This is only a small sample of what's possible. For framework builders, metaclasses offer an opportunity to tightly control what happens during class definition—allowing classes to serve as a kind of domain-specific language.

Historically, metaclasses have been used to accomplish a variety of tasks that are now possible through other means. The __init_subclass__() method, in particular, can be used to address a wide variety of use cases where metaclasses were once applied. This includes registration of classes with a central registry, automatic decoration of methods, and code generation.

7.32   Built-in Objects for Instances and Classes

This section gives some details about the low-level objects used to represent types and instances. This information may be useful in low-level metaprogramming and code that needs to directly manipulate types.

Table 7.1 shows commonly used attributes of a type object cls.

Table 7.1   Attributes of Types

Attribute	Description
cls.__name__	Class name
cls.__module__	Module name in which the class is defined
cls.__qualname__	Fully qualified class name
cls.__bases__	Tuple of base classes
cls.__mro__	Method Resolution Order tuple
cls.__dict__	Dictionary holding class methods and variables
cls.__doc__	Documentation string
cls.__annotations__	Dictionary of class type hints
cls.__abstractmethods__	Set of abstract method names (may be undefined if there aren't any).

The cls.__name__ attribute contains a short class name. The cls.__qualname__ attribute contains a fully qualified name with additional information about the surrounding context (this may be useful if a class is defined inside a function or if you create a nested class definition). The cls.__annotations__ dictionary contains class-level type hints (if any).

Table 7.2 shows special attributes of an instance i.

Table 7.2   Instance Attributes

Attribute	Description
i.__class__	Class to which the instance belongs
i.__dict__	Dictionary holding instance data (if defined)

The __dict__ attribute is normally where all of the data associated with an instance is stored. However, if a user-defined class uses __slots__, a more efficient internal representation is used and instances will not have a __dict__ attribute.

7.33 Final Words: Keep It Simple

This chapter has presented a lot of information about classes and the ways to customize and control them. However, when writing classes, keeping it simple is often the best strategy. Yes, you could use abstract based classes, metaclasses, descriptors, class decorators, properties, multiple inheritance, mixins, patterns, and type hints. However, you could also just write a plain class. There's a pretty good chance that this class is good enough and that everyone will understand what it's doing.

In the big picture, it's useful to step back and consider a few generally desirable code qualities. First and foremost, readability counts for a lot—and it often suffers if you pile on too many layers of abstraction. Second, you should try to make code that is easy to observe and debug, and don't forget about using the REPL. Finally, making code testable is often a good driver for good design. If your code can't be tested or testing is too awkward, there may be a better way to organize your solution.

8

Modules and Packages

Python programs are organized into modules and packages that are loaded with the `import` statement. This chapter describes the module and package system in more detail. The primary focus is on programming with modules and packages, not the process of bundling code for deployment to others. For the latter, consult the latest documentation at `https://packaging.python.org/tutorials/packaging-projects/`.

8.1 Modules and the `import` Statement

Any Python source file can be imported as a module. For example:

```
# module.py

a = 37

def func():
    print(f'func says that a is {a}')

class SomeClass:
    def method(self):
        print('method says hi')

print('loaded module')
```

This file contains common programming elements—including a global variable, a function, a class definition, and an isolated statement. This example illustrates some important (and sometimes subtle) features of module loading.

To load a module, use the statement `import module`. For example:

```
>>> import module
loaded module
>>> module.a
```

```
>>> module.func()
func says that a is 37
>>> s = module.SomeClass()
>>> s.method()
method says hi
>>>
```

In executing an import, several things happen:

1. The module source code is located. If it can't be found, an `ImportError` exception is raised.

2. A new module object is created. This object serves as a container for all of the global definitions contained within the module. It's sometimes referred to as a *namespace*.

3. The module source code is executed within the newly created module namespace.

4. If no errors occur, a name is created within the caller that refers to the new module object. This name matches the name of the module, but without any kind of filename suffix. For example, if the code is found in a file `module.py`, the name of the module is `module`.

Of these steps, the first one (locating modules) is the most complicated. A common source of failure for newcomers is using a bad filename or putting code in an unknown location. A module filename must use the same rules as variable names (letters, digits, and underscore) and have a `.py` suffix—for example, `module.py`. When using `import`, you specify the name without the suffix: `import module`, not `import module.py` (the latter produces a rather confusing error message). The file needs to be placed in one of the directories found in `sys.path`.

The remaining steps are all related to a module defining an isolated environment for the code. All definitions that appear in a module remain isolated to that module. Thus, there is no risk of the names of variables, functions, and classes clashing with identical names in other modules. When accessing definitions in a module, use a fully qualified name such as `module.func()`.

`import` executes all of the statements in the loaded source file. If a module carries out a computation or produces output in addition to defining objects, you will see the result—such as the "loaded module" message printed in the example above. A common confusion with modules concerns accessing classes. A module always defines a namespace, so if a file `module.py` defines a class `SomeClass`, use the name `module.SomeClass` to refer to the class.

To import multiple modules using a single `import`, use a comma-separated list of names:

```
import socket, os, re
```

Sometimes the local name used to refer to a module is changed using the `as` qualifier to `import`. For example:

```
import module as mo
mo.func()
```

This latter style of import is standard practice in the data analysis world. For example, you often see this:

```
import numpy as np
import pandas as pd
import matplotlib as plt
...
```

When a module is renamed, the new name only applies to the context where the import statement appeared. Other unrelated program modules can still load the module using its original name.

Assigning a different name to an imported module can be a useful tool for managing different implementations of common functionality or for writing extensible programs. For example, if you have two modules unixmodule.py and winmodule.py that both define a function func() but involve platform-dependent implementation details, you could write code to selectively import the module:

```
if platform == 'unix':
    import unixmodule as module
elif platform == 'windows':
    import winmodule as module


...
r = module.func()
```

Modules are first-class objects in Python. This means they can be assigned to variables, placed in data structures, and passed around in a program as data. For instance, the module name in the above example is a variable that refers to the corresponding module object.

8.2 Module Caching

The source code for a module is loaded and executed only once, regardless of how often you use the import statement. Subsequent import statements bind the module name to the module object already created by the previous import.

A common confusion for newcomers arises when a module is imported into an interactive session, then its source code is modified (for example, to fix a bug) but a new import fails to load the modified code. The module cache is to blame for this. Python will never reload a previously imported module even if the underlying source code has been updated.

You can find the cache of all currently loaded modules in sys.modules, which is a dictionary that maps module names to module objects. The contents of this dictionary are used to determine whether import loads a fresh copy of a module or not. Deleting a module from the cache will force it to load again on the next import statement. However, this is rarely safe for reasons explained in Section 8.5 on module reloading.

Sometimes you will see `import` used inside a function like this:

```
def f(x):
    import math
    return math.sin(x) + math.cos(x)
```

At first glance, it seems like such an implementation would be horribly slow—loading a module on each invocation. In reality, the cost of the `import` is minimal—it's just a single dictionary lookup, as Python immediately finds the module in the cache. The main objection to having the `import` inside a function is one of style—it's more common to have all module imports listed at the top of a file where they're easy to see. On the other hand, if you have a specialized function that's rarely invoked, putting the function's import dependencies inside the function body can speed up program loading. In this case, you'd only load the required modules if they are actually needed.

8.3   Importing Selected Names from a Module

You can load specific definitions from a module into the current namespace using the `from module import name` statement. It's identical to `import` except that, instead of creating a name referring to the newly created module namespace, it places references to one or more of the objects defined in the module into the current namespace:

```
from module import func    # Imports module and puts func in current namespace
func()                     # Calls func() defined in module
module.func()              # Fails. NameError: module
```

The `from` statement accepts comma-separated names if you want multiple definitions. For example:

```
from module import func, SomeClass
```

Semantically, the statement `from module import name` performs a name copy from the module cache to the local namespace. That is, Python first executes `import module` behind the scenes. Afterwards, it makes an assignment from the cache to a local name, such as `name = sys.modules['module'].name`.

A common misconception is that the `from module import name` statement is more efficient—possibly only loading part of a module. This is not the case. Either way, the entire module is loaded and stored in the cache.

Importing functions using the `from` syntax does not change their scoping rules. When functions look for variables, they only look within the file where the function was defined, not the namespace into which a function is imported and called. For example:

```
>>> from module import func
>>> a = 42
```

```
>>> func()
func says that a is 37
>>> func.__module__
'module'
>>> func.__globals__['a']
37
>>>
```

A related confusion concerns the behavior of global variables. For example, consider this code that imports both func and a global variable a that it uses:

```
from module import a, func
a = 42                    # Modify the variable
func()                    # Prints "func says a is 37"
print(a)                  # Prints "42"
```

Variable assignment in Python is not a storage operation. That is, the name a in this example does not represent some kind of box where a value gets stored. The initial import associates the local name a with the original object module.a. However, the later reassignment a = 42 moves the local name a to a completely different object. At this point, a is no longer bound to the value in the imported module. Because of this, it is not possible to use the from statement in a way that makes variables behave like global variables in a language such as C. If you want to have mutable global parameters in your program, put them in a module and use the module name explicitly using the import statement— for example, module.a.

The asterisk (*) wildcard character is sometimes used to load all the definitions in a module, except those that start with an underscore. Here's an example:

```
# Load all definitions into the current namespace
from module import *
```

The from module import * statement may only be used at the top-level scope of a module. In particular, it is illegal to use this form of import inside a function body.

Modules can precisely control the set of names imported by from module import * by defining the list __all__. Here's an example:

```
# module: module.py
__all__ = [ 'func', 'SomeClass' ]

a = 37                # Not exported

def func():           # Exported
    ...

class SomeClass:      # Exported
    ...
```

When at the interactive Python prompt, using `from module import *` can be a convenient way to work with a module. However, using this style of import in a program is frowned upon. Overuse can pollute the local namespace and lead to confusion. For example:

```
from math import *
from random import *
from statistics import *

a = gauss(1.0, 0.25)          # From which module?
```

It's usually better to be explicit about names:

```
from math import sin, cos, sqrt
from random import gauss
from statistics import mean

a = gauss(1.0, 0.25)
```

8.4 Circular Imports

A peculiar problem arises if two modules mutually import each other. For example, suppose you had two files:

```
# ---------------------------
# moda.py

import modb

def func_a():
    modb.func_b()

class Base:
    pass


# ---------------------------
# modb.py

import moda

def func_b():
    print('B')

class Child(moda.Base):
    pass
```

There is a strange import order dependency in this code. Using `import modb` first works fine, but if you put `import moda` first, it blows up with an error about `moda.Base` being undefined.

To understand what is happening, you have to follow the control flow. `import moda` starts executing the file `moda.py`. The first statement it encounters is `import modb`. Thus, control switches over to `modb.py`. The first statement in that file is `import moda`. Instead of entering a recursive cycle, that import is satisfied by the module cache and control continues on to the next statement in `modb.py`. This is good—circular imports don't cause Python to deadlock or enter a new spacetime dimension. However, at this point in execution, module `moda` has only been partially evaluated. When control reaches the `class Child(moda.Base)` statement, it blows up. The required `Base` class hasn't been defined yet.

One way to fix this problem is to move the `import modb` statement someplace else. For example, you could move the import into `func_a()` where the definition is actually needed:

```
# moda.py

def func_a():
    import modb
    modb.func_b()

class Base:
    pass
```

You could also move the import to a later position in the file:

```
# moda.py

def func_a():
    modb.func_b()

class Base:
    pass

import modb       # Must be after Base is defined
```

Both of these solutions are likely to raise eyebrows in a code review. Most of the time, you don't see module imports appearing at the end of a file. The presence of circular imports almost always suggests a problem in code organization. A better way to handle this might be to move the definition of `Base` to a separate file `base.py` and rewrite `modb.py` as follows:

```
# modb.py

import base
```

```
def func_b():
    print('B')

class Child(base.Base):
    pass
```

8.5 Module Reloading and Unloading

There is no reliable support for reloading or unloading of previously imported modules. Although you can remove a module from `sys.modules`, this does not unload a module from memory. This is because references to the cached module object still exist in other modules that imported that module. Moreover, if there are instances of classes defined in the module, those instances contain references back to their class objects, which in turn hold references to the module in which they were defined.

The fact that module references exist in many places makes it generally impractical to reload a module after making changes to its implementation. For example, if you remove a module from `sys.modules` and use `import` to reload it, this will not retroactively change all of the previous references to the module used in a program. Instead, you'll have one reference to the new module created by the most recent `import` statement, and a set of references to the old module created by imports in other parts of the code. This is rarely what you want. Module reloading is never safe to use in any kind of sane production code unless you are able to carefully control the entire execution environment.

There is a `reload()` function for reloading a module that can be found in the `importlib` library. As an argument, you pass it the already loaded module. For example:

```
>>> import module
>>> import importlib
>>> importlib.reload(module)
loaded module
<module 'module' from 'module.py'>
>>>
```

`reload()` works by loading a new version of the module source code and then executing it on top of the already existing module namespace. This is done without clearing the previous namespace. It's literally the same as you typing new source code on top of the old code without restarting the interpreter.

If other modules had previously imported the reloaded module using a standard `import` statement, such as `import module`, reloading will make them see the updated code as if by magic. However, there's still a lot of peril. First, reloading doesn't reload any of the modules that might be imported by the reloaded file. It's not recursive—it only applies to the single module given to `reload()`. Second, if any module has used the `from module import name` form of import, those imports fail to see the effect of the reload. Finally, if instances of classes have been created, reloading does not update their underlying class definition. In fact, you'll now have two different definitions of the same class in the same program—the old one that remains in use for all existing instances at the time of reloading, and the new one that gets used for new instances. This is almost always confusing.

Finally, it should be noted that C/C++ extensions to Python cannot be safely unloaded or reloaded in any way. No support is provided for this, and the underlying operating system may prohibit it anyways. Your best recourse for that scenario is to restart the Python interpreter process.

8.6 Module Compilation

When modules are first imported, they are compiled into an interpreter bytecode. This code is written to a .pyc file within a special __pycache__ directory. This directory is usually found in the same directory as the original .py file. When the same import occurs again on a different run of the program, the compiled bytecode is loaded instead. This significantly speeds up the import process.

The caching of bytecode is an automatic process that you almost never need to worry about. Files are automatically regenerated if the original source code changes. It just works.

That said, there are still reasons to know about this caching and compilation process. First, sometimes Python files get installed (often accidentally) in an environment where users don't have operating system permissions to create the required __pycache__ directory. Python will still work, but every import now loads the original source code and compiles it to bytecode. Program loading will be a lot slower than it needs to be. Similarly, in deploying or packaging a Python application, it may be advantageous to include the compiled bytecode, as that may significantly speed up program startup.

The other good reason to know about module caching is that some programming techniques interfere with it. Advanced metaprogramming techniques involving dynamic code generation and the exec() function defeat the benefits of bytecode caching. A notable example is the use of dataclasses:

```
from dataclasses import dataclass

@dataclass
class Point:
    x: float
    y: float
```

Dataclasses work by generating method functions as text fragments and executing them using exec(). None of this generated code is cached by the import system. For a single class definition, you won't notice. However, if you have a module consisting of 100 dataclasses, you might find that it imports nearly 20 times slower than a comparable module where you just wrote out the classes in the normal, if less compact, way.

8.7 The Module Search Path

When importing modules, the interpreter searches the list of directories in sys.path. The first entry in sys.path is often an empty string ' ', which refers to the current working directory. Alternatively, if you run a script, the first entry in sys.path is the directory in which the script is located. The other entries in sys.path usually consist of a mix of directory names and .zip archive files. The order in which entries are listed in sys.path determines the search order used when importing modules. To add new entries to the search path, add them to this list. This can be done directly or by setting the PYTHONPATH environment variable. For example, on UNIX:

```
bash $ env PYTHONPATH=/some/path python3 script.py
```

ZIP archive files are a convenient way to bundle a collection of modules into a single file. For example, suppose you created two modules, foo.py and bar.py, and placed them in a file mymodules.zip. The file could be added to the Python search path as follows:

```
import sys
sys.path.append('mymodules.zip')
import foo, bar
```

Specific locations within the directory structure of a .zip file can also be used for the path. In addition, .zip files can be mixed with regular pathname components. Here's an example:

```
sys.path.append('/tmp/modules.zip/lib/python')
```

It is not necessary for a ZIP file to have a .zip file suffix to be used. Historically, it has been common to encounter .egg files on the path as well. .egg files originate from an early Python package management tool called setuptools. However, an .egg file is nothing more than a normal .zip file or directory with some extra metadata added to it (version number, dependencies, and so on).

8.8 Execution as the Main Program

Although this section is about the import statement, Python files are often executed as a main script. For example:

```
% python3 module.py
```

Each module contains a variable, __name__, that holds the module name. Code can examine this variable to determine the module in which they're executing. The top-level module of the interpreter is named __main__. Programs specified on the command line or entered interactively run inside the __main__ module. Sometimes a program may alter its behavior, depending on whether it has been imported as a module or is running in __main__. For example, a module may include code that is executed if the module is used as the main program but not executed if the module is simply imported by another module.

```
# Check if running as a program
if __name__ == '__main__':
    # Yes. Running as the main script
    statements
else:
    # No, I must have been imported as a module
    statements
```

Source files intended for use as libraries can use this technique to include optional testing or example code. When developing a module, you can put debugging code for testing the features of your library inside an if statement as shown, and run Python on your module as the main program. That code won't run for users who import your library.

If you've made a directory of Python code, you can execute the directory if it contains a special __main__.py file. For example, if you make a directory like this:

```
myapp/
    foo.py
    bar.py
    __main__.py
```

You can run Python on it by typing python3 myapp. Execution will start in the __main__.py file. This also works if you turn the myapp directory into a ZIP archive. Typing python3 myapp.zip will look for a top-level __main__.py file and execute it if found.

8.9 Packages

For anything but the simplest programs, Python code is organized into *packages*. A package is a collection of modules that are grouped under a common top-level name. This grouping helps resolve conflicts between the module names used in different applications and keeps your code separate from everyone else's code. A package is defined by creating a directory with a distinctive name and placing an initially empty __init__.py file in that directory. You then place additional Python files and subpackages in this directory as needed. For example, a package might be organized as follows:

```
graphics/
    __init__.py
    primitive/
        __init__.py
        lines.py
        fill.py
        text.py
```

```
. . .
graph2d/
    __init__.py
    plot2d.py
    . . .
graph3d/
    __init__.py
    plot3d.py
    . . .
formats/
    __init__.py
    gif.py
    png.py
    tiff.py
    jpeg.py
```

The `import` statement is used to load modules from a package the same way as it's used for simple modules, except that you now have longer names. For example:

```
# Full path
import graphics.primitive.fill
...
graphics.primitive.fill.floodfill(img, x, y, color)

# Load a specific submodule
from graphics.primitive import fill
...
fill.floodfill(img, x, y, color)

# Load a specific function from a submodule
from graphics.primitive.fill import floodfill
...
floodfill(img, x, y, color)
```

Whenever any part of a package is first imported, code in the `__init__.py` file executes first (if it exists). As noted, this file may be empty, but it can also contain code to perform package-specific initializations. If importing a deeply nested submodule, all `__init__.py` files encountered in traversal of the directory structure are executed. Thus, the statement `import graphics.primitive.fill` would first execute the `__init__.py` file in the `graphics/` directory followed by the `__init__.py` file in the `primitive/` directory.

Astute Python users might observe that a package still seems to work if `__init__.py` files are omitted. This is true—you can use a directory of Python code as a package even if it contains no `__init__.py`. However, what's not obvious is that a directory with a missing `__init__.py` file actually defines a different kind of package known as *namespace package*. This is an advanced feature sometimes used by very large libraries and frameworks to implement broken plugin systems. In the opinion of the author, this is rarely what you want—you should always create proper __init__.py files when creating a package.

8.10 Imports Within a Package

A critical feature of the `import` statement is that all module imports require an absolute or fully qualified package path. This includes `import` statements used within a package itself. For example, suppose the `graphics.primitive.fill` module wants to import the `graphics.primitive.lines` module. A simple statement such as `import lines` won't work—you'll get an `ImportError` exception. Instead, you need to fully qualify the import like this:

```
# graphics/primitives/fill.py

# Fully qualified submodule import
from graphics.primitives import lines
```

Sadly, writing out a full package name like that is both annoying and fragile. For example, sometimes it makes sense to rename a package—maybe you want to rename it so that you can use different versions. If the package name is hardwired into the code, you can't do that. A better choice is to use a package-relative import like this:

```
# graphics/primitives/fill.py

# Package-relative import
from . import lines
```

Here, the `.` used in the statement `from . import lines` refers to the same directory as the importing module. Thus, this statement looks for a module `lines` in the same directory as the file `fill.py`.

Relative imports can also specify submodules contained in different directories of the same package. For example, if the module `graphics.graph2d.plot2d` wants to import `graphics.primitive.lines`, it may use a statement like this:

```
# graphics/graph2d/plot2d.py

from ..primitive import lines
```

Here, the `..` moves up one directory level and `primitive` drops down into a different subpackage directory.

Relative imports can only be specified using the `from module import symbol` form of the `import` statement. Thus, statements such as `import ..primitive.lines` or `import .lines` are a syntax error. Also, `symbol` has to be a simple identifier, so a statement such as `from .. import primitive.lines` is also illegal. Finally, relative imports can only be used from within a package; it is illegal to use a relative import to refer to modules that are simply located in a different directory on the filesystem.

8.11   Running a Package Submodule as a Script

Code that's organized into a package has a different runtime environment than a simple script. There is an enclosing package name, submodules, and the use of relative imports (which only work inside a package). One feature that no longer works is the ability to run Python directly on a package source file. For example, suppose you are working on the graphics/graph2d/plot2d.py file and add some testing code at the bottom:

```
# graphics/graph2d/plot2d.py
from ..primitive import lines, text

class Plot2D:
    ...

if __name__ == '__main__':
    print('Testing Plot2D')
    p = Plot2D()
    ...
```

If you try to run it directly, you get a crash complaining about relative import statements:

```
bash $ python3 graphics/graph2d/plot2d.py
Traceback (most recent call last):
  File "graphics/graph2d/plot2d.py", line 1, in <module>
    from ..primitive import line, text
ValueError: attempted relative import beyond top-level package
bash $
```

You can't move into the package directory and run it there either:

```
bash $ cd graphics/graph2d/
bash $ python3 plot2d.py
Traceback (most recent call last):
  File "plot2d.py", line 1, in <module>
    from ..primitive import line, text
ValueError: attempted relative import beyond top-level package
bash $
```

To run a submodule as a main script, you need to use the -m option to the interpreter. For example:

```
bash $ python3 -m graphics.graph2d.plot2d
Testing Plot2D
bash $
```

-m specifies a module or package as the main program. Python will run the module with the proper environment to make sure that imports work. Many of Python's built-in packages have "secret" features that can be used via -m. One of the most well-known is using python3 -m http.server to run a web server from the current directory.

You can provide similar functionality with your own packages. If the name supplied to python -m name corresponds to a package directory, Python looks for the presence of a __main__.py in that directory and runs that as the script.

8.12 Controlling the Package Namespace

The primary purpose of a package is to serve as a top-level container for code. Sometimes users will import the top-level name and nothing else. For example:

```
import graphics
```

This import doesn't specify any particular submodule. Nor does it make any other part of the package accessible. For example, you'll find that code like this fails:

```
import graphics
graphics.primitive.fill.floodfill(img,x,y,color)  # Fails!
```

When only a top-level package import is given, the only file that imports is the associated __init__.py file. In this example, it's the file graphics/__init__.py file.

The primary purpose of an __init__.py file is to build and/or manage the contents of the top-level package namespace. Often, this involves importing selected functions, classes, and other objects from lower-level submodules. For example, if the graphics package in this example consists of hundreds of low-level functions but most of those details are encapsulated into a handful of high-level classes, then the __init__.py file might choose to expose just those classes:

```
# graphics/__init__.py

from .graph2d.plot2d import Plot2D
from .graph3d.plot3d import Plot3D
```

With this __init__.py file, the names Plot2D and Plot3D would appear at the top level of the package. A user could then use those names as if graphics were a simple module:

```
from graphics import Plot2D

plt = Plot2D(100, 100)
plt.clear()
...
```

This is often much more convenient for the user because they don't have to know how you've actually organized your code. In some sense, you're putting a higher layer of abstraction on top of your code structure. Many of the modules in the Python standard library are constructed in this manner. For example, the popular collections module is actually a package. The collections/__init__.py file consolidates definitions from a few different places and presents them to the user as a single consolidated namespace.

8.13   Controlling Package Exports

One issue concerns the interaction between an __init__.py file and low-level submodules. For example, the user of a package might only want to concern themselves with objects and functions that live in the top-level package namespace. However, the implementor of a package might be concerned with the problem of organizing code into maintainable submodules.

To better manage this organizational complexity, package submodules often declare an explicit list of exports by defining an __all__ variable. This is a list of names that should be pushed up one level in the package namespace. For example:

```
# graphics/graph2d/plot2d.py

__all__ = ['Plot2D']

class Plot2D:
    ...
```

The associated __init__.py file then imports its submodules using an * import like this:

```
# graphics/graph2d/__init__.py

# Only loads names explicitly listed in __all__ variables
from .plot2d import *

# Propagate the __all__ up to next level (if desired)
__all__ = plot2d.__all__
```

This lifting process then continues all the way to the top-level package __init__.py. For example:

```
# graphics/__init__.py

from .graph2d import *
from .graph3d import *

# Consolidate exports
__all__ = [
    *graph2d.__all__,
```

```
    *graph3d.__all__
]
```

The gist is that every component of a package explicitly states its exports using the __all__ variable. The __init__.py files then propagate the exports upwards. In practice, it can get complicated, but this approach avoids the problem of hard-wiring specific export names into the __init__.py file. Instead, if a submodule wants to export something, its name gets listed in just one place—the __all__ variable. Then, by magic, it propagates up to its proper place in the package namespace.

It is worth noting that although using * imports in user code is frowned upon, it is widespread practice in package __init__.py files. The reason it works in packages is that it is usually much more controlled and contained—being driven by the contents of the __all__ variables and not a free-wheeling attitude of "let's just import everything."

8.14 Package Data

Sometimes a package includes data files that need to be loaded (as opposed to source code). Within a package, the __file__ variable will give you location information about a specific source file. However, packages are complicated. They might be bundled within ZIP archive files or loaded from unusual environments. The __file__ variable itself might be unreliable or even undefined. As a result, loading a data file is often not a simple matter of passing a filename to the built-in open() function and reading some data.

To read package data, use pkgutil.get_data(package, resource). For example, is your package looks like this:

```
mycode/
    resources/
        data.json
    __init__.py
    spam.py
    yow.py
```

To load the file data.json from the file spam.py, do this:

```python
# mycode/spam.py

import pkgutil
import json

def func():
    rawdata = pkgutil.get_data(__package__,
                               'resources/data.json')
    textdata = rawdata.decode('utf-8')
    data = json.loads(textdata)
    print(data)
```

The `get_data()` function attempts to find the specified resource and returns its contents as a raw byte string. The `__package__` variable shown in the example is a string holding the name of the enclosing package. Any further decoding (such as converting bytes to text) and interpretation is up to you. In the example, the data is decoded and parsed from JSON into a Python dictionary.

A package is not a good place to store giant data files. Reserve package resources for configuration data and other assorted bits of stuff needed to make your package work.

8.15   Module Objects

Modules are first-class objects. Table 8.1 lists attributes commonly found on modules.

Table 8.1   Module Attributes

Attribute	Description
`__name__`	Full module name
`__doc__`	Documentation string
`__dict__`	Module dictionary
`__file__`	Filename where defined
`__package__`	Name of enclosing package (if any)
`__path__`	List of subdirectories to search for submodules of a package.
`__annotations__`	Module-level type hints

The `__dict__` attribute is a dictionary that represents the module namespace. Everything that's defined in the module is placed here.

The `__name__` attribute is often used in scripts. A check such as `if __name__ == '__main__'` is often done to see if a file is running as a standalone program.

The `__package__` attribute contains the name of the enclosing package if any. If set, the `__path__` attribute is a list of directories that will be searched to locate package submodules. Normally, it contains a single entry with the directory in which a package is located. Sometimes large frameworks will manipulate `__path__` to incorporate additional directories for the purpose of supporting plugins and other advanced features.

Not all attributes are available on all modules. For example, built-in modules may not have a `__file__` attribute set. Similarly, package-related attributes are not set for top-level modules (not contained in a package).

The `__doc__` attribute is the module doc string (if any). This is a string that appears as the first statement in a file. The `__annotations__` attribute is a dictionary of module-level type hints. These look something like this:

```
# mymodule.py

'''
```

```
The doc string
'''

# Type hints  (placed into __annotations__)
x: int
y: float
...
```

As with other type hints, module-level hints change no part of Python's behavior, nor do they actually define variables. They are purely metadata that other tools can choose to look at if they want.

8.16 Deploying Python Packages

The final frontier of modules and packages is the problem of giving your code to others. This is a large topic that has been the focus of active ongoing development over many years. I won't try to document a process that's bound to be out-of-date by the time you read this. Instead, direct your attention to the documentation at `https://packaging.python.org/tutorials/packaging-projects`.

For the purposes of day-to-day development, the most important thing is to keep your code isolated as a self-contained project. All of your code should live in a proper package. Try to give your package a unique name so that it doesn't conflict with other possible dependencies. Consult the Python package index at `https://pypi.org` to pick a name. In structuring your code, try to keep things simple. As you've seen, there are many highly sophisticated things that can be done with the module and package system. There is a time and place for that, but it should not be your starting point.

With absolute simplicity in mind, the most minimalistic way to distribute pure Python code is to use the `setuptools` module or the built-in `distutils` module. Suppose you have written some code and it's in a project that looks like this:

```
spam-project/
    README.txt
    Documentation.txt
    spam/                # A package of code
        __init__.py
        foo.py
        bar.py
    runspam.py           # A script to run as: python runspam.py
```

To create a distribution, create a file `setup.py` in the topmost directory (`spam-project/` in this example). In this file, put the following code:

```
# setup.py
from setuptools import setup

setup(name="spam",
```

```
        version="0.0"
        packages=['spam'],
        scripts=['runspam.py'],
)
```

In the `setup()` call, `packages` is a list of all package directories, and `scripts` is a list of script files. Any of these arguments may be omitted if your software does not have them (for example, if there are no scripts). `name` is the name of your package, and `version` is the version number as a string. The call to `setup()` supports a variety of other parameters that supply various metadata about your package. See the full list at `https://docs.python.org/3/distutils/apiref.html`.

Creating a `setup.py` file is enough to create a source distribution of your software. Type the following shell command to make a source distribution:

```
bash $ python setup.py sdist
...
bash $
```

This creates an archive file, such as `spam-1.0.tar.gz` or `spam-1.0.zip`, in the directory `spam/dist`. This is the file you would give to others to install your software. To install, a user can use a command such as `pip`. For example:

```
shell $ python3 -m pip install spam-1.0.tar.gz
```

This installs the software into the local Python distribution and makes it available for general use. The code will normally be installed into a directory called `site-packages` in the Python library. To find the exact location of this directory, inspect the value of `sys.path`. Scripts are normally installed into the same directory as the Python interpreter itself.

If the first line of a script starts with `#!` and contains the text `python`, the installer will rewrite the line to point to the local installation of Python. Thus, if your scripts have been hardcoded to a specific Python location, such as `/usr/local/bin/python`, they should still work when installed on other systems where Python is in a different location.

It must be stressed that the use of `setuptools` as described here is absolutely minimal. Larger projects may involve C/C++ extensions, complicated package structures, examples, and more. Covering all of the tools and possible ways to deploy such code is beyond the scope of this book. You should consult various resources on `https://python.org` and `https://pypi.org` for the most up-to-date advice.

8.17 The Penultimate Word: Start with a Package

When first starting a new program, it is easy to start with a simple single Python file. For example, you might write a script called `program.py` and start with that. Although this will work fine for throwaway programs and short tasks, your "script" may start growing and adding features. Eventually, you might want to split it into multiple files. It's at that point that problems often arise.

In light of this, it makes sense to get in the habit of starting all programs as a package from the onset. For example, instead of making a file called `program.py`, you should make a program package directory called `program`:

```
program/
    __init__.py
    __main__.py
```

Put your starting code in `__main__.py` and run your program using a command such as `python -m program`. As you need more code, add new files to your package and use package-relative imports. An advantage of using a package is that all of your code remains isolated. You can name the files whatever you want and not worry about collisions with other packages, standard library modules, or code written by your coworkers. Although setting up a package requires a bit more work at the start, it will likely save you a lot of headaches later.

8.18 The Final Word: Keep It Simple

There is a lot of more advanced wizardry associated with the module and package system than what has been shown here. Consult the tutorial "Modules and Packages: Live and Let Die!" at `https://dabeaz.com/modulepackage/index.html` to get an idea of what's possible.

All things considered, however, you're probably better off *not* doing any advanced module hacking. Managing modules, packages, and software distribution has always been a source of pain in the Python community. Much of the pain is a direct consequence of people applying hacks to the module system. Don't do that. Keep it simple and find the power to just say "no" when your coworkers propose to modify `import` to work with the blockchain.

9

Input and Output

Input and output (I/O) is part of all programs. This chapter describes the essentials of Python I/O including data encoding, command-line options, environment variables, file I/O, and data serialization. Particular attention is given to programming techniques and abstractions that encourage proper I/O handling. The end of this chapter gives an overview of common standard library modules related to I/O.

9.1 Data Representation

The main problem of I/O is the outside world. To communicate with it, data must be properly represented, so that it can be manipulated. At the lowest level, Python works with two fundamental datatypes: *bytes* that represent raw uninterpreted data of any kind and *text* that represents Unicode characters.

To represent bytes, two built-in types are used, bytes and bytearray. bytes is an immutable string of integer byte values. bytearray is a mutable byte array that behaves as a combination of a byte string and a list. Its mutability makes it suitable for building up groups of bytes in a more incremental manner, as when assembling data from fragments. The following example illustrates a few features of bytes and bytearray:

```
# Specify a bytes literal (note the b' prefix)
a = b'hello'

# Specify bytes from a list of integers
b = bytes([0x68, 0x65, 0x6c, 0x6c, 0x6f])

# Create and populate a bytearray from parts
c = bytearray()
c.extend(b'world')    # c = bytearray(b'world')
c.append(0x21)        # c = bytearray(b'world!')

# Access byte values
print(a[0])           # --> prints 104
```

```
for x in b:        # Outputs 104 101 108 108 111
    print(x)
```

Accessing individual elements of `byte` and `bytearray` objects produces integer byte values, not single-character byte strings. This is different from text strings, so it is a common usage error.

Text is represented by the `str` datatype and stored as an array of Unicode code points. For example:

```
d = 'hello'        # Text (Unicode)
len(d)             # --> 5
print(d[0])        # prints 'h'
```

Python maintains a strict separation between bytes and text. There is never automatic conversion between the two types, comparisons between these types evaluate as `False`, and any operation that mixes bytes and text together results in an error. For example:

```
a = b'hello'       # bytes
b = 'hello'        # text
c = 'world'        # text

print(a == b)      # -> False
d = a + c          # TypeError: can't concat str to bytes
e = b + c          # -> 'helloworld' (both are strings)
```

When performing I/O, make sure you're working with the right kind of data representation. If you are manipulating text, use text strings. If you are manipulating binary data, use bytes.

9.2 Text Encoding and Decoding

If you work with text, all data read from input must be decoded and all data written to output must be encoded. For explicit conversion between text and bytes, there are `encode(text [,errors])` and `decode(bytes [,errors])` methods on text and bytes objects, respectively. For example:

```
a = 'hello'            # Text
b = a.encode('utf-8')  # Encode to bytes

c = b'world'           # Bytes
d = c.decode('utf-8')  # Decode to text
```

Both `encode()` and `decode()` require the name of an encoding such as `'utf-8'` or `'latin-1'`. The encodings in Table 9.1 are common.

Table 9.1   Common Encodings

Encoding Name	Description
`'ascii'`	Character values in the range [0x00, 0x7f].
`'latin1'`	Character values in the range [0x00, 0xff]. Also known as `'iso-8859-1'`.
`'utf-8'`	Variable-length encoding that allows all Unicode characters to be represented.
`'cp1252'`	A common text encoding on Windows.
`'macroman'`	A common text encoding on Macintosh.

Additionally, the encoding methods accept an optional `errors` argument that specifies behavior in the presence of encoding errors. It is one of the values in Table 9.2.

Table 9.2   Error-Handling Options

Value	Description
`'strict'`	Raises a `UnicodeError` exception for encoding and decoding errors (the default).
`'ignore'`	Ignores invalid characters.
`'replace'`	Replaces invalid characters with a replacement character (U+FFFD in Unicode, b'?' in bytes).
`'backslashreplace'`	Replaces each invalid character with a Python character escape sequence. For example, the character U+1234 is replaced by `'\u1234'` (encoding only).
`'xmlcharrefreplace'`	Replaces each invalid character with an XML character reference. For example, the character U+1234 is replaced by `'&#4660;'` (encoding only).
`'surrogateescape'`	Replaces any invalid byte `'\xhh'` with U+DChh on decoding, replaces U+DChh with byte `'\xhh'` on encoding.

The `'backslashreplace'` and `'xmlcharrefreplace'` error policies represent unrepresentable characters in a form that allows them to be viewed as simple ASCII text or as XML character references. This can be useful for debugging.

The `'surrogateescape'` error handling policy allows degenerate byte data—data that does not follow the expected encoding rules—to survive a roundtrip decoding/encoding cycle intact regardless of the text encoding being used. Specifically, `s.decode(enc, 'surrogateescape').encode(enc, 'surrogateescape') == s`. This round-trip preservation of data is useful for certain kinds of system interfaces where a text encoding is expected but can't be guaranteed due to issues outside of Python's control. Instead of destroying data with a bad encoding, Python embeds it "as is" using surrogate encoding. Here's an example of this behavior with a improperly encoded UTF-8 string:

```
>>> a = b'Spicy Jalape\xf1o'   # Invalid UTF-8
>>> a.decode('utf-8')
Traceback (most recent call last):
  File "<stdin>", line 1, in <module>
UnicodeDecodeError: 'utf-8' codec can't decode byte 0xf1
in position 12: invalid continuation byte
>>> a.decode('utf-8', 'surrogateescape')
'Spicy Jalape\udcf1o'
>>> # Encode the resulting string back into bytes
>>> _.encode('utf-8', 'surrogateescape')
b'Spicy Jalape\xf1o'
>>>
```

9.3   Text and Byte Formatting

A common problem when working with text and byte strings is string conversions and formatting—for example, converting a floating-point number to a string with a given width and precision. To format a single value, use the format() function:

```
x = 123.456
format(x, '0.2f')      # '123.46'
format(x, '10.4f')     # '  123.4560'
format(x, '<*10.2f')   # '123.46****'
```

The second argument to format() is a format specifier. The general format of the specifier is [[fill[align]][sign][0][width][,][.precision][type] where each part enclosed in [] is optional. The width specifies the minimum field width to use, and the align specifier is one of <, >, or ^ for left, right, and centered alignment within the field. An optional fill character fill is used to pad the space. For example:

```
name = 'Elwood'
r = format(name, '<10')    # r = 'Elwood    '
r = format(name, '>10')    # r = '    Elwood'
r = format(name, '^10')    # r = '  Elwood  '
r = format(name, '*^10')   # r = '**Elwood**'
```

The type specifier indicates the type of data. Table 9.3 lists the supported format codes. If not supplied, the default format code is s for strings, d for integers, and f for floats.

The sign part of a format specifier is one of +, -, or a space. A + indicates that a leading sign should be used on all numbers. A - is the default and only adds a sign character for negative numbers. A space adds a leading space to positive numbers.

An optional comma (,) may appear between the width and the precision. This adds a thousands separator character. For example:

Table 9.3 Format Codes

Character	Output Format
d	Decimal integer or long integer.
b	Binary integer or long integer.
o	Octal integer or long integer.
x	Hexadecimal integer or long integer.
X	Hexadecimal integer (uppercase letters).
f, F	Floating point as [-]m.dddddd.
e	Floating point as [-]m.dddddde±xx.
E	Floating point as [-]m.ddddddE±xx.
g, G	Use e or E for exponents less than [nd]4 or greater than the precision; otherwise use f.
n	Same as g except that the current locale setting determines the decimal point character.
%	Multiplies a number by 100 and displays it using f format followed by a % sign.
s	String or any object. The formatting code uses str() to generate strings.
c	Single character.

```
x = 123456.78
format(x, '16,.2f')    # '      123,456.78'
```

The precision part of the specifier supplies the number of digits of accuracy to use for decimals. If a leading 0 is added to the field width for numbers, numeric values are padded with leading 0s to fill the space. Here are some examples of formatting different kinds of numbers:

```
x = 42
r = format(x, '10d')      # r = '        42'
r = format(x, '10x')      # r = '        2a'
r = format(x, '10b')      # r = '    101010'
r = format(x, '010b')     # r = '0000101010'

y = 3.1415926
r = format(y, '10.2f')    # r = '      3.14'
r = format(y, '10.2e')    # r = '   3.14e+00'
r = format(y, '+10.2f')   # r = '     +3.14'
r = format(y, '+010.2f')  # r = '+000003.14'
r = format(y, '+10.2%')   # r = '   +314.16%'
```

For more complex string formatting, you can use f-strings:

```
x = 123.456
```

```
f'Value is {x:0.2f}'          #  'Value is 123.46'
f'Value is {x:10.4f}'         #  'Value is   123.4560'
f'Value is {2*x:*<10.2f}'     #  'Value is 246.91****'
```

Within an f-string, text of the form {expr:spec} is replaced by the value of format(expr, spec). expr can be an arbitrary expression as long as it doesn't include {, }, or \ characters. Parts of the format specifier itself can optionally be supplied by other expressions. For example:

```
y = 3.1415926
width = 8
precision=3

r = f'{y:{width}.{precision}f}'   # r = '   3.142'
```

If you end expr by =, then the literal text of expr is also included in the result. For example:

```
x = 123.456

f'{x=:0.2f}'          # 'x=123.46'
f'{2*x=:0.2f}'        # '2*x=246.91'
```

If you append !r to a value, formatting is applied to the output of repr(). If you use !s, formatting is applied to the output of str(). For example:

```
f'{x!r:spec}'      # Calls (repr(x).__format__('spec'))
f'{x!s:spec}'      # Calls (str(x).__format__('spec'))
```

As an alternative to f-strings, you can use the .format() method of strings:

```
x = 123.456

'Value is {:0.2f}'.format(x)        # 'Value is 123.46'
'Value is {0:10.2f}'.format(x)      # 'Value is   123.4560'
'Value is {val:<*10.2f}'.format(val=x)  # 'Value is 123.46****'
```

With a string formatted by .format(), text of the form {arg:spec} is replaced by the value of format(arg, spec). In this case, arg refers to one of the arguments given to the format() method. If omitted entirely, the arguments are taken in order. For example:

```
name = 'IBM'
shares = 50
price = 490.1

r = '{:>10s} {:10d} {:10.2f}'.format(name, shares, price)
# r = '       IBM         50     490.10'
```

arg can also refer to a specific argument number or name. For example:

```
tag = 'p'
text = 'hello world'

r = '<{0}>{1}</{0}>'.format(tag, text)   # r = '<p>hello world</p>'
r = '<{tag}>{text}</{tag}>'.format(tag='p', text='hello world')
```

Unlike f-strings, the `arg` value of a specifier cannot be an arbitrary expression, so it's not quite as expressive. However, the `format()` method can perform limited attribute lookup, indexing, and nested substitutions. For example:

```
y = 3.1415926
width = 8
precision=3

r = 'Value is {0:{1}.{2}f}'.format(y, width, precision)

d = {
    'name': 'IBM',
    'shares': 50,
    'price': 490.1
}
r = '{0[shares]:d} shares of {0[name]} at {0[price]:0.2f}'.format(d)
# r = '50 shares of IBM at 490.10'
```

`bytes` and `bytearray` instances can be formatted using the `%` operator. The semantics of this operator are modeled after the `sprintf()` function from C. Here are some examples:

```
name = b'ACME'
x = 123.456

b'Value is %0.2f' % x              # b'The value is 123.46'
bytearray(b'Value is %0.2f') % x   # b'Value is 123.46'
b'%s = %0.2f' % (name, x)          # b'ACME = 123.46'
```

With this formatting, sequences of the form `%spec` are replaced in order with values from a tuple provided as the second operand to the `%` operator. The basic format codes (d, f, s, etc.) are the same as those used for the `format()` function. However, more advanced features are either missing or changed slightly. For example, to adjust alignment, you use a `-` character like this:

```
x = 123.456
b'%10.2f' % x    # b'    123.46'
b'%-10.2f' % x   # b'123.46    '
```

Using a format code of `%r` produces the output of `ascii()` which can be useful in debugging and logging.

When working with bytes, be aware that text strings are not supported. They need to be explicitly encoded.

```
name = 'Dave'

b'Hello %s' % name                    # TypeError!
b'Hello %s' % name.encode('utf-8')    # Ok
```

This form of formatting can also be used with text strings, but it's considered to be an older programming style. However, it still arises in certain libraries. For example, messages produced by the `logging` module are formatted in this way:

```
import logging
log = logging.getLogger(__name__)

log.debug('%s got %d', name, value)   # '%s got %d' % (name, value)
```

The `logging` module is briefly described later in this chapter in Section 9.15.12.

9.4 Reading Command-Line Options

When Python starts, command-line options are placed in the list `sys.argv` as text strings. The first item is the name of the program. Subsequent items are the options added on the command line after the program name. The following program is a minimal prototype of manually processing command-line arguments:

```
def main(argv):
    if len(argv) != 3:
        raise SystemExit(
                f'Usage : python {argv[0]} inputfile outputfile\n')
    inputfile  = argv[1]
    outputfile = argv[2]
    ...

if __name__ == '__main__':
    import sys
    main(sys.argv)
```

For better code organization, testing, and similar reasons, it's a good idea to write a dedicated `main()` function that accepts the command-line options (if any) as a list, as opposed to directly reading `sys.argv`. Include a small fragment of code at the end of your program to pass the command-line options to your `main()` function.

`sys.argv[0]` contains the name of the script being executed. Writing a descriptive help message and raising `SystemExit` is standard practice for command-line scripts that want to report an error.

Although in simple scripts, you can manually process command options, consider using the `argparse` module for more complicated command-line handling. Here is an example:

```python
import argparse

def main(argv):
    p = argparse.ArgumentParser(description="This is some program")

    # A positional argument
    p.add_argument("infile")

    # An option taking an argument
    p.add_argument("-o","--output", action="store")

    # An option that sets a Boolean flag
    p.add_argument("-d","--debug", action="store_true", default=False)

    # Parse the command line
    args = p.parse_args(args=argv)

    # Retrieve the option settings
    infile    = args.infile
    output    = args.output
    debugmode = args.debug

    print(infile, output, debugmode)

if __name__ == '__main__':
    import sys
    main(sys.argv[1:])
```

This example only shows the most simple use of the `argparse` module. The standard library documentation provides more advanced usage. There are also third-party modules such as `click` and `docopt` that can simplify writing of more complex command-line parsers.

Finally, command-line options might be provided to Python in an invalid text encoding. Such arguments are still accepted but they will be encoded using `'surrogateescape'` error handling as described in Section 9.2. You need to be aware of this if such arguments are later included in any kind of text output and it's critical to avoid crashing. It might not be critical, though—don't overcomplicate your code for edge cases that don't matter.

9.5   Environment Variables

Sometimes data is passed to a program via environment variables set in the command shell. For example, a Python program might be launched using a shell command such as `env`:

```
bash $ env SOMEVAR=somevalue python3 somescript.py
```

Environment variables are accessed as text strings in the mapping `os.environ`. Here's an example:

```
import os
path = os.environ['PATH']
user = os.environ['USER']
editor = os.environ['EDITOR']
val = os.environ['SOMEVAR']
... etc. ...
```

To modify environment variables, set the `os.environ` variable. For example:

```
os.environ['NAME'] = 'VALUE'
```

Modifications to `os.environ` affect both the running program and any subprocesses created later—for example, those created by the `subprocess` module.

As with command-line options, badly encoded environment variables may produce strings that use the `'surrogateescape'` error handling policy.

9.6   Files and File Objects

To open a file, use the built-in `open()` function. Usually, `open()` is given a filename and a file mode. It is also often used in combination with the `with` statement as a context manager. Here are some common usage patterns of working with files:

```
# Read a text file all at once as a string
with open('filename.txt', 'rt') as file:
    data = file.read()

# Read a file line-by-line
with open('filename.txt', 'rt') as file:
    for line in file:
        ...

# Write to a text file
with open('out.txt', 'wt') as file:
    file.write('Some output\n')
    print('More output', file=file)
```

In most cases, using `open()` is a straightforward affair. You give it the name of the file you want to open along with a file mode. For example:

```
open('name.txt')          # Opens "name.txt" for reading
open('name.txt', 'rt')    # Opens "name.txt" for reading (same)
open('name.txt', 'wt')    # Opens "name.txt" for writing
open('data.bin', 'rb')    # Binary mode read
open('data.bin', 'wb')    # Binary mode write
```

For most programs, you will never need to know more than these simple examples to work with files. However, there are a number of special cases and more esoteric features of `open()` worth knowing. The next few sections discuss `open()` and file I/O in more detail.

9.6.1 Filenames

To open a file, you need to give `open()` the name of the file. The name can either be a fully specified absolute pathname such as `'/Users/guido/Desktop/files/old/data.csv'` or a relative pathname such as `'data.csv'` or `'..\old\data.csv'`. For relative filenames, the file location is determined relative to the current working directory as returned by `os.getcwd()`. The current working directory can be changed with `os.chdir(newdir)`.

The name itself can be encoded in a number of forms. If it's a text string, the name is interpreted according to the text encoding returned by `sys.getfilesystemencoding()` before being passed to the host operating system. If the filename is a byte string, it is left unencoded and is passed as is. This latter option may be useful if you're writing programs that must handle the possibility of degenerate or miscoded filenames—instead of passing the filename as text, you can pass the raw binary representation of the name. This might seem like an obscure edge case, but Python is commonly used to write system-level scripts that manipulate the filesystem. Abuse of the filesystem is a common technique used by hackers to either hide their tracks or to break system tools.

In addition to text and bytes, any object that implements the special method `__fspath__()` can be used as a name. The `__fspath__()` method must return a text or bytes object corresponding to the actual name. This is the mechanism that makes standard library modules such as `pathlib` work. For example:

```
>>> from pathlib import Path
>>> p = Path('Data/portfolio.csv')
>>> p.__fspath__()
'Data/portfolio.csv'
>>>
```

Potentially, you could make your own custom `Path` object that worked with `open()` as long as it implements `__fspath__()` in a way that resolves to a proper filename on the system.

Finally, filenames can be given as low-level integer file descriptors. This requires that the "file" is already open on the system in some way. Perhaps it corresponds to a network socket, a pipe, or some other system resource that exposes a file descriptor. Here is an example of opening a file directly with the os module and then turning it into a proper file object:

```
>>> import os
>>> fd = os.open('/etc/passwd', os.O_RDONLY)     # Integer fd
>>> fd
3
>>> file = open(fd, 'rt')     # Proper file object
>>> file
<_io.TextIOWrapper name=3 mode='rt' encoding='UTF-8'>
>>> data = file.read()
>>>
```

When opening an existing file descriptor like this, the close() method of the returned file will also close the underlying descriptor. This can be disabled by passing closefd=False to open(). For example:

```
file = open(fd, 'rt', closefd=False)
```

9.6.2   File Modes

When opening a file, you need to specify a file mode. The core file modes are 'r' for reading, 'w' for writing, and 'a' for appending. 'w' mode replaces any existing file with new content. 'a' opens a file for writing and positions the file pointer to the end of the file so that new data can be appended.

A special file mode of 'x' can be used to write to a file, but only if it doesn't exist already. This is a useful way to prevent accidental overwriting of existing data. For this mode, a FileExistsError exception is raised if the file already exists.

Python makes a strict distinction between text and binary data. To specify the kind of data, you append a 't' or a 'b' to the file mode. For example, a file mode of 'rt' opens a file for reading in text mode and 'rb' opens a file for reading in binary mode. The mode determines the kind of data returned by file-related methods such as f.read(). In text mode, strings are returned. In binary mode, bytes are returned.

Binary files can be opened for in-place updates by supplying a plus (+) character, such as 'rb+' or 'wb+'. When a file is opened for update, you can perform both input and output, as long as all output operations flush their data before any subsequent input operations. If a file is opened using 'wb+' mode, its length is first truncated to zero. A common use of the update mode is to provide random read/write access to file contents in combination with seek operations.

9.6.3   I/O Buffering

By default, files are opened with I/O buffering enabled. With I/O buffering, I/O operations are performed in larger chunks to avoid excessive system calls. For example, write operations would start filling an internal memory buffer and output would only actually occur when the buffer is filled up. This behavior can be changed by giving a `buffering` argument to `open()`. For example:

```
# Open a binary-mode file with no I/O buffering

with open('data.bin', 'wb', buffering=0) as file:
    file.write(data)
    ...
```

A value of 0 specifies unbuffered I/O and is only valid for binary mode files. A value of 1 specifies line-buffering and is usually only meaningful for text-mode files. Any other positive value indicates the buffer size to use (in bytes). If no buffering value is specified, the default behavior depends on the kind of file. If it's a normal file on disk, buffering is managed in blocks and the buffer size is set to `io.DEFAULT_BUFFER_SIZE`. Typically this is some small multiple of 4096 bytes. It might vary by system. If the file represents an interactive terminal, line buffering is used.

For normal programs, I/O buffering is not typically a major concern. However, buffering can have an impact on applications involving active communication between processes. For example, a problem that sometimes arises is two communicating subprocesses that deadlock due to an internal buffering issue—for instance, one process writes into a buffer, but a receiver never sees that data because the buffer didn't get flushed. Such problems can be fixed by either specifying unbuffered I/O or by an explicit `flush()` call on the associated file. For example:

```
file.write(data)
file.write(data)
...
file.flush()        # Make sure all data is written from buffers
```

9.6.4 Text Mode Encoding

For files opened in text mode, an optional encoding and an error-handling policy can be specified using the `encoding` and `errors` arguments. For example:

```
with open('file.txt', 'rt',
        encoding='utf-8', errors='replace') as file:
    data = file.read()
```

The values given to the `encoding` and `errors` argument have the same meaning as for the `encode()` and `decode()` methods of strings and bytes respectively.

The default text encoding is determined by the value of `sys.getdefaultencoding()` and may vary by system. If you know the encoding in advance, it's often better to explicitly provide it even if it happens to match the default encoding on your system.

9.6.5 Text-Mode Line Handling

With text files, one complication is the encoding of newline characters. Newlines are encoded as '\n', '\r\n', or '\r' depending on the host operating system—for example, '\n' on UNIX and '\r\n' on Windows. By default, Python translates all of these line endings to a standard '\n' character when reading. On writing, newline characters are translated back to the default line ending used on the system. The behavior is sometimes referred to as "universal newline mode" in Python documentation.

You can change the newline behavior by giving a newline argument to open(). For example:

```
# Exactly require '\r\n' and leave intact
file = open('somefile.txt', 'rt', newline='\r\n')
```

Specifying newline=None enables the default line handling behavior where all line endings are translated to a standard '\n' character. Giving newline='' makes Python recognize all line endings, but disables the translation step—if lines were terminated by '\r\n', the '\r\n' combination would be left in the input intact. Specifying a value of '\n', '\r', or '\r\n' makes that the expected line ending.

9.7 I/O Abstraction Layers

The open() function serves as a kind of high-level factory function for creating instances of different I/O classes. These classes embody the different file modes, encodings, and buffering behaviors. They are also composed together in layers. The following classes are defined in the io module:

FileIO(filename, mode='r', closefd=True, opener=None)
>   Opens a file for raw unbuffered binary I/O. filename is any valid filename accepted by the open() function. Other arguments have the same meaning as for open().

BufferedReader(file [, buffer_size])
BufferedWriter(file [, buffer_size])
BufferedRandom(file [, buffer_size])
>   Implements a buffered binary I/O layer for a file. file is an instance of FileIO. buffer_size specifies the internal buffer size to use. The choice of class depends on whether or not the file is reading, writing, or updating data. The optional buffer_size argument specifies the internal buffer size used.

TextIOWrapper(buffered, [encoding, [errors [, newline [, line_buffering [, write_through]]]]])
>   Implements text mode I/O. buffered is a buffered binary mode file, such as BufferedReader or BufferedWriter. The encoding, errors, and newline arguments have the same meaning as for open(). line_buffering is a Boolean flag that forces I/O to be flushed on newline characters (False by default). write_through is a Boolean flag that forces all writes to be flushed (False by default).

Here is an example that shows how a text-mode file is constructed, layer-by-layer:

```
>>> raw = io.FileIO('filename.txt', 'r')       # Raw-binary mode
>>> buffer = io.BufferedReader(raw)        # Binary buffered reader
>>> file = io.TextIOWrapper(buffer, encoding='utf-8') # Text mode
>>>
```

Normally you don't need to manually construct layers like this—the built-in `open()` function takes care of all of the work. However, if you already have an existing file object and want to change its handling in some way, you might manipulate the layers as shown.

To strip layers away, use the `detach()` method of a file. For example, here is how you can convert an already text-mode file into a binary-mode file:

```
f = open('something.txt', 'rt')   # Text-mode file
fb = f.detach()                   # Detach underlying binary mode file
data = fb.read()                  # Returns bytes
```

9.7.1 File Methods

The exact type of object returned by `open()` depends on the combination of file mode and buffering options provided. However, the resulting file object supports the methods in Table 9.4.

Table 9.4   File Methods

Method	Description
`f.readable()`	Returns `True` if file can be read.
`f.read([n])`	Reads at most n bytes.
`f.readline([n])`	Reads a single line of input up to n characters. If n is omitted, this method reads the entire line.
`f.readlines([size])`	Reads all the lines and returns a list. `size` optionally specifies the approximate number of characters to read on the file before stopping.
`f.readinto(buffer)`	Reads data into a memory buffer.
`f.writable()`	Returns `True` if file can be written.
`f.write(s)`	Writes string s.
`f.writelines(lines)`	Writes all strings in iterable `lines`.
`f.close()`	Closes the file.
`f.seekable()`	Returns `True` if file supports random-access seeking.
`f.tell()`	Returns the current file pointer.
`f.seek(offset [, where])`	Seeks to a new file position.
`f.isatty()`	Returns `True` if f is an interactive terminal.
`f.flush()`	Flushes the output buffers.
`f.truncate([size])`	Truncates the file to at most `size` bytes.
`f.fileno()`	Returns an integer file descriptor.

The `readable()`, `writable()`, and `seekable()` methods test for supported file capabilities and modes. The `read()` method returns the entire file as a string unless an optional length parameter specifies the maximum number of characters. The `readline()` method returns the next line of input, including the terminating newline; the `readlines()` method returns all the input file as a list of strings. The `readline()` method optionally accepts a maximum line length, n. If a line longer than n characters is read, the first n characters are returned. The remaining line data is not discarded and will be returned on subsequent read operations. The `readlines()` method accepts a `size` parameter that specifies the approximate number of characters to read before stopping. The actual number of characters read may be larger than this depending on how much data has been buffered already. The `readinto()` method is used to avoid memory copies and is discussed later.

`read()` and `readline()` indicate end-of-file (EOF) by returning an empty string. Thus, the following code shows how you can detect an EOF condition:

```
while True:
    line = file.readline()
    if not line:          # EOF
        break
    statements
    ...
```

You could also write this code as follows:

```
while (line:=file.readline()):
    statements
    ...
```

A convenient way to read all lines in a file is to use iteration with a `for` loop:

```
for line in file:     # Iterate over all lines in the file
    # Do something with line
    ...
```

The `write()` method writes data to the file, and the `writelines()` method writes an iterable of strings to the file. `write()` and `writelines()` do not add newline characters to the output, so all output that you produce should already include all necessary formatting.

Internally, each open file object keeps a file pointer that stores the byte offset at which the next read or write operation will occur. The `tell()` method returns the current value of the file pointer. The `seek(offset [,whence])` method is used to randomly access parts of a file given an integer offset and a placement rule in whence. If whence is os.SEEK_SET (the default), `seek()` assumes that offset is relative to the start of the file; if whence is os.SEEK_CUR, the position is moved relative to the current position; and if whence is os.SEEK_END, the offset is taken from the end of the file.

The `fileno()` method returns the integer file descriptor for a file and is sometimes used in low-level I/O operations in certain library modules. For example, the `fcntl` module uses the file descriptor to provide low-level file control operations on UNIX systems.

The `readinto()` method is used to perform zero-copy I/O into contiguous memory buffers. It is most commonly used in combination with specialized libraries such as numpy—for example, to read data directly into the memory allocated for a numeric array . File objects also have the read-only data attributes shown in Table 9.5.

Table 9.5 File Attributes

Attribute	Description
`f.closed`	Boolean value indicates the file state: `False` if the file is open, `True` if closed.
`f.mode`	The I/O mode for the file.
`f.name`	Name of the file if created using `open()`. Otherwise, it will be a string indicating the source of the file.
`f.newlines`	The newline representation actually found in the file. The value is either `None` if no newlines have been encountered, a string containing `'\n'`, `'\r'`, or `'\r\n'`, or a tuple containing all the different newline encodings seen.
`f.encoding`	A string that indicates file encoding, if any (for example, `'latin-1'` or `'utf-8'`). The value is `None` if no encoding is being used.
`f.errors`	The error handling policy.
`f.write_through`	Boolean value indicating if writes on a text file pass data directly to the underlying binary level file without buffering.

9.8 Standard Input, Output, and Error

The interpreter provides three standard file-like objects, known as standard input, standard output, and standard error, available as `sys.stdin`, `sys.stdout`, and `sys.stderr`, respectively. `stdin` is a file object corresponding to the stream of input characters supplied to the interpreter, `stdout` is the file object that receives output produced by `print()`, and `stderr` is a file that receives error messages. More often than not, `stdin` is mapped to the user's keyboard, whereas `stdout` and `stderr` produce text on screen.

The methods described in the preceding section can be used to perform I/O with the user. For example, the following code writes to standard output and reads a line of input from standard input:

```
import sys
sys.stdout.write("Enter your name: ")
name = sys.stdin.readline()
```

Alternatively, the built-in function `input(prompt)` can read a line of text from `stdin` and optionally print a prompt:

```
name = input("Enter your name: ")
```

Lines read by `input()` do not include the trailing newline. This is different than reading directly from `sys.stdin` where newlines are included in the input text.

If necessary, the values of `sys.stdout`, `sys.stdin`, and `sys.stderr` can be replaced with other file objects, in which case the `print()` and `input()` functions will use the new values. Should it ever be necessary to restore the original value of `sys.stdout`, it should be saved first. The original values of `sys.stdout`, `sys.stdin`, and `sys.stderr` at interpreter startup are also available in `sys.__stdout__`, `sys.__stdin__`, and `sys.__stderr__`, respectively.

9.9 Directories

To get a directory listing, use the `os.listdir(pathname)` function. For example, here is how to print out a list of filenames in a directory:

```
import os

names = os.listdir('dirname')
for name in names:
    print(name)
```

Names returned by `listdir()` are normally decoded according to the encoding returned by `sys.getfilesystemencoding()`. If you specify the initial path as bytes, the filenames are returned as undecoded byte strings. For example:

```
import os

# Return raw undecoded names
names = os.listdir(b'dirname')
```

A useful operation related to directory listing is matching filenames according to a pattern, known as *globbing*. The `pathlib` modules can be used for this purpose. For example, here is an example of matching all `*.txt` files in a specific directory:

```
import pathlib

for filename in path.Path('dirname').glob('*.txt'):
    print(filename)
```

If you use `rglob()` instead of `glob()`, it will recursively search all subdirectories for filenames that match the pattern. Both the `glob()` and `rglob()` functions return a generator that produces the filenames via iteration.

9.10 The `print()` function

To print a series of values separated by spaces, supply them all to `print()` like this:

```
print('The values are', x, y, z)
```

To suppress or change the line ending, use the `end` keyword argument:

```
# Suppress the newline
print('The values are', x, y, z, end='')
```

To redirect the output to a file, use the `file` keyword argument:

```
# Redirect to file object f
print('The values are', x, y, z, file=f)
```

To change the separator character between items, use the `sep` keyword argument:

```
# Put commas between the values
print('The values are', x, y, z, sep=',')
```

9.11 Generating Output

Working directly with files is most familiar to programmers. However, generator functions can also be used to emit an I/O stream as a sequence of data fragments. To do this, use the `yield` statement as you would use a `write()` or `print()` function. Here is an example:

```
def countdown(n):
    while n > 0:
        yield f'T-minus {n}\n'
        n -= 1
    yield 'Kaboom!\n'
```

Producing an output stream in this manner provides flexibility because it is decoupled from the code that actually directs the stream to its intended destination. For example, if you want to route the above output to a file `f`, you can do this:

```
lines = countdown(5)
f.writelines(lines)
```

If, instead, you want to redirect the output across a socket `s`, you can do this:

```
for chunk in lines:
    s.sendall(chunk.encode('utf-8'))
```

Or, if you simply want to capture all of the output in a single string, you can do this:

```
out = ''.join(lines)
```

More advanced applications can use this approach to implement their own I/O buffering. For example, a generator could be emitting small text fragments, but another function would then collect the fragments into larger buffers to create a more efficient single I/O operation.

```
chunks = []
buffered_size = 0
for chunk in count:
    chunks.append(chunk)
    buffered_size += len(chunk)
    if buffered_size >= MAXBUFFERSIZE:
        outf.write(''.join(chunks))
        chunks.clear()
        buffered_size = 0
outf.write(''.join(chunks))
```

For programs that are routing output to files or network connections, a generator approach can also result in a significant reduction in memory use because the entire output stream can often be generated and processed in small fragments, as opposed to being first collected into one large output string or list of strings.

9.12   Consuming Input

For programs that consume fragmentary input, enhanced generators can be useful for decoding protocols and other facets of I/O. Here is an example of an enhanced generator that receives byte fragments and assembles them into lines:

```
def line_receiver():
    data = bytearray()
    line = None
    linecount = 0
    while True:
        part = yield line
        linecount += part.count(b'\n')
        data.extend(part)
        if linecount > 0:
            index = data.index(b'\n')
            line = bytes(data[:index+1])
            data = data[index+1:]
            linecount -= 1
        else:
            line = None
```

In this example, a generator has been programmed to receive byte fragments that are collected into a byte array. If the array contains a newline, a line is extracted and returned. Otherwise, None is returned. Here's an example illustrating how it works:

```
>>> r = line_receiver()
>>> r.send(None)        # Necessary first step
>>> r.send(b'hello')
>>> r.send(b'world\nit ')
b'hello world\n'
>>> r.send(b'works!')
>>> r.send(b'\n')
b'it works!\n''
>>>
```

An interesting side effect of this approach is that it externalizes the actual I/O operations that must be performed to get the input data. Specifically, the implementation of line_receiver() contains no I/O operations at all! This means that it could be used in different contexts. For example, with sockets:

```
r = line_receiver()
data = None
while True:
    while not (line:=r.send(data)):
        data = sock.recv(8192)

    # Process the line
    ...
```

or with files:

```
r = line_receiver()
data = None
while True:
    while not (line:=r.send(data)):
        data = file.read(10000)

    # Process the line
    ...
```

or even in asynchronous code:

```
async def reader(ch):
    r = line_receiver()
    data = None
    while True:
        while not (line:=r.send(data)):
            data = await ch.receive(8192)

        # Process the line
        ...
```

9.13 Object Serialization

Sometimes it's necessary to serialize the representation of an object so it can be transmitted over the network, saved to a file, or stored in a database. One way to do this is to convert data into a standard encoding such as JSON or XML. There is also a common Python-specific data serialization format called *Pickle*.

The `pickle` module serializes an object into a stream of bytes that can be used to reconstruct the object at a later point in time. The interface to `pickle` is simple, consisting of two operations, `dump()` and `load()`. For example, the following code writes an object to a file:

```
import pickle
obj = SomeObject()
with open(filename, 'wb') as file:
    pickle.dump(obj, file)        # Save object on f
```

To restore the object, use:

```
with open(filename, 'rb') as file:
    obj = pickle.load(file)       # Restore the object
```

The data format used by `pickle` has its own framing of records. Thus, a sequence of objects can be saved by issuing a series of `dump()` operations one after the other. To restore these objects, simply use a similar sequence of `load()` operations.

For network programming, it is common to use pickle to create byte-encoded messages. To do that, use `dumps()` and `loads()`. Instead of reading/writing data to a file, these functions work with byte strings.

```
obj = SomeObject()

# Turn an object into bytes
data = pickle.dumps(obj)
...


# Turn bytes back into an object
obj = pickle.loads(data)
```

It is not normally necessary for user-defined objects to do anything extra to work with `pickle`. However, certain kinds of objects can't be pickled. These tend to be objects that incorporate runtime state—open files, threads, closures, generators, and so on. To handle these tricky cases, a class can define the special methods __getstate__() and __setstate__().

The __getstate__() method, if defined, will be called to create a value representing the state of an object. The value returned by __getstate__() is typically a string, tuple, list, or dictionary. The __setstate__() method receives this value during unpickling and should restore the state of an object from it.

When encoding an object, pickle does not include the underlying source code itself. Instead, it encodes a name reference to the defining class. When unpickling, this name is used to perform a source-code lookup on the system. For unpickling to work, the recipient of a pickle must have the proper source code already installed. It is also important to emphasize that pickle is inherently insecure—unpickling untrusted data is a known vector for remote code execution. Thus, pickle should only be used if you can completely secure the runtime environment.

9.14 Blocking Operations and Concurrency

A fundamental aspect of I/O is the concept of *blocking*. By its very nature, I/O is connected to the real world. It often involves waiting for input or devices to be ready. For example, code that reads data on the network might perform a receive operation on a socket like this:

```
data = sock.recv(8192)
```

When this statement executes, it might return immediately if data is available. However, if that's not the case, it will stop—waiting for data to arrive. This is blocking. While the program is blocked, nothing else happens.

For a data analysis script or a simple program, blocking is not something that you worry about. However, if you want your program to do something else while an operation is blocked, you will need to take a different approach. This is the fundamental problem of concurrency—having a program work on more than one thing at a time. One common problem is having a program read on two or more different network sockets at the same time:

```
def reader1(sock):
    while (data := sock.recv(8192)):
        print('reader1 got:', data)

def reader2(sock):
    while (data := sock.recv(8192)):
        print('reader2 got:', data)

# Problem: How to make reader1() and reader2()
# run at the same time?
```

The rest of this section outlines a few different approaches to solving this problem. However, it is not meant to be a full tutorial on concurrency. For that, you will need to consult other resources.

9.14.1 Nonblocking I/O

One approach to avoiding blocking is to use so-called *nonblocking I/O*. This is a special
mode that has to be enabled—for example, on a socket:

```
sock.setblocking(False)
```

Once enabled, an exception will now be raised if an operation would have blocked. For
example:

```
try:
    data = sock.recv(8192)
except BlockingIOError as e:
    # No data is available
    ...
```

In response to a `BlockingIOError`, the program could elect to work on something else.
It could retry the I/O operation later to see if any data has arrived. For example, here's
how you might read on two sockets at once:

```
def reader1(sock):
    try:
        data = sock.recv(8192)
        print('reader1 got:', data)
    except BlockingIOError:
        pass

def reader2(sock):
    try:
        data = sock.recv(8192)
        print('reader2 got:', data)
    except BlockingIOError:
        pass

def run(sock1, sock2):
    sock1.setblocking(False)
    sock2.setblocking(False)
    while True:
        reader1(sock1)
        reader2(sock2)
```

In practice, relying only on nonblocking I/O is clumsy and inefficient. For example,
the core of this program is the `run()` function at the end. It will run in a inefficient busy
loop as it constantly tries to read on the sockets. This works, but it is not a good design.

9.14.2   I/O Polling

Instead of relying upon exceptions and spinning, it is possible to poll I/O channels to see if data is available. The `select` or `selectors` module can be used for this purpose. For example, here's a slightly modified version of the `run()` function:

```
from selectors import DefaultSelector, EVENT_READ, EVENT_WRITE

def run(sock1, sock2):
    selector = DefaultSelector()
    selector.register(sock1, EVENT_READ, data=reader1)
    selector.register(sock2, EVENT_READ, data=reader2)
    # Wait for something to happen
    while True:
        for key, evt in selector.select():
            func = key.data
            func(key.fileobj)
```

In this code, the loop dispatches either `reader1()` or `reader2()` function as a callback whenever I/O is detected on the appropriate socket. The `selector.select()` operation itself blocks, waiting for I/O to occur. Thus, unlike the previous example, it won't make the CPU furiously spin.

This approach to I/O is the foundation of many so-called "async" frameworks such as `asyncio`, although you usually don't see the inner workings of the event loop.

9.14.3   Threads

In the last two examples, concurrency required the use of a special `run()` function to drive the calculation. As an alternative, you can use thread programming and the `threading` module. Think of a thread as an independent task that runs inside your program. Here is an example of code that reads data on two sockets at once:

```
import threading

def reader1(sock):
    while (data := sock.recv(8192)):
        print('reader1 got:', data)

def reader2(sock):
    while (data := sock.recv(8192)):
        print('reader2 got:', data)

t1 = threading.Thread(target=reader1, args=[sock1])
t2 = threading.Thread(target=reader2, args=[sock2])

# Start the threads
```

```
t1.start()
t2.start()

# Wait for the threads to finish
t1.join()
t2.join()
```

In this program, the `reader1()` and `reader2()` functions execute concurrently. This is managed by the host operating system, so you don't need to know much about how it works. If a blocking operation occurs in one thread, it does not affect the other thread.

The subject of thread programming is, in its entirety, beyond the scope of this book. However, a few additional examples are provided in the `threading` module section later in this chapter.

9.14.4 Concurrent Execution with `asyncio`

The `asyncio` module provides a concurrency implementation alternative to threads. Internally, it's based on an event loop that uses I/O polling. However, the high-level programming model looks very similar to threads through the use of special `async` functions. Here is an example:

```
import asyncio

async def reader1(sock):
    loop = asyncio.get_event_loop()
    while (data := await loop.sock_recv(sock, 8192)):
        print('reader1 got:', data)

async def reader2(sock):
    loop = asyncio.get_event_loop()
    while (data := await loop.sock_recv(sock, 8192)):
        print('reader2 got:', data)

async def main(sock1, sock2):
    loop = asyncio.get_event_loop()
    t1 = loop.create_task(reader1(sock1))
    t2 = loop.create_task(reader2(sock2))

    # Wait for the tasks to finish
    await t1
    await t2

...
# Run it
asyncio.run(main(sock1, sock2))
```

Full details of using `asyncio` would require its own dedicated book. What you should know is that many libraries and frameworks advertise support for asynchronous operation. Usually that means that concurrent execution is supported through `asyncio` or a similar module. Much of the code is likely to involve async functions and related features.

9.15   Standard Library Modules

A large number of standard library modules are used for various I/O related tasks. This section provides a brief overview of the commonly used modules, along with a few examples. Complete reference material can be found online or in an IDE and is not repeated here. The main purpose of this section is to point you in the right direction by giving you the names of the modules that you should be using along with a few examples of very common programming tasks involving each module.

Many of the examples are shown as interactive Python sessions. These are experiments that you are encouraged to try yourself.

9.15.1   asyncio **Module**

The `asyncio` module provides support for concurrent I/O operations using I/O polling and an underlying event loop. Its primary use is in code involving networks and distributed systems. Here is an example of a TCP echo server using low-level sockets:

```python
import asyncio
from socket import *

async def echo_server(address):
    loop = asyncio.get_event_loop()
    sock = socket(AF_INET, SOCK_STREAM)
    sock.setsockopt(SOL_SOCKET, SO_REUSEADDR, 1)
    sock.bind(address)
    sock.listen(5)
    sock.setblocking(False)
    print('Server listening at', address)
    with sock:
        while True:
            client, addr = await loop.sock_accept(sock)
            print('Connection from', addr)
            loop.create_task(echo_client(loop, client))

async def echo_client(loop, client):
    with client:
        while True:
            data = await loop.sock_recv(client, 10000)
```

```
                if not data:
                    break
                await loop.sock_sendall(client, b'Got:' + data)
        print('Connection closed')

if __name__ == '__main__':
    loop = asyncio.get_event_loop()
    loop.create_task(echo_server(('', 25000)))
    loop.run_forever()
```

To test this code, use a program such as nc or telnet to connect to port 25000 on your machine. The code should echo back the text that you type. If you connect more than once using multiple terminal windows, you'll find that the code can handle all of the connections concurrently.

Most applications using asyncio will probably operate at a higher level than sockets. However, in such applications, you will still have to make use of special async functions and interact with the underlying event loop in some manner.

9.15.2 binascii **Module**

The binascii module has functions for converting binary data into various text-based representations such as hexadecimal and base64. For example:

```
>>> binascii.b2a_hex(b'hello')
b'68656c6c6f'
>>> binascii.a2b_hex(_)
b'hello'
>>> binascii.b2a_base64(b'hello')
b'aGVsbG8=\n'
>>> binascii.a2b_base64(_)
b'hello'
>>>
```

Similar functionality can be found in the base64 module as well as with the hex() and fromhex() methods of bytes. For example:

```
>>> a = b'hello'
>>> a.hex()
'68656c6c6f'
>>> bytes.fromhex(_)
b'hello'
>>> import base64
>>> base64.b64encode(a)
b'aGVsbG8='
>>>
```

9.15.3 `cgi` **Module**

So, let's say you just want to put a basic form on your website. Perhaps it's a sign-up form for your weekly "Cats and Categories" newsletter. Sure, you could install the latest web framework and spend all of your time fiddling with it. Or, you could also just write a basic CGI script—old-school style. The `cgi` module is for doing just that.

Suppose you have the following form fragment on a webpage:

```
<form method="POST" action="cgi-bin/register.py">
   <p>
   To register, please provide a contact name and email address.
   </p>
   <div>
      <input name="name" type="text">Your name:</input>
   </div>
   <div>
      <input name="email" type="email">Your email:</input>
   </div>
   <div class="modal-footer justify-content-center">
      <input type="submit" name="submit" value="Register"></input>
   </div>
</form>
```

Here's a CGI script that receives the form data on the other end:

```
#!/usr/bin/env python
import cgi
try:
    form = cgi.FieldStorage()
    name = form.getvalue('name')
    email = form.getvalue('email')
    # Validate the responses and do whatever
    ...
    # Produce an HTML result (or redirect)
    print("Status: 302 Moved\r")
    print("Location: https://www.mywebsite.com/thanks.html\r")
    print("\r")
except Exception as e:
    print("Status: 501 Error\r")
    print("Content-type: text/plain\r")
    print("\r")
    print("Some kind of error occurred.\r")
```

Will writing such a CGI script get you a job at an Internet startup? Probably not. Will it solve your actual problem? Likely.

9.15.4 `configparser` **Module**

INI files are a common format for encoding program configuration information in a human-readable form. Here is an example:

```
# config.ini

; A comment
[section1]
name1 = value1
name2 = value2

[section2]
; Alternative syntax
name1: value1
name2: value2
```

The `configparser` module is used to read `.ini` files and extract values. Here's a basic example:

```
import configparser

# Create a config parser and read a file
cfg = configparser.ConfigParser()
cfg.read('config.ini')

# Extract values
a = cfg.get('section1', 'name1')
b = cfg.get('section2', 'name2')
...
```

More advanced functionality is also available, including string interpolation features, the ability to merge multiple `.ini` files, provide default values, and more. Consult the official documentation for more examples.

9.15.5 `csv` **Module**

The `csv` module is used to read/write files of comma-separated values (CSV) produced by programs such as Microsoft Excel or exported from a database. To use it, open a file and then wrap an extra layer of CSV encoding/decoding around it. For example:

```
import csv

# Read a CSV file into a list of tuples
def read_csv_data(filename):
    with open(filename, newline='') as file:
        rows = csv.reader(file)
```

```
    # First line is often a header. This reads it
    headers = next(rows)
    # Now read the rest of the data
    for row in rows:
        # Do something with row
        ...


# Write Python data to a CSV file
def write_csv_data(filename, headers, rows):
    with open(filename, 'w', newline='') as file:
        out = csv.writer(file)
        out.writerow(headers)
        out.writerows(rows)
```

An often used convenience is to use a `DictReader()` instead. This interprets the first line of a CSV file as headers and returns each row as dictionary instead of a tuple.

```
import csv

def find_nearby(filename):
    with open(filename, newline='') as file:
        rows = csv.DictReader(file)
        for row in rows:
            lat = float(rows['latitude'])
            lon = float(rows['longitude'])
            if close_enough(lat, lon):
                print(row)
```

The `csv` module doesn't do much with CSV data other than reading or writing it. The main benefit provided is that the module knows how to properly encode/decode the data and handles a lot of edge cases involving quotation, special characters, and other details. This is a module you might use to write simple scripts for cleaning or preparing data to be used with other programs. If you want to perform data analysis tasks with CSV data, consider using a third-party package such as the popular `pandas` library.

9.15.6 `errno` Module

Whenever a system-level error occurs, Python reports it with an exception that's a subclass of `OSError`. Some of the more common kinds of system errors are represented by separate subclasses of `OSError` such as `PermissionError` or `FileNotFoundError`. However, there are hundreds of other errors that could occur in practice. For these, any `OSError` exception carries a numeric `errno` attribute that can be inspected. The `errno` module provides symbolic constants corresponding to these error codes. They are often used when writing specialized exception handlers. For example, here is an exception handler that checks for no space remaining on a device:

```
import errno

def write_data(file, data):
    try:
        file.write(data)
    except OSError as e:
        if e.errno == errno.ENOSPC:
            print("You're out of disk space!")
        else:
            raise        # Some other error. Propagate
```

9.15.7 `fcntl` Module

The `fcntl` module is used to perform low-level I/O control operations on UNIX using the `fcntl()` and `ioctl()` system calls. This is also the module to use if you want to perform any kind of file locking—a problem that sometimes arises in the context of concurrency and distributed systems. Here is an example of opening a file in combination with mutual exclusion locking across all processes using `fcntl.flock()`:

```
import fcntl

with open("somefile", "r") as file:
    try:
        fcntl.flock(file.fileno(), fcntl.LOCK_EX)
        # Use the file

        ...
    finally:
        fcntl.flock(file.fileno(), fcntl.LOCK_UN)
```

9.15.8 `hashlib` Module

The `hashlib` module provides functions for computing cryptographic hash values such as MD5 and SHA-1. The following example illustrates how to use the module:

```
>>> h = hashlib.new('sha256')
>>> h.update(b'Hello')     # Feed data
>>> h.update(b'World')
>>> h.digest()
b'\xa5\x91\xa6\xd4\x0b\xf4 @J\x01\x173\xcf\xb7\xb1\x90\xd6,e\xbf\x0b\xcd
\xa3+W\xb2w\xd9\xad\x9f\x14n'
>>> h.hexdigest()
'a591a6d40bf420404a011733cfb7b190d62c65bf0bcda32b57b277d9ad9f146e'
>>> h.digest_size
32
>>>
```

9.15.9 http **Package**

The http package contains a large amount of code related to the low-level implementation of the HTTP internet protocol. It can be used to implement both servers and clients. However, most of this package is considered legacy and too low-level for day-to-day work. Serious programmers working with HTTP are more likely to use third-party libraries such as requests, httpx, Django, flask, and others.

Nevertheless, one useful easter egg of the http package is the ability for Python to run a standalone web server. Go a directory with a collection of files and type the following:

```
bash $ python -m http.server
Serving HTTP on 0.0.0.0 port 8000 (http://0.0.0.0:8000/) ...
```

Now, Python will serve the files to your browser if you point it at the right port. You wouldn't use this to run a website, but it can be useful for testing and debugging programs related to the web. For example, the author has used this to locally test programs involving a mix of HTML, Javascript, and WebAssembly.

9.15.10 io **Module**

The io module primarily contains the definitions of classes used to implement the file objects as returned by the open() function. It is not so common to access those classes directly. However, the module also contains a pair of classes that are useful for "faking" a file in the form of strings and bytes. This can be useful for testing and other applications where you need to provide a "file" but have obtained data in a different way.

The StringIO() class provides a file-like interface on top of strings. For example, here is how you can write output to a string:

```
# Function that expects a file
def greeting(file):
    file.write('Hello\n')
    file.write('World\n')

# Call the function using a real file
with open('out.txt', 'w') as file:
    greeting(file)

# Call the function with a "fake" file
import io
file = io.StringIO()
greeting(file)

# Get the resulting output
output = file.getvalue()
```

Similarly, you can create a StringIO object and use it for reading:

```
file = io.StringIO('hello\nworld\n')
while (line := file.readline()):
    print(line, end='')
```

The `BytesIO()` class serves a similar purpose but is used for emulating binary I/O with bytes.

9.15.11   json **Module**

The `json` module can be used to encode and decode data in the JSON format, commonly used in the APIs of microservices and web applications. There are two basic functions for converting data, `dumps()` and `loads()`. `dumps()` takes a Python dictionary and encodes it as a JSON Unicode string:

```
>>> import json
>>> data = { 'name': 'Mary A. Python', 'email': 'mary123@python.org' }
>>> s = json.dumps(data)
>>> s
'{"name": "Mary A. Python", "email": "mary123@python.org"}'
>>>
```

The `loads()` function goes in the other direction:

```
>>> d = json.loads(s)
>>> d == data
True
>>>
```

Both the `dumps()` and `loads()` functions have many options for controlling aspects of the conversion as well as interfacing with Python class instances. That's beyond the scope of this section but copious amounts of information is available in the official documentation.

9.15.12   logging **Module**

The `logging` module is the de facto standard module used for reporting program diagnostics and for print-style debugging. It can be used to route output to a log file and provides a large number of configuration options. A common practice is to write code that creates a `Logger` instance and issues messages on it like this:

```
import logging
log = logging.getLogger(__name__)

# Function that uses logging
def func(args):
    log.debug("A debugging message")
    log.info("An informational message")
```

```
        log.warning("A warning message")
        log.error("An error message")
        log.critical("A critical message")

    # Configuration of logging (occurs one at program startup)
    if __name__ == '__main__':
        logging.basicConfig(
                level=logging.WARNING,
                filename="output.log"
        )
```

There are five built-in levels of logging ordered by increasing severity. When configuring the logging system, you specify a level that acts as a filter. Only messages at that level or greater severity are reported. Logging provides a large number of configuration options, mostly related to the back-end handling of the log messages. Usually you don't need to know about that when writing application code—you use `debug()`, `info()`, `warning()`, and similar methods on some given `Logger` instance. Any special configuration takes place during program startup in a special location (such as a `main()` function or the main code block).

9.15.13 os **Module**

The `os` module provides a portable interface to common operating-system functions, typically associated with the process environment, files, directories, permissions, and so forth. The programming interface closely follows C programming and standards such as POSIX.

Practically speaking, most of this module is probably too low-level to be directly used in a typical application. However, if you're ever faced with the problem of executing some obscure low-level system operation (such as opening a TTY), there's a good chance you'll find the functionality for it here.

9.15.14 os.path **Module**

The `os.path` module is a legacy module for manipulating pathnames and performing common operations on the filesystem. Its functionality has been largely replaced by the newer `pathlib` module, but since its use is still so widespread, you'll continue to see it in a lot of code.

One fundamental problem solved by this module is portable handling of path separators on UNIX (forward-slash /) and Windows (backslash \). Functions such as `os.path.join()` and `os.path.split()` are often used to pull apart filepaths and put them back together:

```
>>> filename = '/Users/beazley/Desktop/old/data.csv'
>>> os.path.split()
('/Users/beazley/Desktop/old', 'data.csv')
>>> os.path.join('/Users/beazley/Desktop', 'out.txt')
```

```
'/Users/beazley/Desktop/out.txt'
>>>
```

Here is an example of code that uses these functions:

```
import os.path

def clean_line(line):
    # Line up a line (whatever)
    return line.strip().upper() + '\n'

def clean_data(filename):
    dirname, basename = os.path.split()
    newname = os.path.join(dirname, basename+'.clean')
    with open(newname, 'w') as out_f:
        with open(filename, 'r') as in_f:
            for line in in_f:
                out_f.write(clean_line(line))
```

The os.path module also has a number of functions, such as isfile(), isdir(), and getsize(), for performing tests on the filesystem and getting file metadata. For example, this function returns the total size in bytes of a simple file or of all of files in a directory:

```
import os.path

def compute_usage(filename):
    if os.path.isfile(filename):
        return os.path.getsize(filename)
    elif os.path.isdir(filename):
        return sum(compute_usage(os.path.join(filename, name))
                   for name in os.listdir(filename))
    else:
        raise RuntimeError('Unsupported file kind')
```

9.15.15 pathlib Module

The pathlib module is the modern way of manipulating pathnames in a portable and high-level manner. It combines a lot of the file-oriented functionality in one place and uses an object-oriented interface. The core object is the Path class. For example:

```
from pathlib import Path

filename = Path('/Users/beazley/old/data.csv')
```

Once you have an instance filename of Path, you can perform various operations on it to manipulate the filename. For example:

```
>>> filename.name
'data.csv'
>>> filename.parent
Path('/Users/beazley/old')
>>> filename.parent / 'newfile.csv'
Path('/Users/beazley/old/newfile.csv')
>>> filename.parts
('/', 'Users', 'beazley', 'old', 'data.csv')
>>> filename.with_suffix('.csv.clean')
Path('/Users/beazley/old/data.csv.clean')
>>>
```

Path instances also have functions for obtaining file metadata, getting directory listings, and other similar functions. Here is a reimplementation of the `compute_usage()` function from the previous section:

```python
import pathlib

def compute_usage(filename):
    pathname = pathlib.Path(filename)
    if pathname.is_file():
        return pathname.stat().st_size
    elif pathname.is_dir():
        return sum(path.stat().st_size
                   for path in pathname.rglob('*')
                   if path.is_file())
        return pathname.stat().st_size
    else:
        raise RuntimeError('Unsupported file kind')
```

9.15.16 re Module

The re module is used to perform text matching, searching, and replacement operations using regular expressions. Here is a simple example:

```
>>> text = 'Today is 3/27/2018. Tomorrow is 3/28/2018.'
>>> # Find all occurrences of a date
>>> import re
>>> re.findall(r'\d+/\d+/\d+', text)
['3/27/2018', '3/28/2018']
>>> # Replace all occurrences of a date with replacement text
>>> re.sub(r'(\d+)/(\d+)/(\d+)', r'\3-\1-\2', text)
'Today is 2018-3-27. Tomorrow is 2018-3-28.'
>>>
```

Regular expressions are often notorious for their inscrutable syntax. In this example, the \d+ is interpreted to mean "one or more digits." More information about the pattern syntax can be found in the official documentation for the re module.

9.15.17 shutil **Module**

The shutil module is used to carry out some common tasks that you might otherwise perform in the shell. These include copying and removing files, working with archives, and so forth. For example, to copy a file:

```
import shutil

shutil.copy(srcfile, dstfile)
```

To move a file:

```
shutil.move(srcfile, dstfile)
```

To copy a directory tree:

```
shutil.copytree(srcdir, dstdir)
```

To remove a directory tree:

```
shutil.rmtree(pathname)
```

The shutil module is often used as a safer and more portable alternative to directly executing shell commands with the os.system() function.

9.15.18 select **Module**

The select module is used for simple polling of multiple I/O streams. That is, it can be used to watch a collection of file descriptors for incoming data or for the ability to receive outgoing data. The following example shows typical usage:

```
import select

# Collections of objects representing file descriptors.  Must be
# integers or objects with a fileno() method.
want_to_read = [ ... ]
want_to_write = [ ... ]
check_exceptions = [ ... ]

# Timeout (or None)
timeout = None

# Poll for I/O
```

```
can_read, can_write, have_exceptions = \
    select.select(want_to_read, want_to_write, check_exceptions, timeout)

# Perform I/O operations
for file in can_read:
    do_read(file)
for file in can_write:
    do_write(file)

# Handle exceptions
for file in have_exceptions:
    handle_exception(file)
```

In this code, three sets of file descriptors are constructed. These sets correspond to reading, writing, and exceptions. These are passed to `select()` along with an optional timeout. `select()` returns three subsets of the passed arguments. These subsets represent the files on which the requested operation can be performed. For example, a file returned in `can_read()` has incoming data pending.

The `select()` function is a standard low-level system call that's commonly used to watch for system events and to implement asynchronous I/O frameworks such as the built-in `asyncio` module.

In addition to `select()`, the `select` module also exposes `poll()`, `epoll()`, `kqueue()`, and similar variant functions that provide similar functionality. The availability of these functions varies by operating system.

The `selectors` module provides a higher-level interface to `select` that might be useful in certain contexts. An example was given earlier in Section 9.14.2.

9.15.19 `smtplib` Module

The `smtplib` module implements the client side of SMTP, commonly used to send email messages. A common use of the module is in a script that does just that—sends an email to someone. Here is an example:

```
import smtplib

fromaddr = "someone@some.com"
toaddrs = ["recipient@other.com" ]
amount = 123.45
msg = f"""From: {fromaddr}
Pay {amount} bitcoin or else.  We're watching.
"""

server = smtplib.SMTP('localhost')
serv.sendmail(fromaddr, toaddrs, msg)
serv.quit()
```

There are additional features to handle passwords, authentication, and other matters. However, if you're running a script on a machine and that machine is configured to support email, the above example will usually do the job.

9.15.20 socket Module

The socket module provides low-level access to network programming functions. The interface is modeled after the standard BSD socket interface commonly associated with system programming in C.

The following example shows how to make an outgoing connection and receive a response:

```python
from socket import socket, AF_INET, SOCK_STREAM

sock = socket(AF_INET, SOCK_STREAM)
sock.connect(('python.org', 80))
sock.send(b'GET /index.html HTTP/1.0\r\n\r\n')
parts = []
while True:
    part = sock.recv(10000)
    if not part:
        break
    parts.append(part)
parts = b''.join(parts)
print(parts)
```

The following example shows a basic echo server that accepts client connections and echoes back any received data. To test this server, run it and then connect to it using a command such as telnet localhost 25000 or nc localhost 25000 in a separate terminal session.

```python
from socket import socket, AF_INET, SOCK_STREAM

def echo_server(address):
    sock = socket(AF_INET, SOCK_STREAM)
    sock.bind(address)
    sock.listen(1)
    while True:
        client, addr = sock.accept()
        echo_handler(client, addr)

def echo_handler(client, addr):
    print('Connection from:', addr)
    with client:
        while True:
            data = client.recv(10000)
```

```
            if not data:
                break
            client.sendall(data)
    print('Connection closed')

if __name__ == '__main__':
    echo_server(('', 25000))
```

For UDP servers, there is no connection process. However, a server must still bind the socket to a known address. Here is a typical example of what a UDP server and client look like:

```
# udp.py

from socket import socket, AF_INET, SOCK_DGRAM

def run_server(address):
    sock = socket(AF_INET, SOCK_DGRAM)      # 1. Create a UDP socket
    sock.bind(address)                      # 2. Bind to address/port
    while True:
        msg, addr = sock.recvfrom(2000)     # 3. Get a message
        # ... do something
        response = b'world'
        sock.sendto(response, addr)         # 4. Send a response back

def run_client(address):
    sock = socket(AF_INET, SOCK_DGRAM)      # 1. Create a UDP socket
    sock.sendto(b'hello', address)          # 2. Send a message
    response, addr = sock.recvfrom(2000)    # 3. Get response
    print("Received:", response)
    sock.close()

if __name__ == '__main__':
    import sys
    if len(sys.argv) != 4:
        raise SystemExit('Usage: udp.py [-client|-server] hostname port')
    address = (sys.argv[2], int(sys.argv[3]))
    if sys.argv[1] == '-server':
        run_server(address)
    elif sys.argv[1] == '-client':
        run_client(address)
```

9.15.21   `struct` **Module**

The `struct` module is used to convert data between Python and binary data structures, represented as Python byte strings. These data structures are often used when interacting with functions written in C, binary file formats, network protocols, or binary communication over serial ports.

As an example, suppose you need to construct a binary message with its format described by a C data structure:

```
# Message format: All values are "big endian"
struct Message {
    unsigned short msgid;       // 16 bit unsigned integer
    unsigned int sequence;      // 32 bit sequence number
    float x;                    // 32 bit float
    float y;                    // 32 bit float
}
```

Here's how you do this using the `struct` module:

```
>>> import struct
>>> data = struct.pack('>HIff', 123, 456, 1.23, 4.56)
>>> data
b'\x00{\x00\x00\x00-?\x9dp\xa4@\x91\xeb\x85'
>>>
```

To decode binary data, use `struct.unpack`:

```
>>> struct.unpack('>HIff', data)
(123, 456, 1.2300000190734863, 4.559999942779541)
>>>
```

The differences in the floating-point values are due to the loss of accuracy incurred by their conversion to 32-bit values. Python represents floating-point values as 64-bit double precision values.

9.15.22   `subprocess` **Module**

The `subprocess` module is used to execute a separate program as a subprocess, but with control over the execution environment including I/O handling, termination, and so forth. There are two common uses of the module.

If you want to run a separate program and collect all of its output at once, use `check_output()`. For example:

```
import subprocess

# Run the 'netstat -a' command and collect its output
try:
    out = subprocess.check_output(['netstat', '-a'])
```

```
except subprocess.CalledProcessError as e:
    print("It failed:", e)
```

The data returned by check_output() is presented as bytes. If you want to convert it to text, make sure you apply a proper decoding:

```
text = out.decode('utf-8')
```

It is also possible to set up a pipe and to interact with a subprocess in a more detailed manner. To do that, use the Popen class like this:

```
import subprocess

# wc is a program that returns line, word, and byte counts
p = subprocess.Popen(['wc'],
                     stdin=subprocess.PIPE,
                     stdout=subprocess.PIPE)

# Send data to the subprocess
p.stdin.write(b'hello world\nthis is a test\n')
p.stdin.close()

# Read data back
out = p.stdout.read()
print(out)
```

An instance p of Popen has attributes stdin and stdout that can be used to communicate with the subprocess.

9.15.23 tempfile Module

The tempfile module provides support for creating temporary files and directories. Here is an example of creating a temporary file:

```
import tempfile

with tempfile.TemporaryFile() as f:
    f.write(b'Hello World')
    f.seek(0)
    data = f.read()
    print('Got:', data)
```

By default, temporary files are open in binary mode and allow both reading and writing. The with statement is also commonly used to define a scope for when the file will be used. The file is deleted at the end of the with block.

If you would like to create a temporary directory, use this:

```
with tempfile.TemporaryDirectory() as dirname:
    # Use the directory dirname
    ...
```

As with a file, the directory and all of its contents will be deleted at the end of the with block.

9.15.24   `textwrap` **Module**

The `textwrap` module can be used to format text to fit a specific terminal width. Perhaps it's a bit special-purpose but it can sometimes be useful in cleaning up text for output when making reports. There are two functions of interest.

`wrap()` takes text and wraps it to fit a specified column width. The function returns a list of strings. For example:

```
import textwrap

text = """look into my eyes
look into my eyes
the eyes the eyes the eyes
not around the eyes
don't look around the eyes
look into my eyes you're under
"""

wrapped = textwrap.wrap(text, width=81)
print('\n'.join(wrapped))
# Produces:
# look into my eyes look into my eyes the
# eyes the eyes the eyes not around the
# eyes don't look around the eyes look
# into my eyes you're under
```

The `indent()` function can be used to indent a block of text. For example:

```
print(textwrap.indent(text, '    '))
# Produces:
#     look into my eyes
#     look into my eyes
#     the eyes the eyes the eyes
#     not around the eyes
#     don't look around the eyes
#     look into my eyes you're under
```

9.15.25 `threading` **Module**

The `threading` module is used to execute code concurrently. This problem commonly arises with I/O handling in network programs. Thread programming is a large topic, but the following examples illustrate solutions to common problems.

Here's an example of launching a thread and waiting for it:

```
import threading
import time

def countdown(n):
    while n > 0:
        print('T-minus', n)
        n -= 1
        time.sleep(1)

t = threading.Thread(target=countdown, args=[10])
t.start()
t.join()        # Wait for the thread to finish
```

If you're never going to wait for the thread to finish, make it daemonic by supplying an extra `daemon` flag like this:

```
t = threading.Thread(target=countdown, args=[10], daemon=True)
```

If you want to make a thread terminate, you'll need to do so explicitly with a flag or some dedicated variable for that purpose. The thread will have to be programmed to check for it.

```
import threading
import time

must_stop = False

def countdown(n):
    while n > 0 and not must_stop:
        print('T-minus', n)
        n -= 1
        time.sleep(1)
```

If threads are going to mutate shared data, protect it with a `Lock`.

```
import threading

class Counter:
    def __init__(self):
        self.value = 0
        self.lock = threading.Lock()
```

```
    def increment(self):
        with self.lock:
            self.value += 1

    def decrement(self):
        with self.lock:
            self.value -= 1
```

If one thread must wait for another thread to do something, use an Event.

```
import threading
import time

def step1(evt):
    print('Step 1')
    time.sleep(5)
    evt.set()

def step2(evt):
    evt.wait()
    print('Step 2')

evt = threading.Event()
threading.Thread(target=step1, args=[evt]).start()
threading.Thread(target=step2, args=[evt]).start()
```

If threads are going to communicate, use a Queue:

```
import threading
import queue
import time

def producer(q):
    for i in range(10):
        print('Producing:', i)
        q.put(i)
    print('Done')
    q.put(None)

def consumer(q):
    while True:
        item = q.get()
        if item is None:
            break
        print('Consuming:', item)
    print('Goodbye')
```

```
q = queue.Queue()
threading.Thread(target=producer, args=[q]).start()
threading.Thread(target=consumer, args=[q]).start()
```

9.15.26 time Module

The time module is used to access system time-related functions. The following selected functions are the most useful:

sleep(seconds)

Make Python sleep for a given number of seconds, given as a floating point.

time()

Return the current system time in UTC as a floating-point number. This is the number of seconds since the epoch (usually January 1, 1970 for UNIX systems). Use localtime() to convert it into a data structure suitable for extracting useful information.

localtime([secs])

Return a struct_time object representing the local time on the system or the time represented by the floating-point value secs passed as an argument. The resulting struct has attributes tm_year, tm_mon, tm_mday, tm_hour, tm_min, tm_sec, tm_wday, tm_yday, and tm_isdst.

gmtime([secs])

The same as localtime() except that the resulting structure represents the time in UTC (or Greenwich Mean Time).

ctime([secs])

Convert a time represented as seconds to a text string suitable for printing. Useful for debugging and logging.

asctime(tm)

Convert a time structure as represented by localtime() into a text string suitable for printing.

The datetime module is more generally used for representing dates and times for the purpose of performing date-related computations and dealing with timezones.

9.15.27 urllib Package

The urllib package is used to make client-side HTTP requests. Perhaps the most useful function is urllib.request.urlopen() which can be used to fetch simple webpages. For example:

```
>>> from urllib.request import urlopen
>>> u = urlopen('http://www.python.org')
```

```
>>> data = u.read()
>>>
```

If you want to encode form parameters, you can use `urllib.parse.urlencode()` as shown here:

```
from urllib.parse import urlencode
from urllib.request import urlopen

form = {
    'name': 'Mary A. Python',
    'email': 'mary123@python.org'
}

data = urlencode(form)
u = urlopen('http://httpbin.org/post', data.encode('utf-8'))
response = u.read()
```

The `urlopen()` function works fine for basic webpages and APIs involving HTTP or HTTPS. However, it becomes quite awkward to use if access also involves cookies, advanced authentication schemes, and other layers. Frankly, most Python programmers would use a third-party library such as `requests` or `httpx` to handle these situations. You should too.

The `urllib.parse` subpackage has additional functions for manipulating URLs themselves. For example, the `urlparse()` function can be used to pull apart a URL:

```
>>> url = 'http://httpbin.org/get?name=Dave&n=42'
>>> from urllib.parse import urlparse
>>> urlparse(url)
ParseResult(scheme='http', netloc='httpbin.org', path='/get', params='',
query='name=Dave&n=42', fragment='')
>>>
```

9.15.28 `unicodedata` Module

The `unicodedata` module is used for more advanced operations involving Unicode text strings. There are often multiple representations of the same Unicode text. For example, the character U+00F1 (ñ) might be fully composed as a single character U+00F1 or decomposed into a multicharacter sequence U+006e U+0303 (n, ~). This can cause strange problems in programs that are expecting text strings that visually render the same to actually be the same in representation. Consider the following example involving dictionary keys:

```
>>> d = {}
>>> d['Jalape\xf1o'] = 'spicy'
>>> d['Jalapen\u0303o'] = 'mild'
```

```
>>> d
{'jalapeño': 'spicy', 'jalapeño': 'mild' }
>>>
```

At first glance, this looks like it should be an operational error—how could a dictionary have two identical, yet separate, keys like that? The answer is found in the fact that the keys consist of different Unicode character sequences.

If consistent processing of identically rendered Unicode strings is an issue, they should be normalized. The `unicodedata.normalize()` function can be used to ensure a consistent character representation. For example, `unicodedata.normalize('NFC', s)` will make sure that all characters in s are fully composed and not represented as a sequence of combining characters. Using `unicodedata.normalize('NFD', s)` will make sure that all characters in s are fully decomposed.

The `unicodedata` module also has functions for testing character properties such as capitalization, numbers, and whitespace. General character properties can be obtained with the `unicodedata.category(c)` function. For example, `unicodedata.category('A')` returns `'Lu'`, signifying that the character is an uppercase letter. More information about these values can be found in the official Unicode character database at `https://www.unicode.org/ucd`.

9.15.29 `xml` Package

The `xml` package is a large collection of modules for processing XML data in various ways. However, if your primary goal is to read an XML document and extract information from it, the easiest way to do it is to use the `xml.etree` subpackage. Suppose you had an XML document in a file `recipe.xml` like this:

```
<?xml version="1.0" encoding="iso-8859-1"?>
<recipe>
   <title>Famous Guacamole</title>
   <description>A southwest favorite!</description>
   <ingredients>
      <item num="4"> Large avocados, chopped </item>
      <item num="1"> Tomato, chopped </item>
      <item num="1/2" units="C"> White onion, chopped </item>
      <item num="2" units="tbl"> Fresh squeezed lemon juice </item>
      <item num="1"> Jalapeno pepper, diced </item>
      <item num="1" units="tbl"> Fresh cilantro, minced </item>
      <item num="1" units="tbl"> Garlic, minced </item>
      <item num="3" units="tsp"> Salt </item>
      <item num="12" units="bottles"> Ice-cold beer </item>
   </ingredients>
   <directions>
   Combine all ingredients and hand whisk to desired consistency.
   Serve and enjoy with ice-cold beers.
```

```
    </directions>
</recipe>
```

Here's how to extract specific elements from it:

```
from xml.etree.ElementTree import ElementTree

doc = ElementTree(file="recipe.xml")
title = doc.find('title')
print(title.text)

# Alternative (just get element text)
print(doc.findtext('description'))

# Iterate over multiple elements
for item in doc.findall('ingredients/item'):
    num = item.get('num')
    units = item.get('units', '')
    text = item.text.strip()
    print(f'{num} {units} {text}')
```

9.16 Final Words

I/O is a fundamental part of writing any useful program. Given its popularity, Python is able to work with literally any data format, encoding, or document structure that's in use. Although the standard library might not support it, you will almost certainly find a third-party module to solve your problem.

In the big picture, it may be more useful to think about the edges of your application. At the outer boundary between your program and reality, it's common to encounter issues related to data encoding. This is especially true for textual data and Unicode. Much of the complexity in Python's I/O handling—supporting different encoding, error handling policies, and so on—is aimed at this specific problem. It's also critical to keep in mind that textual data and binary data are strictly separated. Knowing what you're working with helps in understanding the big picture.

A secondary consideration in I/O is the overall evaluation model. Python code is currently separated into two worlds—normal synchronous code and asynchronous code usually associated with the `asyncio` module (characterized by the use of `async` functions and the `async`/`await` syntax). Asynchronous code almost always requires using dedicated libraries that are capable of operating in that environment. This, in turn, forces your hand on writing your application code in the "async" style as well. Honestly, you should probably avoid asynchronous coding unless you absolutely know that you need it—and if you're not really sure, then you almost certainly don't. Most of the well-adjusted Python-speaking universe codes in a normal synchronous style that is far easier to reason about, debug, and test. You should choose that.

Built-in Functions and Standard Library

This chapter is a compact reference to Python built-in functions. These functions are always available without any `import` statement. The chapter concludes with a brief overview of some useful standard library modules.

10.1 Built-in Functions

`abs(x)`

> Returns the absolute value of x.

`all(s)`

> Returns `True` if all of the values in the iterable s evaluate as `True`. Returns `True` if s is empty.

`any(s)`

> Returns `True` if any of the values in the iterable s evaluate as `True`. Returns `False` if s is empty.

`ascii(x)`

> Creates a printable representation of the object x just like the `repr()`, but only uses ASCII characters in the result. Non-ASCII characters are turned into appropriate escape sequences. This can be used to view Unicode strings in a terminal or shell that doesn't support Unicode.

`bin(x)`

> Returns a string with the binary representation of the integer x.

`bool([x])`

> Type representing Boolean values `True` and `False`. If used to convert x, it returns `True` if x evaluates to true using the usual truth-testing semantics—that is, nonzero number, nonempty list, and so on. Otherwise, `False` is returned. `False` is also the default value returned if `bool()` is called without any arguments. The `bool` class

inherits from int so the Boolean values True and False can be used as integers with values 1 and 0 in mathematical calculations.

breakpoint()

Sets a manual debugger breakpoint. When encountered, control will transfer to pdb, the Python debugger.

bytearray([x])

A type representing a mutable array of bytes. When creating an instance, x may either be an iterable sequence of integers in the range 0 to 255, an 8-bit string or bytes literal, or an integer that specifies the size of the byte array (in which case every entry will be initialized to 0).

bytearray(s, encoding)

An alternative calling convention for creating a bytearray instance from characters in a string s where encoding specifies the character encoding to use in the conversion.

bytes([x])

A type representing an immutable array of bytes.

bytes(s, encoding)

An alternate calling convention for creating bytes from a string s where encoding specifies the encoding to use in conversion.

Table 10.1 shows operations supported by both bytes and byte arrays.

Table 10.1   Operations on Bytes and Bytearrays

Operation	Description
s + t	Concatenates if t is bytes.
s * n	Replicates if n is an integer.
s % x	Formats bytes. x is tuple.
s[i]	Returns element i as an integer.
s[i:j]	Returns a slice.
s[i:j:stride]	Returns an extended slice.
len(s)	Number of bytes in s.
s.capitalize()	Capitalizes the first character.
s.center(width [, pad])	Centers the string in a field of length width. pad is a padding character.
s.count(sub [, start [, end]])	Counts occurrences of the specified substring sub.
s.decode([encoding [, errors]])	Decodes a byte string into text (bytes type only).
s.endswith(suffix [, start [, end]])	Checks the end of the string for a suffix.
s.expandtabs([tabsize])	Replaces tabs with spaces.

Operation	Description
s.find(sub [, start [, end]])	Finds the first occurrence of the specified substring sub.
s.hex()	Converts to a hexadecimal string.
s.index(sub [, start [, end]])	Finds the first occurrence or error in the specified substring sub.
s.isalnum()	Checks whether all characters are alphanumeric.
s.isalpha()	Checks whether all characters are alphabetic.
s.isascii()	Checks whether all characters are ASCII.
s.isdigit()	Checks whether all characters are digits.
s.islower()	Checks whether all characters are lowercase.
s.isspace()	Checks whether all characters are whitespace.
s.istitle()	Checks whether the string is a title-cased string (first letter of each word capitalized).
s.isupper()	Checks whether all characters are uppercase.
s.join(t)	Joins a sequence of strings t using a delimiter s.
s.ljust(width [, fill])	Left-aligns s in a string of size width.
s.lower()	Converts to lowercase.
s.lstrip([chrs])	Removes leading whitespace or characters supplied in chrs.
s.maketrans(x [, y [, z]])	Makes a translation table for s.translate().
s.partition(sep)	Partitions a string based on a separator string sep. Returns a tuple (head, sep, tail) or (s, '', '') if sep isn't found.
s.removeprefix(prefix)	Returns s with a given prefix removed if present.
s.removesuffix(suffix)	Returns s with a given suffix removed if present.
s.replace(old, new [, maxreplace])	Replaces a substring.
s.rfind(sub [, start [, end]])	Finds the last occurrence of a substring.
s.rindex(sub [, start [, end]])	Finds the last occurrence or raises an error.
s.rjust(width [, fill])	Right-aligns s in a string of length width.
s.rpartition(sep)	Partitions s based on a separator sep, but searches from the end of the string.
s.rsplit([sep [, maxsplit]])	Splits a string from the end of the string using sep as a delimiter. maxsplit is the maximum number of splits to perform. If maxsplit is omitted, the result is identical to the split() method.

Operation	Description
`s.rstrip([chrs])`	Removes trailing whitespace or characters supplied in `chrs`.
`s.split([sep [, maxsplit]])`	Splits a string using `sep` as a delimiter. `maxsplit` is the maximum number of splits to perform.
`s.splitlines([keepends])`	Splits a string into a list of lines. If keepends is 1, trailing newlines are preserved.
`s.startswith(prefix [, start [, end]])`	Checks whether a string starts with `prefix`.
`s.strip([chrs])`	Removes leading and trailing whitespace or characters supplied in `chrs`.
`s.swapcase()`	Converts uppercase to lowercase, and vice versa.
`s.title()`	Returns a title-cased version of the string.
`s.translate(table [, deletechars])`	Translates a string using a character translation table `table`, removing characters in `deletechars`.
`s.upper()`	Converts a string to uppercase.
`s.zfill(width)`	Pads a string with zeros on the left up to the specified `width`.

Byte arrays additionally support the methods in Table 10.2.

Table 10.2   Additional Operations on Byte Arrays

Operation	Description
`s[i] = v`	Item assignment
`s[i:j] = t`	Slice assignment
`s[i:j:stride] = t`	Extended slice assignment
`del s[i]`	Item deletion
`del s[i:j]`	Slice deletion
`del s[i:j:stride]`	Extended slice deletion
`s.append(x)`	Appends a new byte to the end.
`s.clear()`	Clears the byte array.
`s.copy()`	Makes a copy.
`s.extend(t)`	Extends s with bytes from `t`.
`s.insert(n, x)`	Inserts byte x at index n.
`s.pop([n])`	Removes and returns byte at index n.
`s.remove(x)`	Removes first occurrence of byte x.
`s.reverse()`	Reverses the byte array in-place.

`callable(obj)`
> Returns True if `obj` is callable as a function.

`chr(x)`
> Converts the integer `x` representing a Unicode code-point into a single-character string.

`classmethod(func)`
> This decorator creates a class method for the function `func`. It is typically only used inside class definitions where it is implicitly invoked using `@classmethod`. Unlike a normal method, a class method receives the class as the first argument, not an instance.

`compile(string, filename, kind)`
> Compiles `string` into a code object for use with `exec()` or `eval()`. `string` is a string containing valid Python code. If this code spans multiple lines, the lines must be terminated by a single newline (`'\n'`) and not platform-specific variants (for example, `'\r\n'` on Windows). `filename` is a string containing the name of the file in which the string was defined (if any). `kind` is `'exec'` for a sequence of statements, `'eval'` for a single expression, or `'single'` for a single executable statement. The resulting code object that is returned can be directly passed to `exec()` or `eval()` in place of a string.

`complex([real [, imag]])`
> Type representing a complex number with real and imaginary components, `real` and `imag`, which can be supplied as any numeric type. If `imag` is omitted, the imaginary component is set to zero. If `real` is passed as a string, the string is parsed and converted to a complex number. In this case, `imag` should be omitted. If `real` is any other kind of object, the value of `real.__complex__()` is returned. If no arguments are given, `0j` is returned.

Table 10.3 shows methods and attributes of `complex`.

Table 10.3 Attributes of `complex`

Attribute/Method	Description
`z.real`	Real component
`z.imag`	Imaginary component
`z.conjugate()`	Conjugates as a complex number.

`delattr(object, attr)`
> Deletes an attribute of an object. `attr` is a string. Same as `del object.attr`.

`dict([m])` **or** `dict(key1=value1, key2=value2, ...)`
> Type representing a dictionary. If no argument is given, an empty dictionary is returned. If `m` is a mapping object (such as another dictionary), a new dictionary

having the same keys and same values as m is returned. For example, if m is a dictionary, dict(m) makes a shallow copy of it. If m is not a mapping, it must support iteration in which a sequence of (key, value) pairs is produced. These pairs are used to populate the dictionary. dict() can also be called with keyword arguments. For example, dict(foo=3, bar=7) creates the dictionary {'foo': 3, 'bar': 7 }.

Table 10.4 shows operations supported by dictionaries.

Table 10.4   Operations on Dictionaries

Operation	Description
m | n	Merges m and n into a single dictionary.
len(m)	Returns the number of items in m.
m[k]	Returns the item of m with key k.
m[k]=x	Sets m[k] to x.
del m[k]	Removes m[k] from m.
k in m	Returns True if k is a key in m.
m.clear()	Removes all items from m.
m.copy()	Makes a shallow copy of m.
m.fromkeys(s [, value])	Creates a new dictionary with keys from sequence s and values all set to value.
m.get(k [, v])	Returns m[k] if found; otherwise, returns v.
m.items()	Returns (key, value) pairs.
m.keys()	Returns the keys.
m.pop(k [, default])	Returns m[k] if found and removes it from m; otherwise, returns default if supplied or raises KeyError if not.
m.popitem()	Removes a random (key, value) pair from m and returns it as a tuple.
m.setdefault(k [, v])	Returns m[k] if found; otherwise, returns v and sets m[k] = v.
m.update(b)	Adds all objects from b to m.
m.values()	Returns the values.

dir([object])

Returns a sorted list of attribute names. If object is a module, it contains the list of symbols defined in that module. If object is a type or class object, it returns a list of attribute names. The names are typically obtained from the object's __dict__ attribute if defined, but other sources may be used. If no argument is given, the names in the current local symbol table are returned. It should be noted that this function is primarily used for informational purposes (for example, used interactively at the command line). It should not be used for formal program analysis because the information obtained may be incomplete. Also, user-defined classes can define a special method __dir__() that alters the result of this function.

`divmod(a, b)`

> Returns the quotient and remainder of long division as a tuple. For integers, the value (`a // b`, `a % b`) is returned. For floats, (`math.floor(a / b)`, `a % b`) is returned. This function may not be called with complex numbers.

`enumerate(iter, start=0)`

> Given an iterable object, `iter`, returns a new iterator (of type `enumerate`) that produces tuples containing a count and the value produced from `iter`. For example, if `iter` produces a, b, c, then `enumerate(iter)` produces (`0,a`), (`1,b`), (`2,c`). The optional `start` changes the initial value of the count.

`eval(expr [, globals [, locals]])`

> Evaluates an expression. `expr` is a string or a code object created by `compile()`. `globals` and `locals` are mapping objects that define the global and local namespaces, respectively, for the operation. If omitted, the expression is evaluated using the values of `globals()` and `locals()` as executed in the caller's environment. It is most common for globals and locals to be specified as dictionaries, but advanced applications can supply custom mapping objects.

`exec(code [, globals [, locals]])`

> Executes Python statements. `code` is a string, bytes, or a code object created by `compile()`. `globals` and `locals` define the global and local namespaces, respectively, for the operation. If omitted, the code is executed using the values of `globals()` and `locals()` as executed in the caller's environment.

`filter(function, iterable)`

> Creates an iterator that returns the items in `iterable` for which `function(item)` evaluates as `True`.

`float([x])`

> Type representing a floating-point number. If x is a number, it is converted to a float. If x is a string, it is parsed into a float. For all other objects, `x.__float__()` is invoked. If no argument is supplied, `0.0` is returned.

Table 10.5 shows methods and attributes of floats.

Table 10.5 Methods and Attributes of Floats

Attribute/Method	Description
`x.real`	Real component when used as a complex.
`x.imag`	Imaginary component when used as a complex.
`x.conjugate()`	Conjugates as a complex number.
`x.as_integer_ratio()`	Converts to numerator/denominator pair.
`x.hex()`	Creates a hexadecimal representation
`x.is_integer()`	Tests if an exact integer value.
`float.fromhex(s)`	Creates from a hexadecimal string. A class method.

`format(value [, format_spec])`

Converts `value` to a formatted string according to the format specification string in `format_spec`. This operation invokes `value.__format__()`, which is free to interpret the format specification as it sees fit. For simple types of data, the format specifier typically includes an alignment character of `'<'`, `'>'`, or `'^'`, a number (which indicates the field width), and a character code of `'d'`, `'f'`, or `'s'` for integer, floating point, or string values, respectively. For example, a format specification of `'d'` formats an integer, a specification of `'8d'` right-aligns an integer in an 8-character field, and `'<8d'` left-aligns an integer in an 8-character field. More details on `format()` and format specifiers can be found in Chapter 9.

`frozenset([items])`

Type representing an immutable set object populated with values taken from `items` which must be an iterable. The values must also be immutable. If no argument is given, an empty set is returned. A `frozenset` supports all of the operations found on `sets` except for any operations that mutate a set in-place.

`getattr(object, name [, default])`

Returns the value of a named attribute of an object. `name` is a string containing the attribute name. `default` is an optional value to return if no such attribute exists; otherwise, `AttributeError` is raised. Same as accessing `object.name`.

`globals()`

Returns the dictionary of the current module that represents the global namespace. When called inside another function or method, it returns the global namespace of the module in which the function or method was defined.

`hasattr(object, name)`

Returns `True` if `name` is the name of an attribute of object. `name` is a string.

`hash(object)`

Returns an integer hash value for an object (if possible). The hash value is primarily used in the implementation of dictionaries, sets, and other mapping objects. The hash value is always the same for any objects that compare as equal. Mutable objects usually don't define a hash value, although user-defined classes can define a method `__hash__()` to support this operation.

`hex(x)`

Creates a hexadecimal string from an integer `x`.

`id(object)`

Returns the unique integer identity of object. You should not interpret the return value in any way (for example, it's not a memory location).

`input([prompt])`

Prints a prompt to standard output and reads a single line of input from standard input. The returned line is not modified in any way. It does not include a line ending (e.g., `'\n'`).

```
int(x [, base])
```
    Type representing an integer. If x is a number, it is converted to an integer by truncating towards 0. If it is a string, it is parsed into an integer value. base optionally specifies a base when converting from a string.

    In addition to their support for common math operations, integers also have a number of attributes and methods listed in Table 10.6.

Table 10.6 Methods and Attributes of Integers

Operation	Description
x.numerator	Numerator when used as a fraction.
x.denominator	Denominator when used as a fraction.
x.real	Real component when used as a complex.
x.imag	Imaginary component when used as a complex.
x.conjugate()	Conjugates as a complex number.
x.bit_length()	Number of bits needed to represent the value in binary.
x.to_bytes(length, byteorder, *, signed=False)	Converts to bytes.
int.from_bytes(bytes, byteorder, *, signed=False)	Converts from bytes. A class method.

```
isinstance(object, classobj)
```
    Returns True if object is an instance of classobj or a subclass of classobj. The classobj parameter can also be a tuple of possible types or classes. For example, isinstance(s, (list, tuple)) returns True if s is a tuple or a list.

```
issubclass(class1, class2)
```
    Returns True if class1 is a subclass of (derived from) class2. class2 can also be a tuple of possible classes, in which case each class will be checked. Note that issubclass(A, A) is True.

```
iter(object [, sentinel])
```
    Returns an iterator for producing items in object. If the sentinel parameter is omitted, the object must either provide the method __iter__(), which creates an iterator, or the object must implement __getitem__(), which accepts integer arguments starting at 0. If sentinel is specified, object is interpreted differently. Instead, object should be a callable object that takes no parameters. The returned iterator object will call this function repeatedly until the returned value is equal to sentinel, at which point iteration will stop. A TypeError will be generated if object does not support iteration.

len(s)

    Returns the number of items contained in s which should be some kind of container such as a list, tuple, string, set, or dictionary.

list([items])

    Type representing a list. items may be any iterable object, the values of which are used to populate the list. If items is already a list, a shallow copy is made. If no argument is given, an empty list is returned.

Table 10.7 shows operations defined on lists.

Table 10.7 List Operators and Methods

Operation	Description
s + t	Concatenation if t is a list.
s * n	Replication if n is an integer.
s[i]	Returns element i of s.
s[i:j]	Returns a slice.
s[i:j:stride]	Returns an extended slice.
s[i] = v	Item assignment.
s[i:j] = t	Slice assignment.
s[i:j:stride] = t	Extended slice assignment.
del s[i]	Item deletion.
del s[i:j]	Slice deletion.
del s[i:j:stride]	Extended slice deletion.
len(s)	Number of elements in s.
s.append(x)	Appends a new element, x, to the end of s.
s.extend(t)	Appends a new list, t, to the end of s.
s.count(x)	Counts occurrences of x in s.
s.index(x [, start [, stop]])	Returns the smallest i where s[i] == x. start and stop optionally specify the starting and ending index for the search.
s.insert(i, x)	Inserts x at index i.
s.pop([i])	Returns the element i and removes it from the list. If i is omitted, the last element is returned.
s.remove(x)	Searches for x and removes it from s.
s.reverse()	Reverses items of s in place.
s.sort([key [, reverse]])	Sorts items of s in place. key is a key function. reverse is a flag that sorts the list in reverse order. key and reverse should always be specified as keyword arguments.

`locals()`

Returns a dictionary corresponding to the local namespace of the caller. This dictionary should only be used to inspect the execution environment—changes made to the dictionary don't have any effect on the corresponding local variables.

`map(function, items, ...)`

Creates an iterator that produces the results of applying `function` to the items in `items`. If multiple input sequences are supplied, `function` is assumed to take that many arguments, with each argument taken from a different sequence. In this case, the result is only as long as the shortest input sequence.

`max(s [, args, ...], *, default=obj, key=func)`

For a single argument, `s`, this function returns the maximum value of the items in `s`, which may be any iterable object. For multiple arguments, it returns the largest of the arguments. If the keyword-only argument `default` is given, it supplies the value to return if `s` is empty. If the keyword-only argument `key` is given, then the value `v` for which `key(v)` returns the maximum value is returned.

`min(s [, args, ...], *, default=obj, key=func)`

The same as `max(s)` except that the minimum value is returned.

`next(s [, default])`

Returns the next item from the iterator `s`. If the iterator has no more items, a `StopIteration` exception is raised unless a value is supplied to the default argument. In that case, `default` is returned instead.

`object()`

The base class for all objects in Python. You can call it to create an instance, but the result isn't especially interesting.

`oct(x)`

Converts an integer, `x`, to an octal string.

`open(filename [, mode [, bufsize [, encoding [, errors [, newline [, closefd]]]]]])`

Opens the file `filename` and returns a file object. The arguments are described in detail in Chapter 9.

`ord(c)`

Returns the integer ordinal value of a single character, `c`. This value usually corresponds to the character's Unicode code-point value.

`pow(x, y [, z])`

Returns `x ** y`. If `z` is supplied, this function returns `(x ** y) % z`. If all three arguments are given, they must be integers and `y` must be non-negative.

```
print(value, ... , *, sep=separator, end=ending, file=outfile)
```
Print a collection of values. As input, you can supply any number of values, all of which are printed on the same line. The sep keyword argument is used to specify a different separator character (a space by default). The end keyword argument specifies a different line ending ('\n' by default). The file keyword argument redirects the output to a file object.

```
property([fget [, fset [, fdel [, doc]]]])
```
Creates a property attribute for classes. fget is a function that returns the attribute value, fset sets the attribute value, and fdel deletes an attribute. doc provides a documentation string. Properties are often specified as a decorator:

```
class SomeClass:
    x = property(doc='This is property x')
    @x.getter
    def x(self):
        print('getting x')

    @x.setter
    def x(self, value):
        print('setting x to', value)

    @x.deleter
    def x(self):
        print('deleting x')
```

```
range([start,] stop [, step])
```
Creates a range object that represents a range of integer values from start to stop. step indicates a stride and is set to 1 if omitted. If start is omitted (when range() is called with one argument), it defaults to 0. A negative step creates a list of numbers in descending order.

```
repr(object)
```
Returns a string representation of object. In most cases, the returned string is an expression that can be passed to eval() to recreate the object.

```
reversed(s)
```
Creates a reverse iterator for sequence s. This function only works if s defines the __reversed__() method or it implements the sequence methods __len__() and __getitem__(). It does not work with generators.

```
round(x [, n])
```
Rounds the result of rounding the floating-point number x to the closest multiple of 10 to the power minus n. If n is omitted, it defaults to 0. If two multiples are equally close, it rounds towards 0 if the previous digit is even and away from 0 otherwise (for example, 0.5 is rounded to 0.0 and 1.5 is rounded to 2).

```
set([items])
```

Creates a set populated with items taken from the iterable object items. The items must be immutable. If items contains other sets, those sets must be of type frozenset. If items is omitted, an empty set is returned.

Table 10.8 shows operations on sets.

Table 10.8 Set Operations and Methods

Operation	Description
s | t	Union
s & t	Intersection
s - t	Difference
s ^ t	Symmetric difference
len(s)	Returns number of items in s.
s.add(item)	Adds item to s. Has no effect if item is already in s.
s.clear()	Removes all items from s.
s.copy()	Makes a copy of s.
s.difference(t)	Set difference. Returns all the items in s, but not in t.
s.difference_update(t)	Removes all the items from s that are also in t.
s.discard(item)	Removes item from s. If item is not a member of s, nothing happens.
s.intersection(t)	Intersection. Returns all the items that are both in s and in t.
s.intersection_update(t)	Computes the intersection of s and t and leaves the result in s.
s.isdisjoint(t)	Returns True if s and t have no items in common.
s.issubset(t)	Returns True if s is a subset of t.
s.issuperset(t)	Returns True if s is a superset of t.
s.pop()	Returns an arbitrary set element and removes it from s.
s.remove(item)	Removes item from s. If item is not a member, KeyError is raised.
s.symmetric_difference(t)	Symmetric difference. Returns all the items that are in s or t, but not in both sets.
s.symmetric_difference_update(t)	Computes the symmetric difference of s and t and leaves the result in s.
s.union(t)	Union. Returns all items in s or t.
s.update(t)	Adds all the items in t to s. t may be another set, a sequence, or any object that supports iteration.

`setattr(object, name, value)`
Sets an attribute of an object. `name` is a string. Same as `object.name = value`.

`slice([start,] stop [, step])`
Returns a slice object representing integers in the specified range. Slice objects are also generated by the extended slice syntax `a[i:i:k]`.

`sorted(iterable, *, key=keyfunc, reverse=reverseflag)`
Creates a sorted list from items in `iterable`. The keyword argument `key` is a single-argument function that transforms values before they are compared. The keyword argument `reverse` is a Boolean flag that specifies whether or not the resulting list is sorted in reverse order. The `key` and `reverse` arguments must be specified using keywords—for example, `sorted(a, key=get_name)`.

`staticmethod(func)`
Creates a static method for use in classes. This function is usually used as a `@staticmethod` decorator.

`str([object])`
Type representing a string. If object is supplied, a string representation of its value is created by calling its `__str__()` method. This is the same string that you see when you print the object. If no argument is given, an empty string is created.

Table 10.9 shows methods defined on strings.

Table 10.9 String Operators and Methods

Operation	Description
`s + t`	Concatenates strings if t is a string.
`s * n`	Replicates a string if n is an integer.
`s % x`	Formats a string. x is tuple.
`s[i]`	Returns element i of a string.
`s[i:j]`	Returns a slice.
`s[i:j:stride]`	Returns an extended slice.
`len(s)`	Number of elements in s.
`s.capitalize()`	Capitalizes the first character.
`s.casefold()`	Converts s to a string usable for a caseless comparison.
`s.center(width [, pad])`	Centers the string in a field of length `width`. pad is a padding character.
`s.count(sub [, start [, end]])`	Counts occurrences of the specified substring sub.
`s.decode([encoding [, errors]])`	Decodes a byte string into text (`bytes` type only).
`s.encode([encoding [, errors]])`	Returns an encoded version of the string (`str` type only).

Operation	Description
s.endswith(suffix [, start [, end]])	Checks the end of the string for a suffix.
s.expandtabs([tabsize])	Replaces tabs with spaces.
s.find(sub [, start [, end]])	Finds the first occurrence of the specified substring sub.
s.format(*args, **kwargs)	Formats s (str type only).
s.format_map(m)	Formats s with substitutions taking from the mapping m (str type only).
s.index(sub [, start [, end]])	Finds the first occurrence or error in the specified substring sub.
s.isalnum()	Checks whether all characters are alphanumeric.
s.isalpha()	Checks whether all characters are alphabetic.
s.isascii()	Checks whether all characters are ASCII.
s.isdecimal()	Checks whether all characters are decimal characters. Does not match superscript, subscripts, or other special digits.
s.isdigit()	Checks whether all characters are digits. Matches superscripts and superscripts, but not vulgar fractions.
s.isidentifier()	Checks whether s is a valid Python identifier.
s.islower()	Checks whether all characters are lowercase.
s.isnumeric()	Checks whether all characters are numeric. Matches all forms of numeric characters such as vulgar fractions, Roman numerals, etc.
s.isprintable()	Checks whether all characters are printable.
s.isspace()	Checks whether all characters are whitespace.
s.istitle()	Checks whether the string is a title-cased string (first letter of each word capitalized).
s.isupper()	Checks whether all characters are uppercase.
s.join(t)	Joins a sequence of strings t using a delimiter s.
s.ljust(width [, fill])	Left-aligns s in a string of size width.
s.lower()	Converts to lowercase.
s.lstrip([chrs])	Removes leading whitespace or characters supplied in chrs.
s.maketrans(x [, y [, z]])	Makes a translation table for s.translate().
s.partition(sep)	Partitions a string based on a separator string sep. Returns a tuple (head, sep, tail) or (s, '', '') if sep isn't found.

Operation	Description
s.removeprefix(prefix)	Returns s with a given prefix removed if present.
s.removesuffix(suffix)	Returns s with a given suffix removed if present.
s.replace(old, new [, maxreplace])	Replaces a substring.
s.rfind(sub [, start [, end]])	Finds the last occurrence of a substring.
s.rindex(sub [, start [, end]])	Finds the last occurrence or raises an error.
s.rjust(width [, fill])	Right-aligns s in a string of length width.
s.rpartition(sep)	Partitions s based on a separator sep, but searches from the end of the string.
s.rsplit([sep [, maxsplit]])	Splits a string from the end of the string using sep as a delimiter. maxsplit is the maximum number of splits to perform. If maxsplit is omitted, the result is identical to the split() method.
s.rstrip([chrs])	Removes trailing whitespace or characters supplied in chrs.
s.split([sep [, maxsplit]])	Splits a string using sep as a delimiter. maxsplit is the maximum number of splits to perform.
s.splitlines([keepends])	Splits a string into a list of lines. If keepends is 1, trailing newlines are preserved.
s.startswith(prefix [, start [, end]])	Checks whether a string starts with a prefix.
s.strip([chrs])	Removes leading and trailing whitespace or characters supplied in chrs.
s.swapcase()	Converts uppercase to lowercase, and vice versa.
s.title()	Returns a title-cased version of the string.
s.translate(table [, deletechars])	Translates a string using a character translation table table, removing characters in deletechars.
s.upper()	Converts a string to uppercase.
s.zfill(width)	Pads a string with zeros on the left up to the specified width.

sum(items [, initial])

Computes the sum of a sequence of items taken from the iterable object items. initial provides the starting value and defaults to 0. This function usually only works with numbers.

`super()`

Returns an object that represents the collective superclasses of the class in which its used. The primary purpose of this object is to invoke methods in base classes. Here's an example:

```
class B(A):
    def foo(self):
        super().foo()    # Invoke foo() defined by superclasses.
```

`tuple([items])`

Type representing a tuple. If supplied, `items` is an iterable object that is used to populate the tuple. However, if `items` is already a tuple, it's returned unmodified. If no argument is given, an empty tuple is returned.

Table 10.10 shows methods defined on tuples.

Table 10.10   Tuple Operators and Methods

Operation	Description
`s + t`	Concatenation if t is a list.
`s * n`	Replication if n is an integer.
`s[i]`	Returns element i of a s.
`s[i:j]`	Returns a slice.
`s[i:j:stride]`	Returns an extended slice.
`len(s)`	Number of elements in s.
`s.append(x)`	Appends a new element, x, to the end of s.
`s.count(x)`	Counts occurrences of x in s.
`s.index(x [, start [, stop]])`	Returns the smallest i where `s[i] == x`. `start` and `stop` optionally specify the starting and ending index for the search.

`type(object)`

The base class of all types in Python. When called as a function, returns the type of `object`. This type is the same as the object's class. For common types such as integers, floats, and lists, the type will refer to one of the other built-in classes such as `int`, `float`, `list`, and so forth. For user-defined objects, the type is the associated class. For objects related to Python's internals, you will typically get a reference to one of the classes defined in the `types` module.

`vars([object])`

Returns the symbol table of `object` (usually found in its __dict__ attribute). If no argument is given, a dictionary corresponding to the local namespace is returned. The dictionary returned by this function should be assumed to be read-only. It's not safe to modify its contents.

```
zip([s1 [, s2 [, ... ]]])
```
Creates an iterator that produces tuples containing one item each from s1, s2, and so on. The nth tuple is (s1[n], s2[n], ...). The resulting iterator stops when the shortest input is exhausted. If no arguments are given, the iterator produces no values.

10.2   Built-in Exceptions

This section describes the built-in exceptions used to report different kinds of errors.

10.2.1   Exception Base Classes

The following exceptions serve as base classes for all the other exceptions:

BaseException
  The root class for all exceptions. All built-in exceptions are derived from this class.

Exception
  The base class for all program-related exceptions. That includes all built-in exceptions except for SystemExit, GeneratorExit, and KeyboardInterrupt. User-defined exceptions should inherit from Exception.

ArithmeticError
  The base class for arithmetic exceptions, including OverflowError, ZeroDivisionError, and FloatingPointError.

LookupError
  The base class for indexing and key errors, including IndexError and KeyError.

EnvironmentError
  The base class for errors that occur outside Python. Is a synonym for OSError.

The preceding exceptions are never raised explicitly. However, they can be used to catch certain classes of errors. For instance, the following code would catch any sort of numerical error:

```
try:
    # Some operation
    ...
except ArithmeticError as e:
    # Math error
```

10.2.2   Exception Attributes

Instances of an exception e have a few standard attributes that can be useful to inspect and/or manipulate it in certain applications.

`e.args`

The tuple of arguments supplied when raising the exception. In most cases, this is a one-item tuple with a string describing the error. For `EnvironmentError` exceptions, the value is a 2-tuple or 3-tuple containing an integer error number, string error message, and an optional filename. The contents of this tuple might be useful if you need to recreate the exception in a different context—for example, to raise an exception in a different Python interpreter process.

`e.__cause__`

Previous exception when using explicit chained exceptions.

`e.__context__`

Previous exception for implicitly chained exceptions.

`e.__traceback__`

Traceback object associated with the exception.

10.2.3 Predefined Exception Classes

The following exceptions are raised by programs:

`AssertionError`

Failed assert statement.

`AttributeError`

Failed attribute reference or assignment.

`BufferError`

Memory buffer expected.

`EOFError`

End of file. Generated by the built-in functions `input()` and `raw_input()`. It should be noted that most other I/O operations such as the `read()` and `readline()` methods of files return an empty string to signal EOF instead of raising an exception.

`FloatingPointError`

Failed floating-point operation. It should be noted that floating-point exception handling is a tricky problem and this exception only gets raised if Python has been configured and built in a way that enables it. It is more common for floating-point errors to silently produce results such as `float('nan')` or `float('inf')`. A subclass of `ArithmeticError`.

`GeneratorExit`

Raised inside a generator function to signal termination. This happens when a generator is destroyed prematurely (before all generator values are consumed) or the `close()` method of a generator is called. If a generator ignores this exception, the generator is terminated, and the exception is silently ignored.

IOError

> Failed I/O operation. The value is an IOError instance with the attributes errno, strerror, and filename. errno is an integer error number, strerror is a string error message, and filename is an optional filename. A subclass of EnvironmentError.

ImportError

> Raised when an import statement can't find a module or when from can't find a name in a module.

IndentationError

> Indentation error. A subclass of SyntaxError.

IndexError

> Sequence subscript out of range. A subclass of LookupError.

KeyError

> Key not found in a mapping. A subclass of LookupError.

KeyboardInterrupt

> Raised when the user hits the interrupt key (usually Ctrl+C).

MemoryError

> Recoverable out-of-memory error.

ModuleNotFoundError

> Module can't be found by the import statement.

NameError

> Name not found in local or global namespaces.

NotImplementedError

> Unimplemented feature. Can be raised by base classes that require derived classes to implement certain methods. A subclass of RuntimeError.

OSError

> Operating system error. Primarily raised by functions in the os module. The following exceptions are subclasses: BlockingIOError, BrokenPipeError, ChildProcessError, ConnectionAbortedError, ConnectionError, ConnectionRefusedError, ConnectionResetError, FileExistsError, FileNotFoundError, InterruptedError, IsADirectoryError, NotADirectoryError, PermissionError, ProcessLookupError, TimeoutError.

OverflowError

> Result of an integer value being too large to be represented. This exception usually only arises if large integer values are passed to objects that internally rely upon fixed-precision machine integers in their implementation. For example, this error can arise with range or xrange objects if you specify starting or ending values that exceed 32 bits in size. A subclass of ArithmeticError.

RecursionError
>   Recursion limit exceeded.

ReferenceError
>   Result of accessing a weak reference after the underlying object has been destroyed (see the `weakref` module).

RuntimeError
>   A generic error not covered by any of the other categories.

StopIteration
>   Raised to signal the end of iteration. This normally happens in the `next()` method of an object or in a generator function.

StopAsyncIteration
>   Raised to signal the end of asynchronous iteration. Only applicable in the context of `async` functions and generators.

SyntaxError
>   Parser syntax error. Instances have the attributes `filename`, `lineno`, `offset`, and `text`, which can be used to gather more information.

SystemError
>   Internal error in the interpreter. The value is a string indicating the problem.

SystemExit
>   Raised by the `sys.exit()` function. The value is an integer indicating the return code. If it's necessary to exit immediately, `os._exit()` can be used.

TabError
>   Inconsistent tab usage. Generated when Python is run with the `-tt` option. A subclass of `SyntaxError`.

TypeError
>   Occurs when an operation or function is applied to an object of an inappropriate type.

UnboundLocalError
>   Unbound local variable referenced. This error occurs if a variable is referenced before it's defined in a function. A subclass of `NameError`.

UnicodeError
>   Unicode encoding or decoding error. A subclass of `ValueError`. The following exceptions are subclasses: `UnicodeEncodeError`, `UnicodeDecodeError`, `UnicodeTranslateError`.

ValueError
>   Generated when the argument to a function or operation is the right type but an inappropriate value.

WindowsError
> Generated by failed system calls on Windows. A subclass of `OSError`.

ZeroDivisionError
> Dividing by zero. A subclass of `ArithmeticError`.

10.3 Standard Library

Python comes with a sizable standard library. Many of these modules have been previously described in the book. Reference material can be found at `https://docs.python.org/library`. That material is not repeated here.

The modules listed below are notable because they are generally useful for a wide variety of applications and for Python programming in general.

10.3.1 `collections` Module

The `collections` module supplements Python with a variety of additional container objects that can be quite useful for working with data—such as a double-ended queue (`deque`), dictionaries that automatically initialize missing items (`defaultdict`), and counters for tabulation (`Counter`).

10.3.2 `datetime` Module

The `datetime` module is where you find functions related to dates, times, and computations involving those things.

10.3.3 `itertools` Module

The `itertools` module provides a variety of useful iteration patterns—chaining iterables together, iterating over product sets, permutations, grouping, and similar operations.

10.3.4 `inspect` Module

The `inspect` module provides functions for inspecting the internals of code-related elements such as functions, classes, generators, and coroutines. It's commonly used in metaprogramming by functions that define decorators and similar features.

10.3.5 `math` Module

The `math` module provides common mathematical functions such as `sqrt()`, `cos()`, and `sin()`.

10.3.6 os **Module**

The os module is where you find low-level functions related to the host operating system—processes, files, pipes, permissions, and similar features.

10.3.7 random **Module**

The random module provides various functions related to random number generation.

10.3.8 re **Module**

The re module provides support for working with text via regular expression pattern matching.

10.3.9 shutil **Module**

The shutil module has functions for performing common tasks related to the shell, such as copying files and directories.

10.3.10 statistics **Module**

The statistics module provides functions for computing common statistical values such as means, medians, and standard deviation.

10.3.11 sys **Module**

The sys module contains a variety of attributes and methods related to the runtime environment of Python itself. This includes command-line options, standard I/O streams, the import path, and similar features.

10.3.12 time **Module**

The time module is where you find various functions related to system time, such as getting the value of the system clock, sleeping, and the number of elapsed CPU seconds.

10.3.13 turtle **Module**

Turtle graphics. You know, for kids.

10.3.14 unittest **Module**

The unittest module provides built-in support for writing unit tests. Python itself is tested using unittest. However, many programmers prefer using third-party libraries such as pytest for testing. This author concurs.

10.4 Final Words: Use the Built-Ins

In the modern world where there are hundreds of thousands of Python packages, it is easy for programmers to seek solutions to small problems in the form of third-party package dependencies. However, Python has long had an extremely useful set of built-in functions and datatypes. Combined with modules from the standard library, a wide range of common programming problems can often be solved using nothing beyond what Python already provides. Given a choice, prefer that.

Index

Photo by izusek/gettyir

Register Your Product at informit.com/register

Access additional benefits and **save 35%** on your next purchase

- Automatically receive a coupon for 35% off your next purchase, valid for 30 days. Look for your code in your InformIT cart or the Manage Codes section of your account page.

- Download available product updates.

- Access bonus material if available.*

- Check the box to hear from us and receive exclusive offers on new editions and related products.

Registration benefits vary by product. Benefits will be listed on your account page under Registered Products.

InformIT.com—The Trusted Technology Learning Source

InformIT is the online home of information technology brands at Pearson, the world's foremost education company. At InformIT.com, you can:

- Shop our books, eBooks, software, and video training
- Take advantage of our special offers and promotions (informit.com/promotions)
- Sign up for special offers and content newsletter (informit.com/newsletters)
- Access thousands of free chapters and video lessons

Connect with InformIT—Visit informit.com/community

inform IT ®
the trusted technology learning source

Addison-Wesley · Adobe Press · Cisco Press · Microsoft Press · Pearson IT Certification · Que · Sams · Peachpit Press

 Pearson